A Fresh Look at Fraud

A Fresh Look at Fraud features psychologists, criminologists, and computer scientists to address the state-of-the-art research on the rising problem of fraud, scams, and financial abuse, stimulating a cross-disciplinary exchange of ideas, theories, methods, and practices.

In this timely volume, Yaniv Hanoch and Stacey Wood bring together leading international researchers to discuss and review state-of-the-art research in fraud research, adopting diverse methodologies (from experimental to neuroimaging), perspectives, and questions. The book addresses topics such as mass marketing fraud, financial exploitation, ageing and cyber fraud, risk factors associated with becoming a fraud victim and online/cryptocurrency fraud. It offers a holistic picture of emerging trends and issues in fraud research and also includes discussion of the 'Next Frontiers' in research and important insights on how to create solutions.

This book will be a crucial read for practitioners and researchers engaged in fraud research and other fields such as Forensic Psychology, Social Psychology, Criminal Behavior, and Criminology, as well as for postgraduates training in these fields.

Yaniv Hanoch is Associate Professor of Risk Management, Southampton University Business School, Southampton University, UK.

Stacey Wood is Molly Mason Jones Professor of Psychology at Scripps College, USA.

A Fresh Look at Fraud

Theoretical and Applied Perspectives

Edited by
YANIV HANOCH
and
STACEY WOOD

Routledge
Taylor & Francis Group
LONDON AND NEW YORK

Cover image: © Getty Images

First published 2022
by Routledge
4 Park Square, Milton Park, Abingdon, Oxon OX14 4RN

and by Routledge
605 Third Avenue, New York, NY 10158

Routledge is an imprint of the Taylor & Francis Group, an informa business

British Library Cataloguing-in-Publication Data
A catalogue record for this book is available from the British Library

Library of Congress Cataloging-in-Publication Data
A catalog record has been requested for this book

ISBN: 978-0-367-86145-2 (hbk)
ISBN: 978-0-367-86144-5 (pbk)
ISBN: 978-1-003-01718-9 (ebk)

DOI: 10.4324/9781003017189

Typeset in Avenir and Dante
by SPi Technologies India Pvt Ltd (Straive)

Yaniv Hanoch would like to dedicate this volume to his parents—Rafi and Sara—for their lifelong inspiration and love.

Stacey Wood would like to dedicate this volume to her husband Mark, her partner in love and work, for his enthusiastic support of this project.

Contents

Acknowledgments

An edited book requires the labour of many authors. Thus, we would like to extend our thank you to all the authors in this volume for their commitment, motivation, engagement, and support throughout the process. This was especially the case with the COVID-19 pandemic impacting every aspect of our lives. Authors not only contributed their respective chapters, but were kind enough to read and provide feedback on other chapters. Without these efforts and kindness, the volume would have not been submitted in a timely fashion. We would also like to thank the publisher and the editorial team—Christina Chronister and Shreya Bajpai—for their encouragement and patience.

Contributors

Keith B. Anderson, Formerly Bureau of Economics, Federal Trade Commission, USA

Rebecca Campbell, Wayne State University, USA

Natalie C. Ebner, University of Florida, USA

Latoya Hall, Wayne State University, USA

S. Duke Han, University of Southern California and Rush University Medical Center, USA

David Hengerer, Claremont Graduate University, USA

Shane Johnson, University College London, UK

Josh Kamps, University College London, UK

Bennett Kleinberg, Tilburg University, The Netherlands

Peter A. Lichtenberg, Wayne State University, USA

David Modic, University of Ljubljana, Slovenia

Didem Pehlivanoglu, University of Florida, USA

Rebecca Polk, University of Florida, USA

Gary R. Turner, York University, Canada

Felix Soldner, University College London, UK

R. Nathan Spreng, McGill University, Canada

Wendy Loken Thornton, Department of Psychology, Simon Fraser University

Arianna Trozze, University College London, UK

Laura C. Walzak, Department of Psychology, Simon Fraser University

1 Introduction

Yaniv Hanoch and Stacey Wood

Introduction

Not a day goes by without news items telling another story about fraud. Indeed, fraud (or scams)[1] have become so frequent and ubiquitous that the United Kingdom National Crime Agency has identified them as the UK's most common crime (National Crime Agency, 2021). According to the National Crime Agency data, close to 3.5 million incidents took place in 2016–2017; however, it also suggests that this number represents only the tip of the iceberg, as it is estimated that less than 20% of incidences are being reported. The high prevalence of fraud also translates into enormous financial losses. A 2019 report estimates that the cost of fraud for businesses and individuals is over $5 trillion per year (Gee & Button, 2019)—about 4 times the UK (about £842 billion) 2019–2020 budget and slightly higher than the US ($4.79 trillion) 2020 budget. These grim financial statistics are further compounded by the emotional and psychological distress that fraud victims experience. In fact, a survey by the European Commission (2020; see also, Modic & Anderson, 2015) has revealed that almost 80% of fraud victims have suffered emotionally and with most victims indicating that the emotional costs of fraud are more distressing than the economic costs. Despite the prevalence of fraud and its substantial impact on individuals and society, there are still many open questions. For example, who is most likely to become a victim of fraud or what preventive measures can be employed to tackle fraud are still awaiting answers (Hanoch & Wood, 2021).

DOI: 10.4324/9781003017189-1

Fraud or scams are not a new phenomenon, as their existence can be traced back to, at least, biblical times. Research by Gregory and Nikiforova (2021), for example, nicely captures the evolution of the so-called Nigerian Prince scam (also known as 419 fraud), revealing that similar techniques and letters were already circulating in Europe in the late 1800s. What has changed dramatically over time is the magnitude and ease by which fraudsters can reach millions of individuals across the globe. Thomas Friedman's notion of a flat world is (unfortunately) a perfect metaphor for the lack of barriers and ease by which fraudsters can reach potential victims anywhere in the world, leading Durkin and Brinkman (2009) to signify fraud as a crime without borders. The international nature of fraud is one reason why fighting it is so difficult, as it often requires national and international cooperation and collaboration—at times between states and agents that might have few formal channels of communication or differing legal or law enforcement procedures and rules.

Given the magnitude and breadth of challenges that fraud raises, no single solution will resolve or fully address this complex problem. Technological innovations have been at the forefront of tackling fraud. Advances in artificial intelligence and computing technology, for instance, have made important inroads into fraudsters nefarious activities—Google, for instance, has been blocking millions of Phishing emails a day (Kumaran & Lugani, 2020). Yet, they have not been able to stop the flood of fraudulent emails, phone calls, texts and other types of solicitations. Likewise, a host of organizations have provided advice on the type of warning signs individuals should pay attention to and how to avoid becoming a victim. Yet people's vulnerabilities and behavior are one of the weakest links. Unlike many other crimes, potential victims play an important and active role in the fraud process, such as providing personal information, transferring funds, clicking on links, and maintaining secrecy. Without victims' cooperation, fraudsters would have little to show for. Thus, understanding what human factors are associated with the tendency to respond and comply with fraudsters solicitations and instructions lies at the heart of any preventive program. It is also the essence of this book.

Fraud susceptibility: contribution factors

The quest to better understand who fall prey has focused on two domains: Demographic factors and individual differences. Identifying demographics variables—such as age and income—as risk factors seems like a promising start, and several researchers have examined the association between demographic variables and falling prey to fraud solicitations. The picture emerging from this line of investigation, however, is somewhat opaque. While some researchers have found old age to be a risk factor (James et al., 2014), others have reported that middle age and even young adults might be at higher risk of becoming a victim (e.g., Mueller et al., 2020). Making things even more complex is the fact that different age groups might fall prey to different types of scams—romance vs. investment—and might be targeted more or less frequently by fraudsters.

How other demographic variables, such as gender, ethnicity, education, and income, impact fraud susceptibility is even less conclusive. Emerging data (e.g., The Office for National Statistics, 2016) indicates that higher income is associated with higher fraud rates, possibly because they have more disposable funds and more likely to report the loss of larger monetary amounts. The European Commission (2020) report, which includes data from countries across Europe, revealed a positive correlation between education, income and being a fraud victim, findings that resonate well with data reported by DeLiema et al. (2020) and Whitty (2019). Other demographic variables, such as race, have received little to no attention rendering any insights or generalizations premature. Furthermore, there are few cross-national, longitudinal, or large-scale studies—aside from the European Commission report mentioned above. Such studies are urgently needed to better elucidate how cultures and other demographics variables might impact response to fraudulent solicitations.

While demographic variables are of clear importance, researchers have also focused on how individual differences might help explain differences in fraud solicitation response. These endeavors have cast a wide net to include a spectrum of measures, such as cognitive ability, emotional intelligence, financial literacy, impulsivity (or self-control), numeracy, and risk-taking, to name a few. Again, the literature is far from offering us a unified narrative about any single individual difference measures. While some studies suggest that cognitive abilities help protect against falling prey to fraud solicitations (Ebner et al., 2018)—at least among adults ages 75–89—others have found little support to the idea that cognitive ability serves as a protective measure (DeLiema et al., 2020; Mueller et al., 2020). Interestingly, Jones et al. (2019) reported that individuals who scored higher on the cognitive reflection task exhibited a somewhat reduced intention to respond to fraud solicitation.

Research that examined the link between impulsivity (or self-control), risk-taking and falling prey to fraud solicitation provides a somewhat clearer picture. An impressive body of work by Anderson (2019) has repeatedly found that self-control is a significant predictor of becoming a victim of mass-marketing fraud. Anderson's findings are further corroborated by Whitty's (2019) investigation of both romance and cyber fraud, Chen et al.'s (2017) examination of online fraud, and Modic and Lea's (2013) studies that evaluated both past and future compliance with fraud solicitation.

Regarding risk-taking, the findings thus far are less conclusive. A study by Mueller et al. (2020), for example, did not find a relation between financial risk tolerance and scam susceptibility. In contrast, Anderson (2019), based on data from a survey by the Federal Trade Commission, showed that risk-taking was associated with a higher probability of being previously defrauded. While risk-taking plays a major role in a host of financial decisions, whether it predicts susceptibility to fraud solicitations remains an open question.

Understating the role of demographic and individual differences measures is central to solving one key puzzle: Why some people fall prey to fraud while others remain resilient. Yet, as eluded to earlier, these issues represent only part of the fraud susceptibility conundrum. Other pertinent concerns revolve around the ecological/external validity of the experimental design in studies examining fraud susceptibility as well as utilizing a wide range of experimental techniques to examine who fall prey and why. To date, few studies have used realistic, ecologically valid, and naturalistic designs. Most, in fact, have relied on abstract or simulated lab designs (but see Ebner et al., 2018). Furthermore, there is a paucity of neuroimaging/physiological studies that focus on fraud. This omission is unfortunate as neuroimaging studies have greatly enriched our understanding of a wide spectrum of decision-making and risk-taking activities and behavior. What is also missing are good theoretical or conceptual models that can steer future research and integrate research from multiple disciplines. Finally, what is also urgently needed are preventive programs or tools. While the advice provided by different sources is valuable, there is an immediate need to develop preventive programs that have been tested and validated and to develop programs that are tailored to the needs of different groups (age, minorities, etc.). Decision aids, for instance, have been employed in a wide range of settings (such as financial [e.g., Aouni et al., 2018] and health decisions [Whelan et al., 2004]), aiding millions of people to make better and more informed decisions. There are no reasons why similar decisions aids cannot be developed to assist people in fighting against fraud solicitations.

The complex nature of fraud, the enormous financial and psychological price tag associated with this crime, and the relatively sparse scientific data that exist, together serve as the main impetus for writing this book. There is a clear need to develop new insights, models, experimental designs, and adopt a multidisciplinary approach. The chapters in this book offer a window into some of the above questions, (partial) answers, and hopefully, inspiration for others to pursue research in this important and applied domain. Law enforcement agencies and other organizations across the world have started to acknowledge the magnitude of the problems and have formed fruitful collaborations and created special task forces that are designed to address this problem. Many high-tech companies have also harnessed their expertise and knowledge to fight fraudsters. While these efforts are necessary to curtail fraudulent activities, they are not sufficient to end fraud—it is still taking place at an unprecedented rate. Behavioral scientists can offer crucial help, and we hope this book plays a part in this process.

The chapters in this book offer a journey into some of the opportunities and challenges that fraud poses to individuals and society alike. The chapters discuss and review state-of-the-art research in the field, adopting diverse methodologies (from experimental to neuroimaging), perspectives, and questions. While we have made every attempt to provide a holistic and diverse approach, a single book can only achieve so much. Given the wide scope of the problem—financial, legal, and psychological—many questions, problems, and issues will remain open and will hopefully be addressed by other volumes and scholars. Furthermore, as fraud research has gained momentum relatively recently, many ideas have only been tested or explored in the laboratory and their applicability and merit will have to be confirmed and tested in real-life situations. We hope, therefore, that this volume serves as an inspiration to researchers in more than one way. It could galvanize and motivate new researchers to explore the topics raised in this volume. At the same time, it could stimulate those who are already working in the field in thinking about the problem with a fresh perspective and explore new avenues and ideas. Research on fraud is much needed, and the chapters that follow will hopefully be utilized by researchers and practitioners alike in seeking a better understanding of the problem and in exploring innovative and creative preventive measures.

Overview of the book

The chapters in this book are mainly focused on the individual level, but many of the ideas and findings surveyed and discussed could be extended and applied to the organizational and governmental levels. Overall, the chapters in the book can be divided into three broad topics: Mass marketing fraud, financial exploitation, and online/cryptocurrency fraud. Together, they intend to offer a holistic, albeit incomplete, picture of emerging trends and issues in fraud research.

Mass marketing scams (MMS) are one of the most prevalent types of fraud consumers face. According to one estimate (Anderson, 2019), in the US alone there were over 60 million mass marketing frauds taking place in just one year. The range and scope of MMS are simply hard to fathom as new ones appear regularly while others seem to be a constant feature in our emails, mail, and phone calls. MMS prevalence is partially due to the ease by which fraudsters can reach large numbers of individuals. While there are clear variations between different MMS, they do share several features in common, such as being unsolicited and often looking very genuine. Over the last decade or so, we have seen an increase in the type and number of MMS; gaining a better understanding of who fall prey to these types of fraud and what can be done to reduce compliance rate are of the utmost importance.

Keith Anderson, the author of Chapter 2, has probably done more than any other researcher in the field in trying to understand the factors involved in responding and falling prey to mass marketing scams. Starting in the early 2000s, Anderson has been exploring and studying consumer fraud in the United States. In Chapter 2 of this book, he summarizes and highlights finding from his two decades of work and research at the Federal Trade Commission, based on some of the most innovative and extensive surveys on mass marketing fraud (we know of no other organization or researcher who has conducted fraud surveys over such an extended length of time). Titled "Mass-Market Consumer Frauds: What the Statistical Data Show", the chapter provides, first, an important historical perspective, an overview of what MMS is, as well as the scope of the problem and the prevalence of different MMS. Next, he examines the role of a wide range of demographics—such as age and race--and individual difference factors—risk-taking and self-control—that might be linked to greater susceptibility to falling prey to MMS. Taken together, the chapter offers one of the most comprehensive treatments of the subject, as well as pinpointing some of the gaps in the extant literature as well as possible new research avenues.

Mass marketing scams have gained further momentum during the COVID-19 pandemic. As we were working on this book, the COVID -19 pandemic was not only causing widespread financial and health havoc but also served as a breeding ground for novel types of mass marketing frauds. Indeed, a report in the *Guardian* in May 2021 revealed that the "UK cybersecurity agency has taken down more scams in the last year than in the previous three years combined, with coronavirus and NHS-themed cybercrime fueling the increase." Likewise, the Federal Trade Commission (2021) has reported over half a million complaints related to COVID-19, costing consumers close to half a billion dollars in 2021 alone. Given the aforementioned issue of the low rate of fraud reporting, these numbers are likely to be an underestimate of the true extent and costs of COVID-19-related fraud. While disasters have often been exploited by fraudsters, there are few (if any) historical precedence to match the magnitude and scale that COVID-19 has presented. In Chapter 3, titled "Scams in the time of COVID-19: Pandemic trends in scams and fraud", Wood, Hengerer and Hanoch explain why the pandemic created a perfect storm for fraud to thrive and appraise some of the key tactics used by scammers, the evolution of COVID-19 scams, and factors associated with responding to MMS. Drawing on literature from persuasion, the authors illustrate how fraudsters have capitalized on key ideas from this line of investigation to construct their MMS. Many COVID-19 scams have exploited, for instance, a sense of scarcity (from personal protective equipment to vaccines), authority (National Health Service in the UK), and time pressure. Likewise, fraudsters have capitalized on the deep uncertainties that COVID-19 created with official messages changing by the day and increased sense of vulnerabilities and emotional distress that many people felt. The chapter, together with Anderson's chapter, also reviews some of the most common COVID-19 scams and fraud trends, though the list is far from being exhaustive as trends can change quite rapidly depending on what government programs and health schemes are being offered in different countries.

Ageing has been of key interest to fraud researchers. Stories in popular media, quite similarly, have often focused on older adults as fraud victims, as it been assumed that older adults are more vulnerable to fraud. This assumption appears to have gained even further momentum during the COVID-19 pandemic, as many older adults were targeted by scammers—and at a noticeably higher rate than other age groups. Anderson, in Chapter 2 and elsewhere (2019), as well as other researchers and data, have come to challenge this pervasive view. This is not to negate the fact that older adults are falling prey to mass marketing fraud, losing larger amounts of money, and are often less computer and internet savvy as compared to their younger counterparts. Ebner and her colleagues in Chapter 4 take on the important task of examining old age and online / cyber fraud, noting the paucity of data and research on cybersecurity among this growing segment of the population. They also highlight the dynamic nature of digital decision-making, where new technologies and environments are introduced frequently. The authors offer a sweeping perspective that incorporates research from a spectrum of disciplines and approaches—drawing on cognitive, emotional, and neurological literature. By integrating this broad literature, the authors develop and offer a novel and interesting biopsychosocial model—termed the *Biopsychosocial Model of Deception Risk in Aging*—to explain and explore the relationship between age on online decision-making. This model provides a much-needed insight into how individual differences might contribute to susceptibility to fraud. Furthermore, it can serve to guide future research in developing decision aids needed to help older adults make better online decisions. They also champion two other complementing ideas. First, the importance of taking a multidisciplinary approach, where researchers from diverse fields (e.g., computer science, criminology, economics, and psychology) collaborate to study and tackle this complex problem. Second, the need to conduct field and ecologically valid studies. Indeed, we concur wholeheartedly with their assertation that fraud research must move from the lab to the field and requires a multidisciplinary approach.

Ebner and colleagues' chapter serves as a nice segue into the next section of the book, encompassing Chapters 5–7, which focus on financial exploitation and ageing. Chapter 5, by Lichtenberg, Campbell, and Hall, examines the psychological mechanism that is associated with becoming a fraud victim, especially among older adults. Titled "Psychological Aspects of Elder Financial Exploitation: Risk Factors, Intervention Approaches, and Case Studies," the chapter offers readers an important perspective on several issues. First, following other chapters in this volume, they discuss risk factors associated with becoming a fraud victim. Second, they discuss a novel, validated scale—called the Financial Exploitation Vulnerability Scale (FEVS)—which is designed to enhance our capacity to capture and evaluate financial exploitation. Given the paucity of tools currently available, this is a welcome addition to the range of tools researchers and practitioners can utilize. Thirdly, Lichtenberg and colleagues offer a window into one of the only preventions and service programs currently available: Successful Aging through Financial Empowerment (SAFE). Through discussion of the program, the authors remind the readers of the immense psychological impact fraud inflicts on victims and of the enormous importance of offering a range of services to fraud victims—both preventive measures and services to help victims deal with the consequences of fraud. Importantly, the authors discuss some of their success stories and how they can be replicated and extended to other communities across the globe. Hopefully, their success will encourage others to pursue similar programs to aid older (but also all) people who have been victims of fraud.

Following Lichtenberg and colleagues, Chapter 6 by Walzak and Thornton further explores risk factors associated with becoming a fraud victim. In their chapter, title "Cognitive and Metacognitive Predictors of Financial Exploitation: Understanding Fraud Susceptibility in Adulthood", the authors provide a review of cognitive and metacognitive factors that could aid in predicting fraud susceptibility. Drawing from a broader perspective, their chapter highlights the role of numeracy. A large corpus of literature has shown the role numeracy plays in a host of financial and medical decisions, and, by extension, it could play a key part in guarding against financial fraud. Similar to Ebner et al., (Chapter 4) and Lichtenberg et al. (Chapter 5), Walzak and Thornton evaluate how cognitive decline might render older adults more vulnerable to fraud. They extend earlier work by introducing the possible impact of Theory of Mind (ToM), an interesting concept that has rarely contributed to the fraud literature. The authors introduce a new experimental tool to study fraud susceptibility: The Everyday Social Decisions task (ESD). The importance of the ESD rests with its reported increased ecological validity, and its coverage of both purchase intention, deceit detection, and decision confidence across a range of scenarios. The ESD represents the type of measure that fraud researchers urgently need: One that mimics the complexity of real-life decision-making. Indeed, the pilot data report by the authors is very encouraging and would allow researchers to expand their experimental tool in investigating susceptibility to fraud. It could also inspire researchers to develop additional tools, as a new type of fraud solicitations constantly emerges.

There is a large body of work examining how neuropsychological factors are involved in a spectrum of decision-making and risk-taking activities. This corpus of data has been indispensable in our advancement of theories, development of prevention aids, and clinical assessment, to name a few. It seems natural, thus, that this line of investigation is extended to the domain of fraud. Chapter 7, by Han, titled "Vulnerability to Financial Exploitation in Older Age: A Neuropsychology Perspective", is offering readers a closer look at how cognitive impairment might impact financial decision and fraud susceptibility, what neuroimaging studies reveal about brain changes and susceptibility to fraud, and, finally, a model that is informed by behavioral neuroscience research. Han's chapter opens the door to other researchers interested in the link between neurological and neuropsychological facets and fraud. They also offer insights into the link between Alzheimer's disease and fraud risk and possibly viewing falling victim as a sign of age-related neuropathology. It gives readers a peek into the clinical work that is deciphering some of the basic neurological mechanisms involved in: financial decisions in general, in financial exploitations and fraud in particular, and why traditional neuropsychological measures may offer an incomplete picture. As advocated by several authors in this volume and elsewhere, figuring out the neurological mechanisms involved in fraud susceptibility can feed into the development of better clinical tools to treat fraud victims and help predict vulnerability to fraud solicitations.

At least one of the authors (YH) of this book has been an avid eBay buyer. Over the years, he has purchased hundreds of items successfully. Yet, in several limited cases, the items won in the auction were never received and, in other instances, the items either did not match the description or were damaged. While in most of these cases, a refund was available, the experience was either time consuming or very frustrating. Unlike many other frauds discussed in this book, many of the scams taking place on auction platforms, such as eBay, cannot necessarily be avoided (seller not sending an item or due to false advertising). Nevertheless, there are cues and information that buyers can pay attention to and use when deciding whether to bid and purchase an item. In Chapter 8, titled "Do not distract me while I am winning this auction: The psychology of auction fraud", Modic examines which cues can help buyers avoid becoming a victim and which personality traits and persuasion techniques are associated with greater compliance with fraudulent offers. Composed of two studies, this chapter is one of the few in this volume to offer primary data. This work shines a light on the type of persuasion techniques and personality traits that are associated with responding to fraudulent auction offers. Whether the findings presented in this chapter are robust enough to predict compliance with other types of fraud (e.g., MMS), is an open and important question. Modic hoped to identify whether certain fraudulent items (e.g., mobile phones) are more likely to solicit interests and response, but the data do not afford any firm conclusions. This is an interesting conundrum, as knowledge about which item is more likely to generate a response can serve to alert or warn potential buyers. Future studies, hopefully, will pick up on this line of investigation to provide consumers with appropriate warning signs.

Data science represents one of the most significant potential tools in fighting online fraud. As with other domains, data science can help researchers (and practitioners) to identify trends, patterns, and specific frauds. Chapter 9, titled "Trends in online consumer fraud: A data science perspective", by Soldner, Kleinberg, and Johnson extends the previous chapter by examining the role data science can play in online consumer fraud—a domain that is characterized by limited (often a single) and short-lived interactions (in contrast to other types of fraud such as MMS and romance fraud which often require multiple interactions over a long period).[2] It extends the discussion, moreover, to the realm of the dark web—where criminal actors and activities often involve the sale of illegal drugs and weapons (the infamous Silk Road, for example). The work by Soldner and colleagues illustrates some of the methodologies that data scientists use to detect and identify fraudulent billing for services or goods, as well as fake websites and fraudulent emails/

texts/phone calls (Google's ability to block millions of Phishing emails is one such example). While some approaches are useful in fighting fraud over the surface web, the dark web is a whole different story—as no identifying information is available (such as IP address). The authors explore some limitations and opportunities that data science offers both in the surface web and deep web—of which the dark web is a segment. One opportunity highlighted by the authors is the possibility for closer collaboration between data science and psychology to identify who falls prey to fraud and why. Multidisciplinary collaborations will be, without a doubt, fruitful.

In June 2021, a story broke about what was deemed to be the biggest ransomware attack to date, bringing hundreds of businesses across the world to a halt. It was reported that the perpetrators demanded $70 million in cryptocurrency. During a few months, the price of Bitcoin, the original cryptocurrency, swung dramatically, reaching a value of over £45K per coin only to lose 50% of its value within a few months. Over the last few years, cryptocurrency has captured the attention of financial institutions and the public alike. Despite its growing interest and use, the nature of cryptocurrency has made it a favorite among criminals. In Chapter 10, titled "Cryptocurrencies: Boons and curses for fraud prevention," Kamps, Trozze and Kleinberg provide insights into this emerging and novel domain of fraud. The chapter starts with a precis of what cryptocurrencies are and how they function. This section is much needed, as some readers might be unfamiliar with the technical facets underlying this type of currency, and it will aid in understanding how fraud is taking place using this type of currency. To some degree, cryptocurrency-related fraud is unlike other types of fraud discussed in this book. For example, in many cases, cryptocurrencies are simply used as a means to transfer funds to fraudsters—what the authors call crypto-enabled. These are needed to be distinguished from crypto-dependent, where the fraud is contingent and dependent on the nature of these currencies rather than simply enabling the fraud to take place. Running through a list of these two types of crypto frauds, the chapter elucidates some of the unique features raised by cryptocurrencies and some of the similarities to other types of fraud. At the same time, one thing is clear. We have only started to understand and fathom the extent and possibilities that cryptocurrencies offer fraudsters.

The chapters in this book offer both pessimistic and optimistic views. On the one hand, they emphasize the wide range and scope of the fraud, one that is carrying an enormous financial, psychological, physical, and social impact worldwide. Bringing these issues to the public and researchers' attention, however, is of key importance. It can galvanize public opinion to illuminate this problem and encourage individuals affected by fraud to report their experience of being a victim of fraud. It could also place pressure on policy-makers to devote more resources to tackling this crime. And, of course, provide an impetus for researchers to examine more closely the factors associated with falling a victim to fraud and providing support to victims. We hope that this book will generate greater interest and curiosity from researchers from across the academic spectrum—computer scientists, criminologists, data scientists, political scientists, and psychologists, to name a few—and encourage collaborations and multidisciplinary approaches. The field would greatly benefit from innovative and creative research as well as with more applied and ecologically valid studies. We are eager to see how this book helps shape the future of the field.

Notes

1 The terms *scam* and *fraud* are used interchangeably throughout this book and are meant to indicate "the deliberate intent to deceive with promises of goods, services, or other financial benefits that in fact do not exist or that were never intended to be provided" (Titus et al., 1995, p. 54). There are, of course, other definitions of fraud and scams and some chapters in this book might adopt a slightly different one.

2 A BBC News story (Fisher, 2021) tell the case of a UK charity worker who had months of face-to-face interactions with a woman before he was swindle out of large amount of money.

References

Anderson, K. B. (2019). *Mass-market consumer fraud in the United States: A 2017 update* [Staff report]. Federal Trade Commission, Bureau of Economics. https://www.ftc.gov/system/files/documents/reports/mass-market-consumer-fraud-united-states-2017-update/p105502massmarketconsumerfraud2017report.pdf

Aouni, B., Doumpos, M., Pérez-Gladish, B., & Steuer, R. E. (2018). On the increasing importance of multiple criteria decision aid methods for portfolio selection. *Journal of the Operational Research Society, 69*(10), 1525–1542. https://doi.org/10.1080/01605682.2018.1475118

Chen, H., Beaudoin, C. E., & Hong, T. (2017). Securing online privacy: An empirical test on Internet scam victimization, online privacy concerns, and privacy protection behaviors. *Computers in Human Behavior, 70*, 291–302. https://doi.org/10.1016/j.chb.2017.01.003

DeLiema, M., Deevy, M., Lusardi, A., & Mitchell, O. S. (2020). Financial fraud among older Americans: Evidence and implications. *The Journal of Gerontology B: Social Sciences, 75*(4), 861–868. https://doi.org/10.1093/geronb/gby151

Durkin, K. F., & Brinkman, R. (2009). 419 Fraud: A crime without borders in a postmodern world. *International Review of Modern Sociology, 35*, 271–283.

Ebner, N. C., Ellis, D. M., Lin, T., Rocha, H. A., Yang, H., Dommaraju, S., Soliman, A., Woodard, D. L., Turner, G. R., Spreng, R. N., & Oliveira, D. S. (2018). Uncovering susceptibility risk to online deception in aging. *The Journal of Gerontology B: Psychological Sciences, 75*(3), 522–533.

European Commission. (2020). *Survey on "scams and fraud experienced by consumers": Final report*. https://ec.europa.eu/info/sites/info/files/aid:development_cooperation_fundamental_rights/ensuring_aid:effectiveness/documents/survey_on_scams_and_fraud_experienced_by_consumers_-_final_report.pdf

Federal Trade Commission. (2021). *FTC COVID-19 and stimulus report*. https://public.tableau.com/app/profile/federal.trade.commission/viz/COVID-19andStimulusReports/Map

Fisher, J. (June 22, 2021). A fake wedding, and a $250,00 scam. *BBC News*. https://www.bbc.co.uk/news/world-europe-57358241

Gee, J., & Button, M. (2019). *The financial cost of fraud 2019*. http://www.crowe.ie/wp-content/uploads/2019/08/The-Financial-Cost-of-Fraud-2019.pdf

Gregory, W. D., & Nikiforova, B. (2021). A sweetheart of a deal: How people get hooked and reeled. *Journal of Behavioral Finance & Economics*, 2, 96–122.

Hanoch, Y., & Wood, S. (2021). The scams among us: Who falls prey and why. *Current Direction in Psychological Science, 30*, 260–266.

James, B. D., Boyle, P. A., & Bennett, D. A. (2014). Correlates of susceptibility to scams in older adults without dementia. *Journal of Elder Abuse & Neglect, 26*(2), 107–122. https://doi.org/10.1080/08946566.2013.821809

Jones, H. S., Towse, J. N., Race, N., & Harrison, T. (2019). Email fraud: The search for psychological predictors of susceptibility. *PLOS ONE, 14*(1), e0209684. https://doi.org/10.1371/journal.pone.0209684

Kumaran, N., & Lugani, S. (April 6, 2020). Protecting businesses against cyber threats during COVID-19 and beyond. *Google Cloud*. https://cloud.google.com/blog/products/identity-security/protecting-against-cyber-threats-during-covid-19-and-beyond

Lichtenberg, P. A., Sugarman, M. A., Paulson, D., Ficker, L. J., & Rahman-Filipiak, A. (2016). Psychological and functional vulnerability predicts fraud cases in older adults: Results of a longitudinal study. *Clinical Gerontologist: The Journal of Aging and Mental Health, 39*(1), 48–63. https://doi.org/10.1080/07317115.2015.1101632

Modic, D., & Anderson, R. (2015). It's all over but the crying: The emotional and financial impact of Internet fraud. *IEEE Security & Privacy, 13*(5), 99–103. https://doi.org/10.1109/MSP.2015.107

Modic, D., & Lea, S. E. G. (2013). *Scam compliance and the psychology of persuasion. SSRN*. https://doi.org/10.2139/ssrn.2364464

Mueller, E. A., Wood, S. A., Hanoch, Y., Huang, Y., & Reed, C. (2020). Older and wiser: Age differences in susceptibility to financial fraud: The protective role of emotional intelligence. *Journal of Elder Abuse & Neglect, 32*(2), 152–172. https://doi.org/10.1080/08946566.2020.1736704

National Crime Agency. (July 2, 2021). *The threat from fraud*. https://www.nationalcrimeagency.gov.uk/what-we-do/crime-threats/fraud-and-economic-crime

Office for National Statistics. (2016). *Overview of fraud statistics: Year ending Mar 2016*. https://www.ons.gov.uk/peoplepopulationandcommunity/crimeandjustice/articles/overviewoffraudstatistics/yearendingmarch2016

Titus, R. M., Heinzelmann, F., & Boyle, J. (1995). Victimization of persons by fraud. *Crime & Delinquency*, *41*(1), 54–72.

Whelan, T., Levine, M., Willan, A., Gafni, A., Sanders, K., Mirsky, D., et al. (2004). Effect of a decision ai on knowledge and treatment decision making for breast cancer surgery. *JAMA*, *292*, 435–441.

Whitty, M. T. (2019). Predicting susceptibility to cyber-fraud victimhood. *Journal of Financial Crime*, *26*(1), 277–292. https://doi.org/10.1108/JFC-10-2017-0095

Wood, S., Liu, P.-J., Hanoch, Y., Xi, P. M., & Klapatch, L. (2018). Call to claim your prize: Perceived benefits and risk drive intention to comply in a mass marketing scam. *Journal of Experimental Psychology: Applied*, *24*(2), 196–206. https://doi.org/10.1037/xap0000167

Mass-Market Consumer Frauds: What the Statistical Data Show

2

Keith B. Anderson[1]

In this chapter, we consider what we know about mass-market consumer frauds. First, what do we mean by a mass-market consumer fraud? How many consumers are victims of such frauds? Are there characteristics of consumers that make them more or less likely to become victims? In seeking to answer these questions, we draw heavily on the findings of four surveys of consumer experiences with fraud that have been conducted for the U.S. Federal Trade Commission ("FTC") over the past 20 years (the "FTC Fraud Surveys," Anderson, K. B., 2004, 2007, 2013, 2019). We also consider a study by staff of the FTC that looked at what participants said about the likelihood that they would purchase a product that was advertised in likely-fraudulent ways (the "Internet Panel Study," Anderson, K. B., 2016).

Before turning to these questions, however, it may be useful to place the issue of consumer fraud in an historical context.

Consumer Frauds Are Not a New Problem

The offering of fraudulent products is hardly a new problem. While the evidence of consumer fraud in earlier times is limited, a prime example is the sale of patent medicines, nostrums that generally failed to provide the promised relief. From the earliest days of the republic through the early part

DOI: 10.4324/9781003017189-2

of the 20th century, all kinds of nostrums were offered for sale with widely exaggerated claims of their healing powers. These products had names like "Stanley Snake Oil Liniment" (which caught the attention of Upton Sinclair and led to the passage of the Pure Food and Drug Act and later the establishment of the Food and Drug Administration (Milano, 2017)), "Ayer's Cherry Pectoral," "Hamlin's Wizard Oil," "Kick-a-poo Indian Sagwa" and "Buxton's Rheumatic CureAll" (which drew the attention of the Federal Trade Commission (1933)). In 1858, one catalog of patent medicines listed 1,500 products (Anderson, A., 2000. See also Kang & Pedersen, 2017). From the 1920s to the 1940s, bogus potions and cures were marketed containing—or at least claiming to contain—radioactive ingredients (Dotinga, 2020).

In the late 19th and early 20th centuries, one potion, "Warner's Safe Cure," was promoted as being "the only remedy that can effectually expel the Uric Acid waste" and thereby cure, among other things:

> Congestion of the Kidneys, Back-ache, Inflammation of the Kidneys, Bladder and Urinary Organs, Catarrh of the Bladder, Gravel, Stone, Dropsy, Enlarged Prostate Gland, Impotency or General Debility, Bright's Disease. The uric acid also causes Heart Disease, Rheumatism, Apoplexy, Paralysis, Insanity and Death. Warner's Safe Cure relieves the kidneys of surplus blood, and restores their natural action.
>
> (Anderson, A., 2000, p. 5)

Indeed, the history of sellers of fraudulent medical remedies can be traced back even further in Europe, back at least to the medieval European mountebank (Anderson, A., 2000).

While fraudulent products have long been around, recent years have seen significant changes in how fraudsters operate their scams. As the U.K. Office of National Statistics has observed:

> The first established laws on fraud were set out in the First Statute of Westminster in 1275. While fraud is not a new offence, methods of committing it have evolved a great deal over recent times with the rise of new technology, in particular the internet, providing opportunities for fraudsters to commit crime on an industrial scale.
>
> (Flatley, 2016, "How is fraud defined and measured?" section. See also Angell as quoted in U.K. Office of Fair Trade, 2006, p. 6)

Today, promoters of fraudulent products can blast out millions of robocalls—automated calls delivering pre-recorded messages rather than calls handled by a live operator—within a few minutes and at negligible cost. Alternatively, bogus marketers promote and sell their products on the Internet. Obviously, fraudsters are not the only users of these sales channels. Indeed, if legitimate sellers did not use these sales techniques, they would not be as attractive to fraudsters, because fraudsters want to convince consumers that they really are legitimate marketers selling legitimate products.

The impact of these new technologies on the sale of frauds cannot be overstated. The advent of the Internet and modern telecommunications technology has greatly reduced the cost of marketing products—both legitimate and fraudulent. And this makes it profitable to promote things that would not have been profitable even at the end of the 20th century. The cost of making robocalls is so low that it is profitable to market an offering even if the response rate is miniscule.

These new technologies also offer enhanced opportunities to the would-be fraudster. Knock-off products can now readily be marketed at lower cost and covering a much wider area via a website, where the seller can use stolen pictures of the original product rather than showing the low-quality knock-off. In addition, marketing on the Internet increases the opportunities available to those who would offer a product but never deliver it (Bhattarai, 2019).

The availability of inexpensive telephonic services—often using the Internet to originate massive numbers of robocalls—makes it possible for someone half-way around the world to call consumers in the United States and represent that they are with the Social Security Administration, the Internal Revenue Service, or Microsoft. The technology even allows callers to cause the consumer's phone to display a false Caller ID number ("spoofing")—often displaying a number that makes it look like the call is from a government agency or that the caller is located near the person being called. In many cases, the fraudsters convince their victims to transfer thousands of dollars to them using gift cards (Fletcher, 2018), and in some cases are even able to convince their victims to transfer all of their assets to the fraudster's accounts for "safe keeping" (Baker, 2020; Krouse, 2019).

The new technologies also provide increased anonymity for both sellers and their would-be victims—no face-to-face interaction. It is also likely that would-be fraudsters find it much easier to lie in a web advertisement or to have their telephone sale persons lie in a telemarketing call, than to lie in a face-to-face encounter with a potential victim. Potential victims also are more isolated when engaged in a possible fraudulent transaction when it occurs online or in telemarketing—no one is there to caution them from engaging in a problematic transaction.

What Is Mass Market Consumer Fraud?

Consumers may have problems any time they engage in a market transaction. If they order a pizza to be delivered, it may not arrive as quickly or be as hot as they expected. If they order a shirt online, the actual shirt may not be the color they saw in the picture on their laptop.

If any of these problems occur, the consumer may be injured—i.e., be less well off than they would have been if the problem had not occurred. And, the consumer may feel that they have a valid reason to complain to someone. However, these are not, I suspect, examples of what most consumers would consider a fraud.

On the other hand, consumers may well feel defrauded if they agree to purchase pills to help them lose weight or cure a serious disease and find that the product does not function as promised. Similarly, consumers who purchase and pay for a product but never receive it may feel defrauded, particularly if they cannot locate the seller to inquire about the transaction or are refused a refund.

So, how does one draw the line between a fraudulent transaction and something that might be just a bad buying experience? There is no widely accepted answer to this question. However, drawing on an initial definition of fraud by Titus et al. (1995), Beals et al. (2015) define consumer fraud as

> Intentionally and knowingly deceiving the victim by misrepresenting, concealing or omitting facts about promised goods or services, or other benefits and consequences that are nonexistent, unnecessary, never intended to be provided, or deliberately distorted for the purpose of monetary gain.
>
> (p. 7)

The authors then elaborate on this definition, noting:

> How we intend to differentiate fraud from other forms of consumer deception … is that in cases of fraud, scam artists *knowingly* and *deliberately* deceive consumers by convincing them to engage in a transaction that no reasonable person would agree to if he or she had been told the truth.
>
> (p. 7, emphasis in the original)

This successfully captures the types of transactions that should be considered fraudulent. No consumers would have agreed to purchase the pills if they knew that they would not help them lose weight or cure the disease.

Similarly, no consumer would agree to pay for a product knowing that they would never receive it.

So, what does it mean to say that we are focusing on mass-market frauds? Mass-market frauds are those frauds that are generally marketed by media that reach large numbers of consumers, often in widely divergent areas. We are talking about fraudulent offers promoted by social media or by making vast numbers of telemarketing calls to consumers who are not existing customers ("cold-calls"). They may be advertised on an Internet web page or be pitched in late night television infomercials. The victim and the fraudster never meet in person (Baker, 2020; U.S. Department of Justice, 2017). We are not talking about offers that are only promoted in local settings—such as an auto mechanic who recommends repairs that are not needed or a salesman who goes door-to-door falsely telling residents that their homes need repairs such as a new roof. No doubt, frauds can be promoted in these kinds of local settings. However, they are not what we call mass-market frauds.

How Big a Problem Is Mass-Market Consumer Fraud?

In order to measure the magnitude of the problem of mass-marketed consumer fraud in the United States, the Federal Trade Commission ("FTC") has commissioned four consumer surveys. The first survey was conducted in 2003 and the most recent in 2017 ("FTC Fraud Surveys," Anderson, K. B. 2004, 2007, 2013, 2019). The three most recent surveys each involved telephone interviews with between 3,600 and 3,900 randomly chosen U.S. consumers aged 18 and over.

As will be apparent from the previous discussion, it would be very difficult, if not impossible, to rely on consumers to interpret whether or not their experiences meet the definition of fraud. Consumers have no way of knowing the seller's intentions in any transaction. Additionally, relying on consumers to decide whether they had been a victim of fraud would inevitably introduce considerable variation in responses, as different consumers would interpret the same experience differently. Some consumers would think that a particular problem was a fraud while others would write it off as a bad purchase decision. To avoid these problems, rather than asking participants whether they had experienced any mass-market consumer frauds, the FTC Fraud Surveys focused on asking questions about experiences that FTC staff have found generally to be fraudulent experiences.

In the most recent survey, questions about 18 different types of consumer fraud were asked. (The included frauds are set forth in Table 2.1.)

Table 2.1 Types of Fraud Included in the 2017 FTC Survey of Mass-Market Consumer Fraud

Fraud	*Description*
Charged and paid for an item that the consumer had not agreed to purchase[a]	Billed or charged for a product or service that the consumer had not agreed to purchase.
Paid for something that was never received	Paid for a product, but never received it.
Fraudulent weight-loss products	Purchased a weight-loss product that was promoted as making it easy to lose weight or to lose weight without diet or exercise. Only lost a little of the weight anticipated or lost no weight.
Fraudulent computer repair	Paid for computer repairs after someone with whom you had not previously done business contacted you and told you either that your computer had viruses or security vulnerabilities and/or that the seller needed to remotely access your computer.
Falsely told that you owed money to the government	Paid money to someone after receiving a telephone call claiming that they owed money to the government or a government agency or that a court case had been filed against them and they needed to make a payment in connection with that case.
Fraudulent prize promotions	Paid money, made a purchase, or attended a sales presentation to receive a promised prize or lottery winnings. Did not receive the prize or winnings or the prize was not as promised.
Fraudulent work-at-home programs	Purchased a work-at-home program. Did not earn at least half of the promised level of earnings.
Fraudulent business opportunities	Purchased a business opportunity. Did not earn at least half as much as promised or did not receive promised assistance.
Fraudulent credit repair	Paid someone who promised to remove negative, but accurate, information from credit report or promised to provide information on how to establish a new credit record that would not contain negative information in current credit report.
Fraudulent grant offers	Paid someone who promised to obtain a grant either from the government or from someone else. No grant was received.
Debt relief fraud	Paid someone who promised to arrange to pay off credit card debts for less than the amount owed or to arrange a lower interest rate on current credit card debt and then failed to provide the promised services.
Fraudulent pyramid schemes	Purchased a membership in a pyramid scheme. Did not earn at least half of the amount the promoter promised would be earned.

Fraud	Description
Counterfeit check fraud	Received a check and sent some of the money back to the sender or to someone else. Later learned that the check was counterfeit.
Fraudulent credit card insurance	Purchased insurance against the misuse of a lost or stolen credit card.
Fraudulent advance fee loans and credit cards	Paid an advance fee to obtain a promised or guaranteed loan or credit card. Promised credit was not received.
Fraudulent mystery shopper jobs	Paid someone to obtain work as a mystery shopper. Did not earn at least half of the amount the promoter promised you would earn.
Fraudulent promises of government jobs	Made a payment to someone who falsely represented that the purchaser would receive a government job.
Fraudulent mortgage relief	Made an advance payment to someone other than a mortgager or mortgage servicer to obtain a mortgage modification. The modification was either not received or the terms offered were significantly worse than what had been promised.

Source. Anderson, K. B. (2019)

[a] Combines the following four categories from Anderson, K. B. (2019)—Unauthorized Billing for Buyers' Club Memberships, Unauthorized Billing for an Item for a Cell Phone, Unauthorized Billing for Internet Services, and Unauthorized Billing for a Product Or Service Other Than Buyers' Clubs, Cell Phone Products, Or Internet Services.

These problems were mainly selected because they were the subject of frequent complaints found in the Federal Trade Commission's Consumer Sentinel database and, in most cases, the FTC had brought cases based on these types of problems. (For additional detail on the structure of the most recent survey, see Anderson, K. B. 2019, Chapter 2.)

Figure 2.1 and Table 2.2 show estimates of the prevalence of each of the types of fraud included in the 2017 FTC survey. Of participants in the 2017 survey, 15.9%—representing 40.0 million U.S. adults—reported that they had been victims of one or more of the types of fraud covered by the survey ("Any Fraud Included in the Survey") during the one-year period before they were interviewed. There were an estimated 61.8 million incidents of these types of fraud during the year because some victims experienced more than one incident of fraud during the year (Anderson, K. B., 2019). Because the survey did not ask about all kinds of fraud that consumers experienced, this is a lower-bound estimate on the prevalence of consumer fraud in the U.S. economy.[2] To place these figures in context, it is worth noting that, according to the FBI, there were 8.9 million incidents of violent or property crimes in 2017 (FBI, 2017). That is, there were something like nine incidents of fraud for each incident of violent or property crime.

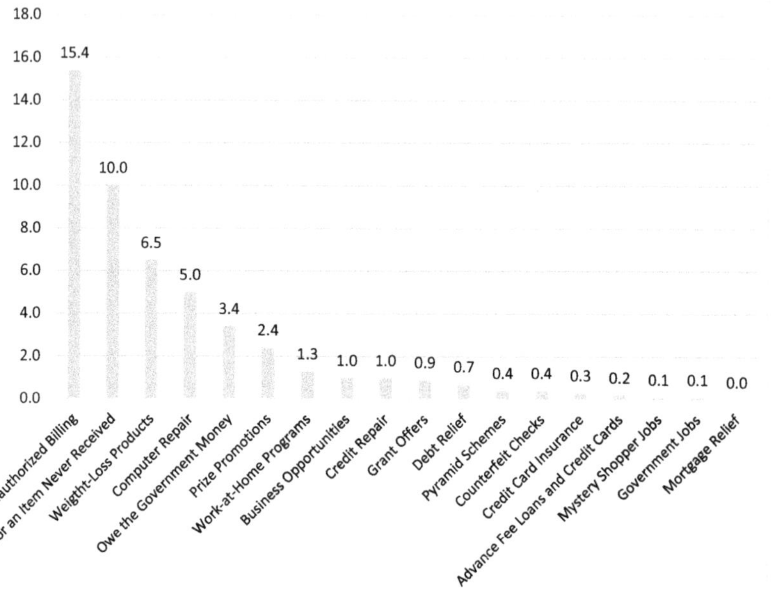

Figure 2.1 Surveyed frauds by number of victims, 2017.
Source. Anderson, K. B. (2019).

Table 2.2 Estimated Number of Adults Who Were Victims of Mass-Market Consumer Frauds, 2017

Type of Fraud	*Number of Victims (Millions)*	*Victims as Percent of Adult Americans*
Any fraud included in the survey	40.0 (36.0–44.1)[a]	15.9% (14.3%–17.5%)[a]
Charged and paid for an item that the consumer had not agreed to purchase[b]	15.4 (12.9–17.9)	6.1% (5.1%–7.1%)
Items for a cell phone	2.5 (1.4–3.7)	1.0% (0.6%–1.5%)
Buyers' club membership	2.5 (1.3–3.8)	1.0% (0.5%–1.5%)
Internet services	1.5 (0.7–2.4)	0.6% (0.3%–1.0%)
Something else	9.7 (7.8–11.6)	3.9% (3.1%–4.6%)
Paid for something that was never received	10.0 (7.7–12.3)	4.0% (3.1%–4.9%)
Fraudulent weight-loss products	6.5 (4.6–8.3)	2.6% (1.8%–3.3%)
Fraudulent computer repair	5.0 (3.5–6.4)	2.0% (1.4%–2.5%)
Falsely told that you owed money to the government	3.4 (2.0–4.9)	1.4% (0.8%–2.0%)
Fraudulent prize promotions	2.4 (1.2–3.5)	0.9% (0.5%–1.4%)
Fraudulent work-at-home programs	1.3 (0.5–2.1)	0.5% (0.2%–0.8%)
Fraudulent business opportunities	1.0 (0.4–1.6)	0.4% (0.2%–0.6%)
Fraudulent credit repair	1.0 (0.2–1.7)	0.4% (0.1%–0.7%)

Type of Fraud	*Number of Victims (Millions)*	*Victims as Percent of Adult Americans*
Fraudulent grant offers	0.9 (0.1–1.7)	0.4% (0.0%–0.7%)
Debt relief fraud	0.7 (0.2–1.3)	0.3% (0.1%–0.5%)
Fraudulent pyramid schemes	0.4 (0.0–0.7)	0.2% (0.0%–0.3%)
Counterfeit check fraud	0.4 (0.0–0.7)	0.1% (0.0%–0.3%)
Fraudulent credit card insurance	0.3 (0.0–0.7)	0.1% (0.0%–0.3%)
Fraudulent advance fee loans and credit cards	0.2 (0.0–0.5)	0.1% (0.0%–0.2%)
Fraudulent mystery shopper jobs	0.1 (0.0–0.3)	0.1% (0.0%–0.1%)
Fraudulent promises of government jobs	0.1 (0.0–0.2)	0.0% (0.0%–0.1%)
Fraudulent mortgage relief	(z)[c]	(z)[c]

Source. Anderson, K. B. (2019).

Numbers are rounded to the nearest 0.1 million and percentages to the nearest 0.1%. 0.0 denotes a value of less than 0.05 million. 0.0% denotes a value of less than 0.05%.

Amounts in individual categories will not sum to totals because some individuals are victims of more than one of the listed frauds.

Projections are based on estimated U.S. population of 252.06 million adults—18 and over—as of July 1, 2017. (See U.S. Census Bureau, Population Division, Estimates of the Total Resident Population and Resident Population Age 18 Years and Older for the United States, States, and Puerto Rico: July 1, 2017 (SCPRC-EST2017-18+POP-RES).)

Interviews were conducted between June 8 and July 30, 2017, with 101 pre-test interviews being conducted between April 4 and April 20, 2017. The survey was designed to inquire about consumer experiences during the one-year period prior to when the interview was conducted. Thus, interviews included in the data could cover periods ranging from April 1, 2016, to April 1, 2017, to July 30, 2016, to July 30, 2017.

The results reported here are based on the responses of those who participated in the survey. If survey participants either over- or under-reported that they had been victims of any of the included frauds, the reported figures will differ from the actual values. In addition, if the experiences of those who refused to participate in the survey differed from those who did participate, this can introduce error in the estimates. Errors may also arise if participants did not understand and answer the questions in the way that was intended. Unfortunately, there is no way to measure or adjust for these types of problems. The confidence intervals reported here reflect uncertainty arising from the number of people interviewed and the way the sample was selected. However, they do not reflect uncertainty resulting from any non-response or wording problems.

[a] Figures in parentheses are 95% confidence intervals.

[b] These figures combine the results for four separate types of fraud involving unauthorized billing in Anderson, K. B. (2019)—Unauthorized Billing for Buyers' Club Memberships, Unauthorized Billing for an Item for a Cell Phone, Unauthorized Billing for Internet Services, and Unauthorized Billing for a Product or Service Other than Buyers' Clubs, Cell Phone Products, or Internet Services.

[c] (z) = zero. No survey participants indicated that they had been victims of this type of fraud during 2017.

Unauthorized Billing

The most prevalent type of fraud reported by participants in the 2017 FTC survey was being charged or billed—and paying the bill—for a product or service that the consumer had not agreed to purchase. As is noted in the survey questions, "This could include a situation where you were offered a free trial of the product or service and were subsequently billed even though you had not agreed to continue beyond the end of the free trial." Free-trial offers are a problem frequently seen by the FTC. The consumer agrees to accept a free trial of a product assuming that, while the seller certainly hopes that the free sample will lead the consumer to buy more, they would have to contact the seller and arrange for additional shipments if they want to keep receiving the product. Sellers, particularly shady sellers, however, treat the consumer's agreement to take the free trial as authorizing additional shipments and billing for the shipments, unless the consumer contacts the seller and indicates that they do not want any more. And, they do not disclose that this is the case—or disclose it only in a way that is unlikely to be seen or understood by the consumer.

Being charged for an item the consumer had not agreed to purchase was reported by 6.1% of survey participants—representing 15.4 million adults in the United States. There were an estimated 18.2 million incidents of this type of fraud in 2017. There were an estimated 4.5 million incidents of unauthorized billing for health care products and services, 2.8 million incidents involving items for a cell phone, and 2.5 million incidents involving buyers' clubs.[3]

Paying for an Item That Was Never Received

The second most commonly reported type of fraud covered by the survey was having paid for an item and then not receiving it. This type of fraud was reported by 4.0% of survey participants—representing 10.0 million adults in the United States.[4] More than three-quarters—78%—of items consumers never received after having paid for them were ordered on the Internet. (In comparison, in 2017, only 9.1% of all retail purchases were ordered on the Internet (U.S. Bureau of the Census, 2019). Across all types of fraud included in the survey, 62% of purchases were by the Internet.) Orders placed by telephone accounted for another 19% of instances in which a consumer paid for an item but never received it. In total, these two types of indirect purchasing were responsible for 97% of this problem.

Purchases of clothing, shoes, or accessories accounted for 29% of situations in which a consumer paid for an item but never received it. Health care products or services were the item involved in 11% of such incidents, while toys or games were involved in 9% of incidents.

Weight-Loss Products

The purchase of weight-loss products that did not work as promised was the next most commonly reported type of fraud included in the 2017 FTC survey. The sellers of bogus weight-loss products promised that using their product would make it easy to lose weight or that the purchaser could lose weight without reducing what they ate or increasing the amount of exercise in which they engaged. However, victims only lost a little of the weight that they thought they would lose or did not lose any weight at all. Around 2.6% of survey participants, representing 6.5 million adults, purchased such weight-loss products that did not deliver as promised.

Of all purchasers of weight-loss products, only 20% indicated that they had lost at least half of the weight they had expected to lose. (These consumers are not considered to have been victims.) Twenty-one percent of purchasers indicated that they had only lost a little of the weight they expected to lose, while 38% did not lose any weight and may have actually gained weight. (An additional 20% reported that they had not used the product.)

Computer Repair

Fraudulent computer repair services were the next most frequently reported of the frauds covered by the 2017 FTC survey, being reported by 2.0% of those interviewed. This represents 5.0 million U.S. consumers. This type of fraud involves consumers paying someone with whom they had not previously done business to perform computer repairs. In order to make the sale, the seller told them that viruses or security vulnerabilities had been detected on the computer, and the computer needed to be fixed immediately. Consumers are also counted as victims if they paid someone with whom they had not previously done business where that person told them that they needed to access the consumer's computer remotely. Consumers often become victims of this type of fraud after receiving a message on their computer screen—such as a pop-up message—telling them that problems have been detected. In other instances, consumers receive telephone calls informing them that the call is coming from a well-known computer company, such as Microsoft, and that their computers purportedly have problems, which the caller can fix.[5]

Falsely Told That Money Was Owed to the Government

Almost 1.5% of those interviewed reported that they had paid money after being told that they owed money to the government or a government agency, or that a court case had been filed against them and they needed to make a payment in connection with that case. Frequently callers represent themselves as being with the Internal Revenue Service and claim the consumer owes back taxes. Callers may also claim to be calling from a court and that the consumer needs to make a payment to avoid being arrested.

Of those making this kind of payment, 38% reported that they had been told that they needed to make the payment because of taxes they owed. Twenty-two percent said that they were told that they needed to make a payment to keep from being arrested or to avoid having to go to court, while 20% indicated that it was because of a traffic ticket.

Who Is More Likely to Have Been a Victim?

In this section, we explore whether the existing statistical data suggest that consumers with certain characteristics are more likely than others to be victims of mass-market consumer frauds. Are older consumers more likely to become victims? How about racial and ethnic minorities? How about consumers who are more skeptical or are overconfident about what they know?[6]

Age

It is widely believed, at least among those who have not studied the issue, that older consumers are more likely to be victims of mass-market consumer fraud. Indeed, a 2016 survey conducted by the Better Business Bureau found that 80% of participants believed that most victims of consumer fraud were over 65 years of age (Fletcher & Pessanha, 2016).

Most research looking at the relationship between age and the prevalence of victimization, however, finds a very different story. The FTC Fraud Surveys have consistently found that those aged 55 and over were less likely than younger consumers to have been victims (Anderson, K. B., 2004, 2007, 2013, 2019). Pooling the results from the three most recent surveys, we find that those between 55 and 64 were 4.8 percentage points less likely to report being a victim of one or more of the covered frauds than those between 35 and 54.

Those between 65 and 74 were an estimated 6.6 percentage points less likely to have been a victim, while those 75 and over were 9.7 percentage points less likely to report. These differences are statistically significant ($p = 0.000$) and are large and meaningful. Averaging across the three surveys, 13.4% of U.S. adult consumers appear to have been victims of one or more of the frauds covered by the surveys. Other researchers who have looked at how victimization rates differ across age groups have similarly found that older consumers are less—not more—likely to have been victims (DeLiema, 2015; DeLiema et al., 2019; Fletcher & Pessanha, 2016; Holtfreter, Reisig, & Pratt, 2008; Mueller et al., 2020; Schoepfer & Piquerro, 2009; Titus et al., 1995; Van Wyk & Benson, 1997; Wood et al., 2018).[7]

While seniors appear to be less likely than younger consumers to be victims, there are some data suggesting that the risk they face may be increasing (Financial Crimes Enforcement Network (2019). Further, if they do become victims, their losses may be greater than for younger consumers. Examining fraud complaints in the Federal Trade Commission's Consumer Sentinel database, the median loss reported by victims between 30 and 39 years of age was $379 in 2019 (Figure 2.2). For older consumers the median reported loss was $600 for those 60 to 69, $800 for those 70 to 79, and $1,600 for those 80 and over (Federal Trade Commission, 2020).

While older consumers appear to be less likely, on average, to become victims of fraud, it would not be surprising to find that some older consumers are more likely to become victims. While not directly looking at fraud, a recent paper by Mazzonna and Peracchi (2020) suggests one characteristic that may identify those who are more vulnerable to fraudulent offers. Mazzona and Peracchi examine the effect of cognitive decline on consumers' wealth management. They find that consumers who have suffered a severe cognitive decline but appear to be unaware of this are more likely to suffer significant losses in the value of their financial portfolios than are those who are aware of declining abilities or have not suffered a severe decline. Mazzona and Peracchi suggest that consumers who are not aware of their cognitive decline may be overconfident about their abilities in financial markets. It seems quite possible that this set of seniors would also be more vulnerable to fraudulent offers.

Overconfidence

Overconfidence is a characteristic that may affect the likelihood of becoming a victim of consumer fraud. Consumers who are overconfident may be more

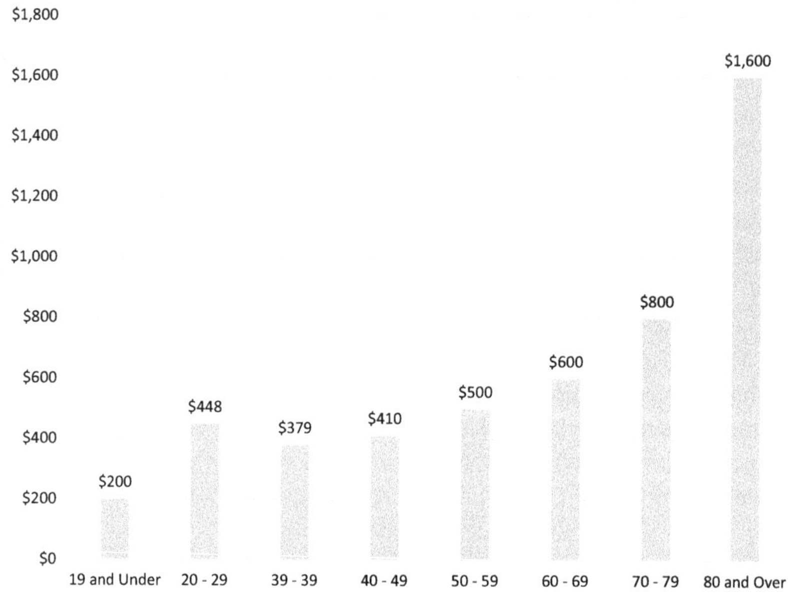

Figure 2.2 Median losses from an incident of fraud, by age.
Source. Federal Trade Commission (2020).

likely to become victims because they believe that they are particularly adept at spotting a bogus claim and can therefore avoid becoming a victim.

The correlation between overconfidence and the likelihood of becoming a victim of consumer fraud is explored in the "Internet Panel Study" (Anderson, K. B., 2016). In this study, which drew participants from a commercial survey firm's online panel, participants were shown mock print ads. Some of the ads included claims that appeared sufficiently outrageous that they would only be found in the promotion of a fraudulent product, while other ads were limited to more plausible claims. After reviewing an ad, participants were asked several questions about the credibility of the ad, as well as how likely they would be to purchase such a product if they saw the ad promoting an actual product. The principal variable of interest in the analysis is whether the participant indicated that they would be "very likely" to purchase the product if it was actually offered.[8] While not directly a measure of actually being a victim of consumer fraud, those who indicate that they would be very likely to purchase one of the fraudulent products included in the study would seem to be more likely to become a victim.

Participants were also asked a series of questions designed to identify which consumers had certain characteristics of interest. The study sought to determine whether the probability that participants said that they were very likely to purchase the product was correlated with the various characteristics considered.

Overconfidence was measured by asking participants to answer a series of six math questions. After answering the questions, participants were asked how many of the questions they thought they had answered correctly and how that number compared to the number of questions other participants had answered correctly. The measure of relative overconfidence was then operationalized by asking participants whether they thought the number of questions they had answered correctly would put them in the first, second, third, or fourth quartile of all participants in the study. Participants' self-ranking was then compared to the quartile in which their answers actually fell.

As has been found in other studies (Dunning et al., 1990; Klayman et al., 1999), on average participants were overconfident about their performance. While over half of all participants—57%—correctly identified the quartile within which their performance fell, 41% said that they were in a higher quartile than they actually were. Only 2% indicated that their answers would put them in a lower quartile.

Those who were overconfident were significantly more likely to indicate that they would be very likely to purchase the product. Participants who said that their answers put them one quartile above where they actually fell—e.g., said that they fell in the second quartile, when their answers actually placed them in the third quartile—were 1.9 percentage points more likely to indicate that they would be very likely to purchase the product than were those who properly placed their performance ($p = 0.003$).

Consumer Literacy

Consumer literacy has attracted considerable attention in the economic literature in recent years. Concern has been expressed that consumers lacking sufficient consumer literacy are ill prepared to make financial decisions and, as a result, do not make good decisions (Allgood & Walstad, 2013; Brown et al., 2017; Lusardi & Mitchell, 2014; Stango & Zinman, 2009). It seems natural, therefore, to ask whether better consumer literacy is associated with a reduced likelihood of becoming a victim of consumer fraud.

The Internet Panel study included seven questions related to consumer literacy. Four of the seven were drawn from the National Financial Capability

Study conducted by the FINRA Investor Education Foundation (FINRA Investor Education Foundation, 2012). The remaining three questions were drawn from questions used in a previous FTC staff study (McAlvanah et al., 2015) and from FTC staff's general knowledge of consumer protection issues. Each of these questions was in a multiple-choice format and participants were allowed to answer that they did not know the answer to a question. Two variables—the number of the seven questions that were answered correctly and the number of questions for which the participant indicated that they did not know the answer—were constructed.

Answering one additional consumer literacy question correctly reduced the likelihood of saying that one would be very likely to purchase a likely-fraudulent product by 0.87 percentage points. This effect was highly significant ($p = 0.009$). Interestingly, answering that one did not know the answer to an additional question also significantly reduced the probability of being very likely to make a purchase ($p = 0.004$).[9] (The effect of answering that one did not know the answer to an additional question is actually greater—1.34 percentage points. However, the difference between the two estimates is not statistically significant.)

What seems to matter is whether or not a question is answered incorrectly. It does not matter whether the question is answered correctly or the participant just says that they do not know that answer. As Mark Twain once observed "It ain't what you don't know that gets you in trouble. It's what you know for sure that just ain't so." One possible explanation for this result may be that it is another manifestation of overconfidence. Those who answer incorrectly may believe that have more knowledge than they in fact do.

Skepticism

One might also hypothesize that consumers who are less skeptical would be more susceptible to fraud because they, inappropriately, trust the honesty of the seller. On the other hand, those who are more skeptical in general would be more skeptical of the claims being made by the perpetrator of a fraudulent offer and thereby be better able to protect themselves from becoming victims of fraud.

Questions designed to measure skepticism were also included in the Internet Panel Study. Two different types of skepticism were considered. The first sought to measure whether participants had the ability to differentiate between problematic marketing situations where extra caution is needed and those where less caution may be needed. The second, drawing on work by Obermiller & Spangenberg (1998), sought to measure the participants' skepticism about advertising claims in general. These two measures of skepticism were each then found to be negatively correlated with the likelihood of being a very likely purchaser ($p = 0.007$). Those who were more skeptical were, as anticipated, less likely to say that they would be very likely to purchase.

Race and Ethnicity

The analysis of the FTC Fraud Surveys showed that racial and ethnic minorities were more likely to report having been victims than were non-Hispanic whites. Again, combining the data from the 2005, 2011, and 2017 FTC surveys, African Americans were 6.8 percentage points more likely to report having been a victim than were non-Hispanic whites, while Hispanics were 4.2 percentage points more likely to so report. These differences are statistically significant ($p = 0.000$ for African Americans and 0.005 for Hispanics).[10]

One possible explanation for the finding that Hispanics are more likely to report being victims might be that they may have been less comfortable doing business in English. To test this possibility, participants in the FTC surveys were asked whether they used any languages other than English in conducting personal business. Those who said that they used a language other than English were asked "if you were engaged in a somewhat complicated transaction, such as trying to buy a home, rent an apartment or purchase a car, would you be comfortable conducting the transaction in English?"

Separating Hispanics by whether they would be uncomfortable doing business in English showed that Hispanics who indicated that they were not comfortable doing business in English were *less* likely to have reported being a victim than were those who said that they were comfortable doing so. Hispanics who said that they were not comfortable in English were 3.5 percentage points *less* likely to have reported being a victim of any of the frauds covered by the survey than were non-Hispanic whites, though this difference was not statistically significant ($p = 0.130$). Hispanics who said that they were comfortable doing business in English, however, were 6.3 percentage points more likely than non-Hispanic whites to report having been a victim ($p = 0.000$). Again, one wonders if this is another manifestation of overconfidence. Are those who say that they are comfortable doing business in English less facile in the language than they may think?

Routine Activity

Numerous authors in recent years have suggested that two theories in criminology—routine activity theory and self-control theory—provide useful insights into who is victimized by frauds (DeLiema, Shadel, & Pak, 2020; Holtfreter, Reisig, & Pratt, 2008; Reisig & Holtfreter, 2013; van Wilsem, 2013; Pratt, Holtfreter, & Reisig, 2010).

In proposing their routine activity theory and seeking to explain changing trends in the commission of crimes, Cohen and Felson (1979) noted that crime requires the convergence of three elements: "(1) motivated offenders, (2) suitable targets and (3) the absence of capable guardians against a violation." While Cohen and Felson were seeking to explain where violent crimes were more likely to occur and how this might change over time, the theory also provides insights for understanding which consumers are most at-risk of being victimized by mass-market consumer fraud.

Perpetrators of mass-market consumer fraud can easily find "suitable targets" for their schemes—whether by making fraudulent claims in advertising on the Internet, via social media, or in cold-call telephone calls. (Indeed, it has been suggested that fraudsters may intentionally make obvious grammatical errors or make claims that most consumers will not find credible so as to weed out those who read closely enough to notice the mistakes as these people are unlikely to fall victim to the scam (Herley, 2012; Steinberg, 2019).) Such solicitations—particularly telemarketing calls—may also limit access to capable guardians who could steer the victim away from falling for the perpetrator's scheme. Perpetrators of mass-market fraud also generally sell their products in a setting where the purchaser has no opportunity to examine the items before purchasing or to take the item home with them.

We therefore identify those most likely to fall victim to a mass-market consumer fraud as those who have purchased an item from someone with whom they have not previously done business after learning about the product via a mass-market media. The purchase was made as a result of a telemarketing call, after receiving an unsolicited commercial ("SPAM") email, or after seeing a television advertisement or infomercial. And, the purchase was made without visiting the seller's store or other place of business.[11] We identify those who have made such a purchase as having engaged in Risky Purchasing Practices.

Using this definition, the data from the three FTC Fraud Surveys show that those who have made risky purchases were 13.4 percentage points more likely to have reported being a victim of a mass-market consumer fraud ($p = 0.000$). Looking separately at the effects of making such a purchase as a result of a telemarketing call, after receiving a SPAM email, or after seeing a television ad or infomercial, we find that those who made such a purchase as a result of a telemarketing call were 31.0 percentage points more likely to have reported being a victim. Those who made the purchase in response to a SPAM email were 12.2 percentage points more likely, while those who did so after seeing a television ad or infomercial were 10.7 percentage points more likely. (For all three of these estimates $p = 0.000$.).

Self-Control

As originally formulated, the theory of self-control explained the tendency to commit crime, not to be victimized by it (Hirschi & Gottfredson, 1993; Pratt & Cullen, 2000). People with low self-control were seen as availing themselves of the immediate gratification afforded by engaging in crime and ignoring the long-term consequences of committing a criminal act. Schreck (1999), however, extended the theory to victimization, suggesting that those with less self-control were less likely to defer immediate enjoyment to make certain that they protected themselves from the risks associated with an immediately enjoyable action (see also Bossler & Holt, 2010).

Only one of the FTC surveys directly asked questions that can be used as measures of the participants' self-reported extent of self-control. The 2011 survey asked a number of questions about how participants saw themselves. These included questions about whether the person would describe themselves as a planner, as impulsive, as self-controlled, and as enjoying spending money. After creating a single measure of self-control by summing the responses to the four questions after reversing the responses to impulsivity and enjoying spending money, 11.8% of those classified as having low self-control reported having been a victim in the previous year. This compared to 10.3% among those classified as having medium self-control and 10.6% of those with high self-control. Thus, the relationship here has the correct sign. However, none of these differences is statistically significant ($p = 0.642$) (Anderson, K. B., 2013).

The Internet Panel Study also included these four questions asking consumers to rate their self-control. Of these four measures, only rating oneself as more impulsive was significantly correlated with being more likely to indicate that one was very likely to purchase a fraudulent product ($p = 0.000$).

In addition to the self-reported measures, data from the FTC Fraud Surveys provide several behavioral measures of self-control. The surveys asked about behavioral characteristics—such as the general willingness to take risks or having too much debt—that may be associated with self-control. Finding a positive correlation between a higher probability of being a victim and the value of the behavioral measure consistent with low self-control would therefore support the theory of self-control.

In the two most recent surveys, participants were asked how willing they were to take risks. Self-control theory may suggest that those who are more willing to take risk have less self-control, being less willing to give up the immediate gratification from taking the risk. Consistent with that theory, we find that those with a high self-described willingness to take risks are 8.4 percentage points more likely to report having been a victim of one of the mass-market frauds covered by the survey than those with a low willingness. Those with low-moderate or high-moderate willingness to take risks were 2.5 percentage points and 3.6 percentage points more likely to report having been victims than those with a low willingness. (Overall the relationship was highly significant, $p = 0.000$.).

The Internet Panel Study also asked about a participant's general willingness to take risks. The results of that study also showed that those who described themselves as being more willing to take risks were more likely to indicate that they would be very likely to purchase a likely-fraudulent product. However, the effect here was only significant at the 10% level ($p = 0.059$).

The second measure is drawn from a question included in all three surveys that asked survey participants to describe their current amount of personal debt. Participants were asked whether: (i) Their current debt was more than they could handle financially, (ii) Their current debt was about as much as they could handle, (iii) They could handle additional debt, or (iv) They did not have any personal debt. At least in some cases, those with more debt than they could handle may be people with limited self-control, having exhibited an inability to control their current consumption to limit the pain of having excessive debt in the future. And, consistent with the self-control theory, those who characterized themselves as having more debt than they could handle financially were 10.9 percentage points more likely to report having been a victim than those who indicated that they had about as much debt as they could handle. Those who said that they could handle more debt and those who said that they did not have any debt were 1.1 percentage points and 3.4 percentage points, respectively, less likely than those who had about as much debt as they could handle to report having been a victim. (The overall relationship between the amount of debt a person had and the likelihood of reporting being a victim was highly significant $p = 0.000$.).

Also in the 2011 and 2017 surveys, participants were asked whether, during the previous two years, they had experienced a "serious negative life event, such as a divorce, the death of a family member or close friend, a serious injury or illness in your family, or the loss of a job". Whether one experiences a serious negative life event may not depend on whether one has high and low self-control. However, it may be that even those who normally have a high degree of self-control have less self-control in the aftermath of a negative life event. They are distracted by the event.

We therefore examine the correlation between having experienced a serious negative life event in the preceding two years and the likelihood of having reported being a victim of one or more of the frauds covered by the FTC surveys. What we find is that, pooling the data for the 2011 and 2017 surveys, those who reported having experienced such a negative event were 8.5 percentage points more likely to report having been a victim than were those who had not. The difference is highly statistically significant ($p = 0.000$).

In sum, the evidence from the FTC Fraud Surveys suggests that self-control is correlated with fraud victimization. An index of self-reported characteristics measuring self-control does not appear to provide strong support for the hypothesis. However, looking at other behavioral characteristics that seem likely to be associated with self-control suggests that those with low self-control are significantly more likely to report having been victims.

Conclusion and Discussion

Mass-market consumer fraud is not a new problem. However, technological improvements in telecommunications and transportation networks have provided enhanced opportunities for fraudsters. Today, those seeking to promote fraudulent offerings can cheaply market to the entire world and do so with considerable anonymity. This allows them to market existing fraudulent offerings more intensively and also to market offerings that would not previously have been economic.

A significant share of the U.S. population reports having fallen victim to a fraudulent offer each year. Looking at just 18 types of fraud, a 2017 survey commissioned by the Federal Trade Commission found that an estimated 15.9% of participants in a survey of U.S. adults reported having been victims of fraud during the previous year.

While everyone is a potential victim of fraud, the existing data show that some consumers appear to be at greater risk. Contrary to popular belief, older consumers are less, rather than more, likely to report having been victims. Being overconfident is correlated with a higher prevalence of victimization, as is answering more questions about consumer literacy incorrectly.

(Answering correctly and indicating that one does not know the answer both appear to provide protection.) Greater skepticism is correlated with a reduced risk of reporting being a victim. African American and Hispanic minorities are more likely to report having been victims. Finally, data from the FTC Fraud Surveys and the Internet Panel Study offer some support for the routine activity and self-control models of victimization.

Future Work

The prevalence of mass-market consumer fraud and the types of fraud being perpetrated do not appear to change quickly. However, fraudsters, unsurprisingly, take advantage of new opportunities as they arise. Two of the five most prevalent types of fraud found in the 2017 FTC survey—Fraudulent Computer Repair and being Falsely Told That You Owed Money to the Government—were not sufficiently on the radar to be included in the earlier surveys. New fraud surveys probably are not needed every year. However, updated surveys, perhaps with changes to incorporate the changing landscape of fraud, will continue to be needed—probably something like every five or six years.

It is important to recognize that the survey work discussed here does not cover all types of fraud. In particular, frauds related to passive investments—for example, purchases of stocks or bonds—are not included. It would be nice to see future research that is better able to incorporate some of the types of fraud that have not been included to date. It should also be noted that the analysis reported here is based on surveys that only included consumers in the United States.

It would also be interesting to see whether alternative characteristics, such as measures of personality or measures of cognitive decline among the elderly—are correlated with victimization. It would also be interesting to see alternative measures of some of the concepts that are analyzed here—ideally measures that have been previously discussed and validated in the literature—used in future studies.

Notes

1 Formerly Economist, Bureau of Economics, Federal Trade Commission, Washington, D.C. The views expressed here are only the views of the author and do not necessarily reflect the views of the Federal Trade Commission or any of its Commissioners. I thank Scott Syms for excellent research assistance and Emma Fletcher, Jan Pappalardo, Patti Poss, Dave Schmidt, and Felix Soldner for helpful comments.

2 Types of fraud that were not covered included frauds that involved passive investments, such as the purchase of stocks or bonds. Grandparent scams and romance scams were also not included. The Better Business Bureau has published a series of studies on a number of other frauds that were not directly covered by the survey, including puppy scams (Baker, 2017), online romance scams (Baker, 2018), and rental listing scams (Baker, 2019).

3 Because these figures are from a consumer survey, the prevalence of frauds will be under-reported if consumers who experience the various included problems do not recognize that something has happened to them. This seems particularly likely to be a problem in the case of unauthorized billing. If consumers did not recognize that they were being billed, for example on their credit cards, for something they had not authorized, they will not be able to report it in the interview.

In some instances, an unauthorized bill may be sent by mistake rather than as part of an attempt to defraud consumers. Such incidents should not be considered to be incidents of fraud. In order to minimize the risk of including such instances in the measure of fraud, survey participants who reported never having received an unauthorized bill were asked whether they had attempted to obtain a refund and, if so, whether the seller had been willing to provide a refund or other adjustment that had satisfied the consumer. Where a refund had been sought and obtained, the incident was not considered to be fraudulent.

4 As with unauthorized billing, in some instances, the failure to fulfill an order may be the result of a problem in a seller's order fulfillment process or in the shipment of the product. Again, such incidents should not be considered to be incidents of fraud. As with unauthorized billing, the survey included questions asking those who reported having never received an item whether they had sought and received a refund or other adjustment.

5 Consumers who took their computers to a store to get them fixed or who dealt with someone with whom they had previously done business are not considered to be victims.

6 The results in this section of the chapter are drawn either from analyses of the data from the FTC surveys or the Internet Panel Study (Anderson, 2016).

Where the FTC Fraud Surveys are the source, the reported statistics are based on an analysis pooling the data from the three most-recent FTC surveys. (Differences between the initial and the later surveys make pooling across all four surveys infeasible.) While there are significant differences in the overall victimization rates across the three included surveys, the effects of different characteristics do not differ significantly across the surveys. Therefore, the results from the three surveys are pooled after controlling for the survey from which the observation came. Separate analyses were performed for each characteristic. The reported results, therefore, do not control for the effect of other characteristics that may be correlated with the characteristic under consideration. However, as reported in the reports on the different individual surveys, the results for the univariate analyses are generally similar to the results when one controls for the other characteristics for which data are available (Anderson, 2007, 2013, 2019).

The analysis in Anderson (2016), including the results reported here, consisted of a probit regression that controlled simultaneously for all of the included variables and included all of the ads that had been used—both the likely-fraudulent and the more-plausible ones.

7 Raval (2020) finds that victimization is higher in communities where the median age is older. More specifically, communities with a median age of 55 have higher rates of victimization than those with a median age of 25.

8 Participants rated the likelihood of buying the product on a 7-point Likert scale where a 1 indicated that the participant would be "Extremely Likely" to purchase the product, while a 7 indicated that a purchase was "Extremely Unlikely." Those who rated the likelihood of purchase as a 1 or a 2 were considered to be very likely to purchase the product if it was available.

9 McAlvanah et al. (2015) also found that those who answered more of the consumer literacy questions correctly rated the likely-fraudulent ads as being less credible. However, there was no significant relationship between indicating that the participant did not know the answer to a question and credibility.

10 Raval (2020) also finds that communities that are heavily African American have higher rates of victimization. However, he finds that communities that are heavily Hispanic have reduced victimization rates.

11 Of course, not all purchases that meet these criteria are fraudulent. For example, consumers may have placed an order online for something sold by a well-known firm, but with whom they have not previously done business. Such a purchase would not seem to present a substantial risk of becoming a victim of a mass-market consumer fraud even if it was placed after seeing a television ad.

References

Allgood, S., & Walstad, W. (2013). Financial literacy and credit card behavior: A cross-sectional analysis by age. *Numeracy: Advancing Education in Quantitative Literacy*, *6*(2), 3. DOI: 10.5038/1936-4660.6.2.3.

Anderson, A. (2000). *Snake oil, hustlers, and hambones: The American medicine show*. McFaland & Company, North Carolina.

Anderson, K. B. (2004). *Consumer fraud in the United States: An FTC survey*. Retrieved from: https://www.ftc.gov/sites/default/files/documents/reports/consumer-fraud-united-states-ftc-survey/040805confraudrpt.pdf

Anderson, K. B. (2007). *Consumer fraud in the United States: The second FTC survey*. Retrieved from: https://www.ftc.gov/sites/default/files/documents/reports/consumer-fraud-united-states-second-federal-trade-commission-survey-staff-report-federal-trade/fraud.pdf

Anderson, K. B. (2013). *Consumer fraud in the United States, 2011: The third FTC survey*. Retrieved from: https://www.ftc.gov/sites/default/files/documents/reports/consumer-fraud-united-states-2011-third-ftc-survey/130419fraudsurvey_0.pdf

Anderson, K. B. (2016). *Mass-market consumer fraud: Who Is most susceptible to becoming a victim?* Working Paper No. 332, Bureau of Economics, Federal Trade Commission. Retrieved from: https://www.ftc.gov/system/files/documents/reports/mass-market-consumer-fraud-who-most-susceptible-becoming-victim/working_paper_332.pdf

Anderson, K. B. (2019). *Mass-market consumer fraud in the United States: A 2017 update*. Retrieved from: https://www.ftc.gov/system/files/documents/reports/mass-market-consumer-fraud-united-states-2017-update/p105502massmarketconsumerfraud2017report.pdf

Baker, C. S. (2017). *Puppy scams: How fake online pet sellers steal from unsuspecting pet buyers*. Better Business Bureau International Investigations Initiative. Retrieved from: https://

www.bbb.org/globalassets/article-library/puppy-scam-study/puppy-scams-bbb-study-20170901.pdf

Baker, C. S. (2018). *Online romance scams: A better business bureau study on how scammers use impersonation, blackmail and trickery to steal from unsuspecting daters*. Better Business Bureau International Investigations Initiative. Retrieved from: https://www.bbb.org/globalassets/local-bbbs/council-113/media/scam-studies/bbb-study-online-romance-scams-study.pdf

Baker, C. S. (2019). *Is that rental listing real?: A BBB study of rental scams involving apartments, houses and vacation properties*. Better Business Bureau International Investigations Initiative. Retrieved from: https://www.bbb.org/globalassets/local-bbbs/council-113/rentalscams/rentalscamstudy.pdf

Baker, C. S. (2020). *Baker fraud report*. Retrieved from: https://bakerfraudreport.com/

Beals, M., DeLiema, M., & Devey, M. (2015). *Framework for a taxonomy of fraud*. Stanford Center on Longevity. Retrieved from: http://longevity3.stanford.edu/wp-content/uploads/2015/7/FFRC_Taxonomy_FullReport_7-22-15.pdf

Bhattarai, A. (December 25, 2019). As more people shop online, fake stores have snowballed. *The Washington Post*, p. A16.

Bossler, A. M., & Holt, T. J. (2010). The effect of self-control on victimization in the cyberworld. *Journal of Criminal Justice*, *38*(3), 227–236. DOI: 10.1016/j.jcrimjus.2010.03.001.

Bracken, S. (2020). Declaration of Samuel Bracken. filed in U.S. v. Nicholas Palumbo, et al., 1:20-cv-00473 (ED. New York, filed January 28, 2020). Retrieved from: https://www.justice.gov/opa/press-release/file/1240026/download

Brown, J. R., Kapteyn, A., Luttmer, E. F. P., Mitchell, O. S. (2017). Cognitive constraints on valuing annuities. *Journal of the European Economic Association*, *15*(2), 429–462. DOI: 10.1093/jeea/jvw009.

Cohen, L. E., & Felson, M. (1979). Social change and crime rate trends: A routine activity approach. *American Sociological Review*, *44*(4), 588–608. DOI: 10.2307/2094589.

DeLiema, M. (2015). *Using mixed methods to identify the characteristics of older fraud victims*. PhD Dissertation, University of Southern California. Retrieved from: http://digitallibrary.usc.edu/cdm/ref/collection/p15799coll3/id/537449

DeLiema, M., Fletcher, E., Kieffer, C. N., Mottola, G. R., Pessanha, R., & Tumpower, M. (2019). *Exposed to scams: What separates victims from non-victims?* FINRA Investor Education Foundation, BBB Institute for Marketplace Trust, Stanford Center on Longevity. Retrieved from: https://www.finrafoundation.org/sites/finrafoundation/files/exposed-to-scams-what-separates-victims-from-non-victims_0_0.pdf

DeLiema, M., Shadel, D., & Pak, K. (2020). Profiling victims of investment fraud: Mindsets and risky behaviors. *Journal of Consumer Research*, *46*(5), 904–914. DOI: 10.1093/jcr/ucz020.

Dotinga, R. (February 18, 2020). Toxic legacy of radiation quackery. *The Washington Post*, pp. E1, E5.

Dunning, D., Griffin, D. W., Milojkovic, J. D., & Ross, L. (1990). The overconfidence effect in social prediction. *Journal of Personality and Social Psychology*, *58*(4), 658–681. DOI: 10.1037/0022-3514.58.4.568.

Federal Bureau of Investigation, Criminal Justice Information Services Division (2017) *Crime in the United States*. Table 1. Retrieved from: https://ucr.fbi.gov/crime-in-the-u.s/2017/crime-in-the-u.s.-2017/topic-pages/tables/table-1.

Federal Trade Commission (1933). *In the Matter of D.H. Buxton, trading as Buxton Medicine Co.*, 18 FTC 561 (December 8).

Federal Trade Commission (2020). *Consumer Sentinel Network data book 2019*. Retrieved from: https://www.ftc.gov/system/files/documents/reports/consumer-sentinel-network-data-book-2019/consumer_sentinel_network_data_book_2019.pdf

Financial Crimes Enforcement Network (2019). *Elders face increased financial threat from domestic and foreign actors*. Retrieved from: https://www.fincen.gov/sites/default/files/shared/FinCEN%20Financial%20Trend%20Analysis%20Elders_FINAL%20508.pdf

FINRA Investor Education Foundation (2012). "2012 national financial capability study state-by-state survey instrument." Retrieved from: https://www.usfinancialcapability.org/downloads/NFCS_2012_State_by_State_Qre.pdf

Fletcher, E. (2018). "Scammers increasingly demand payment by gift card." Federal Trade Commission Data Consumer Protection Data Spotlight. Retrieved from: https://www.ftc.gov/news-events/blogs/data-spotlight/2018/10/scammers-increasingly-demand-payment-gift-card.

Flatley, J. (2016). *Overview of fraud statistics: Year ending Mar 2016*. Office of National Statistics. Retrieved from: https://www.ons.gov.uk/peoplepopulationandcommunity/crimeandjustice/articles/overviewoffraudstatistics/yearendingmarch2016

Fletcher, E., & Pessanha, R. (2016). *Cracking the invulnerability illusion: Stereotypes, optimism bias, and the way forward for marketplace scam education*. BBB Institute for Marketplace Trust. Retrieved from: https://www.bbb.org/globalassets/shared/media/truth-about-scams/bbb-scamprogram-whitepaper-08-digital-0630.pdf

Herley, C. (2012). Why do Nigerian scammers say they are from Nigeria?. *Proceedings of the Workshop on the Economics of Information Security*. Retrieved from: https://www.microsoft.com/en-us/research/wp-content/uploads/2016/02/WhyFromNigeria.pdf

Hirschi, T., & Gottfredson, M. (1993). Commentary: Testing the general theory of crime. *Journal of Research in Crime and Delinquency, 30*(1), 47–54. DOI: 10.1177%2F0022427893030001004.

Holtfreter, K., Reisig, M. D., & Pratt, T. C. (2008). Low self-control, routine activities, and fraud victimization. *Criminology, 46*(1), 189–220. DOI: 10.1111%2Fj.1745-9125.2008.00101.x.

Kang, L., & Pedersen, N. (2017). *Quackery: A brief history of the worst ways to cure everything*, Workman Publishing, New York.

Klayman, J., Soll, J. B., Gonzalez-Vallejo, C., & Barlas, S. (1999). Overconfidence: It depends on how, what and whom you ask. *Organizational Behavior and Human Decision Processes, 79*(3), 216–247. DOI: 10.1006/obhd.1999.2847.

Krouse, S. (November 21, 2019). Robocall scams exist because they work—One woman's story shows how. *The Wall Street Journal*.

Lusardi, A., & Mitchell, O. S. (2014). The economic importance of financial literacy: Theory and evidence. *Journal of Economic Literature, 52*(1), 5–44. DOI: 10.1257/jel.52.1.5.

Mazzonna, F., & Peracchi, F. (2020). *Are older people aware of their cognitive decline? Misperception and financial decision making*. IZA DP 13725. Retrieved from: https://www.iza.org/publications/dp/13725/are-older-people-aware-of-their-cognitive-decline-misperception-and-financial-decision-making

McAlvanah, P., Anderson, K. B., Letzler, R., & Mountjoy, J. (2015). *Fraudulent advertising susceptibility: An experimental approach*. Working Paper No. 325, Bureau of Economics, Federal Trade Commission. Retrieved from: https://www.ftc.gov/system/files/

documents/reports/fraudulent-advertising-susceptibility-experimental-approach/wp325.pdf
Milano, D. (2017). "Marketing stories: Snake oil and truth in advertising." Retrieved from: https://www.ceros.com/originals/strange-true-marketing-stories-snake-oil-truth-advertising/.
Mueller, E., Wood, S., Hanoch, Y, Huang, Y., & Reed, C. (2020). Older and wiser: Age differences in susceptibility to investment fraud: The protective role of emotional intelligence. *Journal of Elder Abuse & Neglect*, *32*(2), 152–172. DOI: 10.1080/08946566.2020.1736704.
Obermiller, C., & Spangenberg, E. R. (1998). Development of a scale to measure consumer skepticism toward advertising. *Journal of Consumer Psychology*, *7*(2), 159–186. DOI: 10.1207/s15327663jcp0702_03.
Pratt, T. C., & Cullen, F. T. (2000). The empirical status of Gottfredson and Hirschi's general theory of crime: A meta-analysis. *Criminology*, *38*(3), 931–964. DOI: 10.1111/j.1745-9125.2000.tb00911.x.
Pratt, T. C., Holtfreter, K., & Reisig, M. D. (2010). Routine online activity and internet fraud targeting: Extending the generality of routine activity theory. *Journal of Research in Crime and Delinquency*, *47*(3). DOI: 10.1177/0022427810365903.
Raval, D. (2020). Who is victimized by fraud? Evidence from consumer protection cases. *Journal of Consumer Policy*. DOI: 10.1007/s10603-020-09466-w.
Reisig, M. D., & Holtfreter, K. (2013). Shopping fraud victimization among the elderly. *Journal of Financial Crime*, *20*(3), 324–337. DOI: 10.1108/JFC-03-2013-0014.
Schoepfer, A., & Piquerro, N. L. (2009). Studying the correlates of fraud victimization and reporting. *Journal of Criminal Justice*, *37*(2), 209–215. DOI: 10.1016/j.jcrimjus.2009.02.003.
Schreck, C. (1999). Criminal victimization and low self-control: An extension and test of a general theory of crime. *Justice Quarterly*, *16*(3), 633–654. DOI: 10.1080/07418829900094291.
Stango, V., & Zinman, J. (2009). Exponential growth bias and household finance. *The Journal of Finance*, *64*(6), 2807–2849. DOI: 10.1111/j.1540-6261.2009.01518.x.
Steinberg, J. (2019). *Why scammers make spelling and grammar "mistakes."* Retrieved from: https://josephsteinberg.com/why-scammers-make-spelling-and-grammar-mistakes
Titus, R. M., Heinzelmann, F., & Boyle, J. M. (1995). Victimization of persons by fraud. *Crime & Delinquency*, *41*(1), 54–72. DOI: 10.1177%2F0011128795041001004.
U.K. Office of Fair Trade (2006). "Research on impact of mass marketed scams: A summary of research into the impact of scams on UK consumers," Report OFT883.
U.S. Bureau of the Census (2019). *E-Stats 2017: Measuring the electronic economy*. Retrieved from: https://www.census.gov/content/dam/Census/library/publications/2017/econ/e17-estats1.pdf
U.S. Department of Justice (2017). *Mass marketing fraud*. Retrieved from: https://www.justice.gov/criminal-fraud/mass-marketing-fraud
van Wilsem, J. (2013). "Bought it, but never got it": Assessing risk factors for online consumer fraud victimization. *European Sociological Review*, *29*(2), 168–178. DOI: 10.1093/esr/jcr05.
Van Wyk, J., & Benson, M. (1997). Fraud victimization: Risky business or just bad luck?. *American Journal of Criminal Justice*, *21*, 163–179. DOI: 10.1007/BF02887448.
Wood, S., Liu, P., Hanoch, Y., Xi, P., & Klapatch, L. (2018). Call to claim your prize: Perceived benefits and risk drive intention to comply in a mass marketing scam. *Journal of Experimental Psychology: Applied*, *24*(2), 196–206. DOI: 10.1037/xap0000167.

3 Scams in the Time of COVID-19: Pandemic Trends in Scams and Fraud

Stacey Wood, David Hengerer, and Yaniv Hanoch

Unfortunately, natural disasters happen all too regularly. In 2005, Hurricane Katrina struck the Gulf Coast of the United States, causing major damage to infrastructure and the loss of many lives. A year earlier, on Boxing Day 2004, one of the most destructive earthquakes and tsunamis originated from the Indian Ocean, leading to unparalleled devastation and loss of life. In both cases, financial contributions and aid poured in from every corner of the earth, in a clear manifestation of human generosity. At the same time, however, disasters have long been a fertile ground for scammers. Following Hurricane Katrina, a surge in scams was reported similar to other disasters (i.e. see https://www.theguardian.com/world/2006/jun/15/hurricanekatrina.usa; https://www.govtech.com/em/disaster/Hurricane-Katrina-Fraud-Task.htm). The COVID-19 pandemic is no different. While many acts of kindness have been reported, scam incidents across the globe have risen to new heights. It is currently untapped territory in terms of understanding the types of techniques scammers employ, and how they use them to capitalize on major disasters Here, we examine some of the main approaches used by scammers, as well as the possible consequences.

We (the authors) were working on this book volume when the COVID-19 pandemic broke out and were witness to the pandemic of scams, cons, and

DOI: 10.4324/9781003017189-3

fraud that came along with it. The Federal Trade Commission (FTC) received more than 18,000 coronavirus complaints from January 2020 to April 15, 2020 (Carrns, 2020), and Google reported an unprecedented number of scam emails, having to block over 18 million a day. In the UK, likewise, a wide range of scams have circulated, trying to lure individuals via emails, false websites, phone calls, and many other techniques, leading most news outlets to raise alarm and inform the wider public. During periods of social isolation, feelings of loneliness increase and people are turning to social media and online platforms to fulfil their social needs (Le Couteur et al., 2020) as well as perform activities of daily life (e.g., banking, submission of medical forms, etc.). These shifting behaviors—from face-to-face to online banking and shopping, coupled with increased calls for donation and governmental provision of funds and tax rebates, have all created a fertile ground for scammers to take advantage of people and organizations. This was even further exacerbated by the increasing sense of confusion and uncertainty. Understanding how scammers work and lure potential victims is the first step to reducing the rate of scams and fraud under such conditions. The goal of this chapter is to play witness to this phenomenon, discuss tactics, psychological factors, and contextual factors that may be activated during times of extreme uncertainty that benefit scammers, document trends in scams that have been occurring during the COVID-19 pandemic, and review the rapidly emerging literature produced during this time.

Tactics Employed by Scammers

Scarcity

In the field of persuasion, there are well-documented tactics that are used by legitimate marketers and scammers alike (see Cialdini, 2006). Scammers employ well-known tactics to lure consumers—perhaps foremost among them, the principles of scarcity and authority. Indeed, it is an aspect of human nature to perceive items that are scarce to be more valuable. As a marketing tactic, scarcity is used by legitimate vendors all the time ("only one seat left!", "sale ends today!") to motivate consumers to purchase their items—just think of Black Friday. However, *perceived* scarcity and *actual* scarcity of some items (such as toilet paper, masks) have created excessive demand. Scammers can capitalize on these fears in a number of ways: by marketing fake products, by price gouging, or by not sending any product at all. As the pandemic rages on, these scams expanded to the domains of contact tracing, treatments, government aid, donations, and vaccine access.

Authority

Individuals across the UK have received emails and texts telling them that "Someone who came in contact with you tested positive or has shown symptoms for Covid-19 & recommends you self-isolate/get tested." They were then asked to click on a link that asked them to provide personal information that was later used to access their bank accounts. It is little wonder that scammers have used the NHS, as it is one of the most highly trusted institutions in the UK. Scholars of persuasion techniques will not be surprised by this approach, therefore, as scammers make use of the perception of authority to abuse individuals (Cialdini, 2006). Research from the persuasion literature has demonstrated that consumers find "authoritative" sources to be more credible and therefore more persuasive in their messaging. The term "authority" can also refer to any source of influence. Often consumers look to a brand, website, or an influencer that they trust when making decisions around purchasing items or acquiring and acting on information regarding a crisis. Scammers frequently impersonate a legitimate website or brand, or, in some cases, co-opt the authority of others (posting a bogus ad on actual Facebook or Amazon) and profit until they are caught. We are also seeing the impersonation of government agencies, such as the World Health Organization (WHO), the Centers for Disease Control and Prevention (CDC), and the Internal Revenue Service (IRS) by scammers with COVID-related scams. In normal daily life, getting a text message from the CDC would be quite unlikely, but during the present crisis, such a text message may be viewed as more credible.

Time Pressure

As COVID-19 has been associated with serious negative health outcomes and even death, responding quickly to symptoms can be a lifesaver. It is no wonder that many scams have pretended to offer testing and treatments. The U.S. Department of Health and Human Services Office of Inspector General, in fact, has issued a specific warning for Medicare beneficiaries (typically older adults) who have been offered faster COVID-19 testing. In this case, scammers are taking advantage of what Nobel-winning economist Daniel Kahneman describes as "System One thinking"—that which is automatic, fast, and emotional. Indeed, under conditions of heightened or deep uncertainties, reverting to System One processing is typical (Kahneman, 2013). Hence, for scammers, if people do not read ads carefully (such as noticing the URLs), if consumers do not pay attention to peripheral information (such as spelling mistakes), or if the public's fear of the pandemic overcomes reasoning (such as feeling the need to stock toilet paper), they are more likely to fall prey to scammers. Individuals should make every effort to verify the source of the offers they get, whether by Googling and checking the legitimacy of the website—a key tool in reducing the likelihood of falling prey to scammers—or, when relevant, by speaking to their physicians about any medical treatments and tests they are considering. Misinformation and biased media coverage are often the sources of fear and panic, so it is important that individuals do not forget to take the time to fact check.

Psychological Factors Linked to Scam Vulnerability

Uncertainty

The COVID-19 pandemic is being described as a so-called "black swan" or "once in 100 years" event. The combination of lack of personal history with such an event created a great deal of uncertainty among individuals. Furthermore, COVID-19 has created unparalleled impact on almost all facets of life, such that uncertainty now prevails in most day-to day activities. Are stores going to be open and will have they have enough products? Will schools be open? Will I be able to work? Is my business going to survive? Will live entrainment (such as dance, concerts, plays, etc.) be back? These levels of uncertainty go far beyond the normal uncertainties that have existed prior to COVID-19, and their impact has not yet been determined. We know, however, that uncertainty is associated with a host of negative psychological outcomes. McEvoy and Mahoney (2011) have found that intolerance of uncertainty was partially associated with anxiety and depression. Others have shown a link between intolerance of uncertainty and worry (Dugas et al., 2012). Specifically, there are growing indications (e.g., Altig et al., 2020) that COVID-19 has had an enormous impact on economic uncertainties, suggesting that both organizations and individuals might be placed at a precarious financial position. Fueling further the sense of uncertainty was the lack of unified message from the authorities regarding the pandemic (whether federal or local). Indeed, often federal and local messages would be competing and conflicting, and at times there was also simply a lack of vital information.

One group that has taken advantage of the current situation is phishing scammers. One type of fraud that has been very prevalent is the business email compromise (BEC) scam, otherwise known as CEO fraud. In general, BEC scams are a type of phishing scam where a cybercriminal pretends to be an executive at a company and sends an email to a lower-level employee, typically someone who works in a finance department. In these communications the scammer directs them to transfer funds to a fake account. During the pandemic, emails from corporate executives containing "critical" information became more plausible. Time pressure is often used in conjunction with BEC scams.

Increase in Psychological Disorders and Vulnerabilities

The coronavirus pandemic is an epidemiological and psychological crisis with many individuals living in isolation, facing financial hardship, and at high risk of developing psychological disorders including anxiety and depression. All of these factors have been linked to increased risk of financial fraud in older adults (Liu et al., 2017; Wang & Dong, 2018).

For example, Lichtenberg et al. (2013) developed a model of fraud susceptibility based upon three factors: depression, changes in social-needs fulfilment, and financial satisfaction. Social-needs fulfilment refers to humans' needs for status, validation, and affection, all of which may have been impacted by forces within the pandemic: Individuals who are isolated may not experience as much affection; those who have lost jobs will have lost status and opportunity for external validation; and financial satisfaction may have also been dealt a blow during the pandemic with record-high levels of unemployment, furloughs, and downsizing.

Depression as a risk factor for fraud and financial exploitation has extensive empirical support (Beach et al., 2010). Lichtenberg et al. (2016) reported that a diagnosis of depression significantly increased the likelihood of fraud vulnerability using the health and retirement survey data in a large sample. Depression and loneliness were also found to be independent predictors of financial exploitation in older adults in a study of 395 community-dwelling participants (Liu et al., 2017). Social isolation has also been related to depression (Antonucci et al., 1997).

The pandemic has increased psychological distress across age groups. Overall, given the data suggesting that depression and isolation have increased during the pandemic (Huang & Zhao, 2020; Salari et al., 2020), it is reasonable to assume an increase in psychological vulnerability to fraud and scams across the lifespan.

Boredom

During quarantine, many leisure activities have been curtailed and consumers had little to do. As a result, consumers have been more available to carefully go through the mail, read every junk email, answer phone calls from unknown callers, and join dating apps. The dating app Tinder president, Elie Siedman, reported that on Sunday March 29, Tinder recorded more than 3 billion "swipes" on the platform, the highest single-day activity volume in the app's history (Cao, 2020). Robocalls have also been reported to be spiking related to the pandemic, including those that target specific products related to the pandemic such as treatment, cures, COVID testing, and financial relief (O'Brien, 2020). Furthermore, there is a body of work linking boredom with heightened levels of risk taking (Kılıç et al., 2019; Yakobi & Danckert, 2020) and the pursuit of new goals and experiences (Bench & Lench, 2013). Given that many routine and leisure activities have stopped, engaging with new (although unsolicited) offers might seem more lucrative compared to "normal" times. All these behaviors raise the risk of exposure to potentially fraudulent offers and increase risk of victimization.

Common Scams during the COVID Epidemic

Scammers quickly adapted to target consumers fears regarding the pandemic and these schemes evolved as the pandemic raged on to new niches of potential interest by consumers. Below we describe some of the most common scams documented during the pandemic.

Fake Cures/Treatment

At the time of writing, there is no cure for the coronavirus. However, that has not stopped scammers from claiming to have found a cure/treatment. As early as April 14, 2020, the Federal Trade Commission (FTC) had sent over 43 warning letters to companies to companies selling homeopathic drugs, cannabinol, essential oils, colloidal silver, traditional Chinese Medicine, and salt therapy (Skiba, 2020).

In-Demand Products

The shortage of items such as face masks led to a large number of fake ads (no product sent or product switched after purchase) on Facebook and Amazon. Other consumers reported items either that were delayed for long periods of time or that when they did arrive the items were of low quality. Other medical products (gloves, sanitizer) were also targets for consumers (i.e. https://www.fbi.gov/news/pressrel/press-releases/

fbi-warns-health-care-professionals-of-increased-potential-for-fraudulent-sales-of-covid-19-related-medical-equipment).

Phishing Emails

Phishing emails, including those pretending to be from "the CDC" and "WHO," use "Authority" to trick consumers into clicking a link in order to install malware or making a fraudulent bitcoin payment.

BEC Scams

According to Help Net Security (2020), there was a 200% increase in invoice and payments fraud BEC attacks in April and May 2020 in the U.S. Generally, during payment and invoice processing, BEC attackers pose as vendors, suppliers, and customers in order to steal money using tactics such as initiating fraudulent wire transfers or redirecting vendor payments. While these transfers were not necessarily COVID-related, they did occur during the massive transition to working remotely and took advantage of a time of disruption in typical corporate practices.

Financial Relief Imposters

During the pandemic, many Americans received stimulus checks or enhanced unemployment benefits. Employers could receive benefits through the CARES Act to continue to keep employees on the payroll (Paycheck Protection Program, or PPP). Some fraudsters applied for funding claiming to have many employees on payroll, but fabricated that information. For example, David Stavely and David Butziger were sentenced to federal prison related to their fraudulent application for $500,000 (Mangan, 2020). In a larger scheme in Florida, scammers submitted their own fraudulent paperwork and, once approved, assisted others with their fraudulent applications garnering a kickback. This scheme ultimately generated more than $17 million (Roustan, 2020).

Work from Home/Money Mule Scams Increasing

The *New York Times* reported an increase in online human resource schemes of 295% in comparison to 2019 (Popper, 2020). In these schemes, fraudulent funds are "laundered" through apparently legitimate accounts and then sent to other "vendors." Potential mules are instructed to deposit checks in their account, keep some of the funds and then send off a certain amount often to overseas accounts. Alternatively, stolen goods are shipped to the mule's home and the mule is instructed to repackage and reship the products. These positions are often advertised on legitimate job boards. At a time of record unemployment, and with many individuals searching for remote work, such schemes have increased dramatically (Popper, 2020).

Charity Scams

A charity scam happens when a thief poses as a real charity or makes up the name of a charity that sounds real to get money from you. Scammers texting or calling pretending to be a charity organization increased during the pandemic. One typical tactic was to call "following-up" on a donation pledge made in the past (Scheithe, 2020).

Contact Tracing Text Message Scams

Typically, contract tracers are usually hired by the state's department of public health to identify any individual they may work with or come into close contact with while possibly infectious. In some states, an exposed individual will receive a text letting them know a health worker will be calling and that then one may receive health message texts for a 14-day period reminding you to self-isolate and monitor your health. The scammers take advantage of this system by sending text messages that closely resemble legitimate messages. However, the spam texts contain a link to click on. Once that link is clicked, it will download software onto a machine or device giving scammers access to your personal and financial information (Tressler, 2020).

Pet Scams

During this time of social distancing, working remotely, and social isolation there has been an increase in interest in pet adoption (Better Business Bureau, 2020). Owning a pet can provide health benefits and companionship. However, online pet scams were very common before the pandemic where scammers will use cute pet images from stock photos to sell non-existent pets. It is best for consumers to try to meet the pet in person before wiring or sending money (Kasumpa, 2020).

Emerging Research on COVID Scams

FTC COVID-19 Fraud Tracker

As mentioned earlier, the FTC receives and records reports of many different types of fraud—one of these happens to be reports of fraud specifically related to the COVID-19 pandemic (e.g., fake personal protective equipment, the impersonation of medical or public health personnel, theft of or advance fee fraud related to government stimulus checks, etc.). The FTC also keeps an active tracker and data visualization tool for documenting and exploring all of these fraud reports via its public Tableau site (Federal Trade Commission, 2020). All data for this section were taken from the aforementioned FTC Tableau site, specifically from the "FTC COVID-19 and Stimulus Reports" visualization. The site appears to be updated at least on a monthly basis with additional COVID-19 fraud reports (Fall, 2020). But it is also likely that the overall trends are the same. Or, at the very least, it should be interesting to serve as a piece of evidence in the ultimate tale of how fraud evolved over the course of the COVID-19 pandemic and the changed world that will eventually emerge from it.

COVID-19 Fraud Reports and Total Fraud Losses

Some of the top-line data from the FTC's COVID-19 visualization will be summarized here. From January 1, 2020 to November 4, 2020, there were a total of 242,857 COVID-19-related self-reports to the FTC. Of those 242,857 reports, 128,480 (52.9%) were of the subtype "Fraud", and these were collectively responsible for $177,320,000.00 in fraud losses over the same time period. For reference, the overall reported "Fraud" losses to the FTC for the same time period in 2020 were $990,234,113.86, so COVID-19-specific fraud accounts for around 17.91% of all fraud losses reported across the majority of 2020.

Sources of COVID-19 Fraud

The single largest segment of those 128,480 COVID-19 specific fraud reports were related to "Online Shopping" (n = 34,449, 26.8%), which accounted for $24,140,000.00 in fraud losses, whereas the single largest segment of the $177,320,000.00 in COVID-19-specific fraud losses was "Vacation and Travel" (n = 28,170, 21.92%), at $52,370,000.00 in fraud losses. Perhaps something about being required to stay indoors and not travel led people to be more susceptible to dream getaway scams or to seek out homes outside of urban areas. Additional large sources of reports were "Diet Products, Plans & Centers" (n = 6,951, 5.41%, $980,000.00), "Unsolicited Text Messages" (n = 5,285, 4.11%, $2,030,000.00), and "Government Imposters" (n = 4,161, 3.23%, $4,440,000.00), with the remaining 49,464 (38.49%) being divided over a large number of categories, each of which having relatively few reports.

Contact Methods Used for COVID-19 Fraud

Of all fraud reports indicating any form of monetary loss, 16.8% (n = 21,532) indicated the contact method by which the fraud occurred. The most common method was "E-mail," which accounted for 10,870 (50.48%) of the contact-indicating reports, and $24,960,000.00 in fraud losses. The second most common method of contact was "Consumer Initiated"; it accounted for 7,941 (36.87%) of the contact-indicated reports, and $14,090,000.00 in fraud losses. Other, less frequently reported methods of contact were "Other" (n = 1,330, 6.17%, $7,590,000.00), "Mail" (n = 918, 4.26%, $1,890,000.00), "Websites/Others" (n = 455, 2.11%, $1,970,000.00), and "Phone" (n = 18, 0.00008%, $100,000.00). Email has been a known source of fraud since shortly after its inception, and has well-known schemas for fraudulent activity (Nigerian Prince fraud emails, phishing, and the notorious email chains of the late 1990s and early 2000s come to mind, for example), so its position as the most frequent source of contact for fraud is understandable, if not expected. Of some concern, however, is the second most common method being consumer-initiated contact.

Payment Methods Used for COVID-19 Fraud

Of all fraud reports indicating any form of monetary loss, 92.6% indicated the payment method used in the fraud transaction. The most common payment method was "Credit Cards" (n = 11,010), credit cards accounted for $16,870,000.00 in fraud losses. The next most common methods of payment were "Bank Account Debit" (n = 5,837, $9,270,000.00), "Internet/Mobile" (n = 4,412, $6,430,000.00), and of note—"Wire Transfer" (n = 2,717, $36,780,000.00 in fraud losses). Less frequently reported payment methods were "Cash/Cash Advance" (n = 937, $7,880,000.00), "Check" (n = 471, $4,440,000.00), and "Money Order" (n = 139, $1,590,000.00).

Similarly, credit card fraud is not unexpected. The bigger surprise here is the sheer magnitude of fraud losses in US dollars for wire transfer relative to the number of reports of fraud involving wire transfer. Each of the 2,717 wire transfers was, on average, $13,536.99 in fraud losses, which is a truly staggering amount of money for most individuals to lose in a single fraudulent transaction. For comparison, the average credit card fraud loss was $1,532.24—in itself not an insignificant loss (approximately 5 weeks' work at $7.50/hour, 40 hours/week), but a full *order of magnitude* less than the average wire transfer transaction.

Age and COVID-19 Fraud

Of the 128,480 COVID-19-specific fraud reports to the FTC, 33.2% (n = 42,606) included information pertaining to the age of the complainant. In summary, although overall rates of fraud were lower in older consumers, the average monetary loss was much larger (Table 3.1).

COVID-19 Fraud as Compared to Overall Fraud in 2020

We also examined how COVID-19-specific fraud compares to 2020 fraud overall using the same data set. There are a few different metrics that can be used, here we focus on median fraud loss, total fraud loss, and reports to the FTC here. Please note, the FTC does not collect data on the 19 and under age group for its general fraud report database, so all comparisons are done after removing that group.

Table 3.1 Fraud Trends by Age Group 2020

Age (Years)	*Number of Reports*	*Rate of Fraud (%)*	*Total Reported Losses ($)*	*Median Reported Loss ($)*
≤19	1,467 (3.44%)	66.8	800,000	100
20–29	6,443 (15.12%)	62.5	8,300,000	262
30–39	8,829 (20.72%)	63.7	15,900,000	207
40–49	8,081 (18.97%)	60.5	18,100,000	228
50–59	7,232 (16.97%)	55.5	19,500,000	234
60–69	6,575 (15.43%)	48.2	17,300,000	239
70–79	3,158 (7.41%)	45.2	8,400,000	360
≥80	821 (1.93%)	36.1	4,100,000	700

Median Fraud Loss

Although there are differences in value, such that 2020 fraud overall are much higher median value than are COVID-19-specific fraud losses—the pattern of median losses by age group is similar for both subsets of fraud. There is a fairly static ~$200 range for all age groups median fraud value, with a noticeable increase in median value for the 70–79 age group and then the 80+ group median fraud loss essentially doubling that of the 70–79 median fraud loss.

Total Fraud Loss

Comparing COVID-19-specific fraud to overall fraud in 2020 is a bit difficult, as the overall magnitude of fraud losses is at least one order of magnitude greater for all age groups for 2020 overall fraud than it is for COVID-19-specific fraud losses. So we once again can't compare directly, but, as before, we can look at the pattern of losses across age groups for both glimpses of fraud. One interesting thing to note right away is that the 80+ category has the lowest total losses in both COVID-19-specific fraud and 2020 fraud overall. A large proportion of all fraud losses occur in the 50–59 and 60–69 age groups, a comparatively smaller proportion of all losses occur in the 20–29 age group. Of note, the 30–39, 40–49, 50–59, and 60–69 age groups total values are much closer together (and higher, relatively) for COVID-19-specific fraud than they are for 2020 fraud overall, which might indicate heightened susceptibility to or interaction with COVID-19-specific fraud for those age groups.

Reports of Fraud

This is perhaps the trickiest of all, as the FTC collects and documents reports in raw numbers for COVID-19-specific fraud, but in averages per 100k people for 2020 overall fraud reports. The easiest way to compare them, then, is just to look at the relative proportions of all fraud reports for each COVID-19-specific fraud and 2020 fraud overall.

If we assume that COVID-19 fraud affects people of different ages much the same as fraud in general does, we would in turn expect to see similar proportions of fraud reporting for the age groups for COVID-19-specific fraud that we see for 2020 fraud overall. But that is not in fact what we see at all. Instead, it appears as though the oldest of older adults (70–79, 80+), and to a slightly lesser extent 20–29 year olds, are under-represented in COVID-19-specific fraud. In other words, they make up for less COVID-19 fraud reporting than we would expect given their rate of fraud reporting for 2020 overall. Further, the other age groups (30–29, 40–49, 50–59, 60–69) are over-represented in COVID-19-specific fraud, i.e. they make up more of COVID-19 fraud reporting than they do of 2020 fraud reporting overall. When taken in conjunction with the previous data about total losses for these age groups, it appears as though there indeed may be increased exposure to or susceptibility towards COVID-19-specific fraud for people aged 30–69.

Consumer Susceptibility to COVID Scams

In a recent study, Nolte et al. (2021) assessed consumers' ratings of age differences in vulnerability to COVID-19 scams and factors that might help explain them. In a within-subjects design, an adult lifespan sample (18–84 years) was asked to indicate their intentions to respond to, or interact with, five solicitations based on real-life COVID-19 product or phishing scams. It was hypothesized that a higher intention to act on a COVID-19 solicitation would be predicted by lower risk perceptions, higher benefit perceptions, and higher genuineness ratings associated with each of the solicitations (e.g., Hanoch et al., 2006; Schoepfer & Piquero, 2009; Wood et al., 2018). Sixty-eight younger adults (18–40 years, M = 25.67, SD = 5.93), 79 middle-aged adults (41–64 years, M = 49.86, SD = 7.20), and 63 older adults (65–84 years, M = 69.87, SD = 4.50) were recruited through the online platform Prolific. Participants responded to the five COVID-19 solicitations, as well as psychological measures and demographic questions.

Overall, middle-aged adults, rather than older or younger adults, exhibited greater vulnerability to COVID-19 scams. Yet, for all age groups, risk and benefit perceptions were the key factors associated with intention to respond to scams similar to other types of solicitations.

Conclusions

At the time of this writing, the COVID pandemic is still ongoing. During this time of disruption, scams and fraud increased to take advantage of consumers' increase in vulnerability. We observed that the tactics/type of scams morphed over time from an initial focus on testing/ scarce items to targeting financial relief packages from the US government, to contact tracing type scams.

Based on secondary analysis of the FTC data and emerging empirical literature, it appears that middle-aged adults were the most likely to report being scammed and demonstrated the highest vulnerability to scams. It is important to note that while representing a smaller proportion of the overall sample of victims, the older adults reported much larger average losses. Whether this undue impact on individuals over 70 years old is due to targeting or reporting issues is unclear, but warrants future work.

Unfortunately, Covid-19 will be with us for some time. These scams will likely evolve over time and become more elaborate, possibly including fake vaccinations, charity frauds, work-at-home schemes, biotech investment schemes, and online learning opportunities for children stuck at home. All consumers should be wary, and sadly we predict older consumers will be particularly targeted given the increased risk for greatest financial losses. Though easier said than done right now, taking the time to carefully read ads, examining their legitimacy, being hyper-vigilant, and staying calm can be helpful during this uncertain time.

References

200% Increase in Invoice and Payment Fraud BEC Attacks. (June 20, 2020). *Help Net Security*. Retrieved October 7, 2020, from https://www.helpnetsecurity.com/2020/06/30/payment-fraud-bec-attacks/

Altig, D., Baker, S., Barrero, J.M., Bloom, N., Bunn, P., Chen, S., Davis, S.J., Leather, J., Meyer, B., Mihaylov, E., Mizen, P., Paker, N., Renault, T., Smietanka, P., & Thwaites, G. (2020). Economic uncertainty before and during the COVID-19 pandemic. *Journal of Public Economics, 191*, 104274. https://doi.org/10.1016/j.jpubeco.2020.104274

Antonucci, T., Fuhrer, R., & Dartigues, J.F. (1997). Social relations and depressing symptomatology in a sample of community-dwelling French older adults. *Psychology and Aging, 12*(1), 189–195. https://doi.org/10.1037/0882-7974.12.1.189

Beach, S.R., Schulz, R., Castle, N.G., & Rosen, J. (2010). Financial exploitation and psychological mistreatment among older adults: Differences between African Americans and non-African Americans in a population-based survey. *The Gerontologist, 50*(6), 744–757. https://doi.org/10.1093/geront/gnq053

Bench, S.W., & Lench, H.C. (2013). On the function of boredom. *Behavioral Sciences, 3*(3), 459–472. https://doi.org/10.3390/bs3030459

Better Busniness Bureau. (December 2, 2020). *Online puppy scams rising sharply in 2020, BBB warns*. https://www.bbb.org/article/news-releases/23354-bbb-study-update-puppy-scams-rising-in-2020.

Cao, S. (May 21, 2020). *Tinder CEO reveals how Coronavirus has affected online dating*. Observer. https://observer.com/2020/05/coroanvirus-impact-online-dating-app-tinder-ceo-interview/.

Carrns, A. (April 17, 2020). *Bogus vaccines. Faking testing sites. Virus frauds are flourishing*. New York Times. https://www.nytimes.com/2020/04/17/your-money/coronavirus-fraud.html

Cialdini, R. B. (2006). *Influence: The Psychology of Persuasion* (revised ed.). Harper Business.

COVID-19 and Stimulus Reports. (June, 2020). *Tableau Public*. Retrieved October 7, 2020, from https://public.tableau.com/profile/federal.trade.commission#!/vizhome/COVID-19andStimulusReports/Map

Dugas, M.J., Laugesen, N., & Bukowski, W.M. (2012). Intolerance of uncertainty, fear of anxiety, and adolescent worry. *Journal of Abnormal Child Psychology*, *40*, 863–870. https://doi.org/10.1007/s10802-012-9611-1

Federal Trade Commission. (2020). *Federal Trade Commission*. Tableau Public. Retrieved December 4, 2020, from https://public.tableau.com/profile/federal.trade.commission#!/

Hanoch, Y., Johnson, J.G., & Wilke, A. (2006). Domain specificity in experimental measures and participant recruitment: An application to risk-taking behavior. *Psychological Science*, *17*(4), 300–304. https://doi.org/10.1111/j.1467-9280.2006.01702.x

Huang, Y., & Zhao, N. (2020). Generalized anxiety disorder, depressive symptoms and sleep quality during COVID-19 outbreak in China: A web-based cross-sectional survey. *Psychiatry Research*, *288*, 112954. https://doi.org/10.1016/j.psychres.2020.112954

Kahneman, D. (2013). *Thinking, Fast and Slow*. New York: Farrar, Straus and Giroux.

Kasumpa, N. (May 20, 2020). *Finding a Furry Friend in the Era of COVID-19*. FTC Consumer Information. https://www.consumer.ftc.gov/blog/2020/05/finding-furry-friend-era-covid-19

Kılıç, A., van Tilburg, W.A.P., & Igou, E.R. (2019). Risk-taking increases under boredom. *Journal of Behavioral Decision Making*, *33*(3), 257–269. https://doi.org/10.1002/bdm.2160

Le Couteur, D.G., Anderson, R.M., & Newman, A.B. (2020). COVID-19 through the lens of gerontology. *The Journals of Gerontology: Series A, Biological Sciences and Medical Sciences*, *75*(9). https://doi.org/10.1093/gerona/glaa077

Lichtenberg, P.A., Stickney, L., & Paulson, D. (2013). Is psychological vulnerability related to the experience of fraud in older adults?. *Clinical Gerontologist*, *36*(2), 132–146. https://doi.org/10.1080/07317115.2012.749323

Lichtenberg, P.A., Sugarman, M.A., Paulson, D., Ficker, L.J., & Rahman-Filipiak, A. (2016). Psychological and functional vulnerability predicts fraud cases in older adults: Results of a longitudinal study. *Clinical Gerontologist*, *39*(1), 48–63. https://doi.org/10.1080/07317115.2015.1101632

Liu, P.J., Wood, S., Xi, P., Berger, D.E., & Wilber, K. (2017). The role of social support in elder financial exploitation using a community sample. *Innovation in Aging*, *1*(1), igx016, https://doi.org/10.1093/geroni/igx016

Mangan, D. (May 5 2020). *Coronavirus Fraud: Two New England Men Are First to be Charged with Scamming Small Business Loan Program*. CNBC. https://www.cnbc.com/2020/05/05/coronavirus-men-charged-with-fraud-over-cares-act-ppp-small-business-aid.html

McEvoy, P.M., & Mahoney, A.E.J. (2011). To be sure, to be sure: Intolerance of uncertainty mediates symptoms of various anxiety disorders and depression. *Behavior Therapy*, *43*(3), 533–545. https://doi.org/10.1016/j.beth.2011.02.007

Nolte, J., Hanoch, Y., Wood, S.A., & Hengerer, D. (2021). Susceptibility to COVID-19 scams: The Roles of Age, Individual Difference Measures, and Scam- Related Perceptions. *Frontiers in Psychology*, 15 December 2021; https://doi.org/10.3389/fpsyg.2021.789883

O'Brien, S. (May19, 2020). *Robocalls Are Spiking as Fraudsters Prey on COVID-19 Fears*. CNBC. https://www.cnbc.com/2020/05/19/robocalls-are-spiking-as-fraudsters-prey-on-covid-19-fears.html

Popper, N. (September 15, 2020). *A job that isn't hard to get in a pandemic: Swindlers' unwitting helper*. New York Times. https://www.nytimes.com/2020/09/15/technology/money-mules-fraud-pandemic.html

Psychological Impact of COVID-19: Know the Signs of Anxiety, Panic Attacks, Depression and Suicide. (April 14, 2020). American Psychological Association. Retrieved October 7, 2020, from http://www.apa.org/topics/covid-19/psychological-impact

Roustan, W.K. (August 7, 2020). *3 more South Floridians charged in $24 million PPP loan scheme*. Sun Sentinel. https://www.sun-sentinel.com/local/broward/miramar/fl-ne-covid-fraud-scheme-20200807-3xfzzj4qijbn5fkcrixq334rc4-story.html

Salari, N., Hosseinian-Far, A., Jalali, R., Vaisi-Raygani, A., Rasoulpoor, S., Mohammadi, M., Rasoulpoor, S., & Khaledi-Paveh, B. (2020). Prevalence of stress, anxiety, depression among the general population during the COVID-19 pandemic: A systematic review and meta-analysis. *Globalization and Health*, *16*(57). https://doi.org/10.1186/s12992-020-00589-w

Scheithe, E. (May 15, 2020). *Beware of Scams Related to the Coronavirus*. CFPB. https://www.consumerfinance.gov/about-us/blog/beware-coronavirus-related-scams/

Schoepfer, A., & Piquero, N.L. (2009). Studying the correlates of fraud victimization and reporting. *Journal of Criminal Justice*, *37*(2), 209–215. https://doi.org/10.1016/j.jcrimjus.2009.02.003

Skiba, K. (April 14, 2020). *FTC Cracks down on Companies Pitching Fake COVID-19 Cures*. AARP. https://www.aarp.org/money/scams-fraud/info-2020/ftc-more-warnings-coronavirus-cures.html

Tressler, C. (May 19, 2020). *COVID-19 Contact Tracing Text Message Scams*. FTC Consumer Information. https://www.consumer.ftc.gov/blog/2020/05/covid-19-contact-tracing-text-message-scams.

Wang, B., & Dong, X. (2018). Gender differences in loneliness and risk of elder abuse in a Chinese community population. *Innovation in Aging*, *2*(1), 526. https://doi.org/10.1093/geroni/igy023.1943

Wood, S., Liu, P.J., Hanoch, Y., Xi, P.M., & Klapatch, L. (2018). Call to claim your prize: Perceived benefits and risk drive intention to comply in a mass marketing scam. *Journal of Experimental Psychology: Applied*, *24*(2), 196–206. http://dx.doi.org/10.1037/xap0000167

Yakobi, O., & Danckert, J. (2020). Risk taking and impulsivity in boredom: An EEG investigation. *Cognitive Science Society*. https://cognitivesciencesociety.org/cogsci20/papers/0838/0838.pdf

4 Aging online: Rethinking the aging decision-maker in a digital era

Natalie C. Ebner, Didem Pehlivanoglu, Rebecca Polk, Gary R. Turner, and R. Nathan Spreng

Introduction: the aging individual in cyberspace

An increasingly digitalized and globally connected world confronts the aging individual with drastically new decision-making contexts. The new challenges require a profound reconceptualization and reassessment of the aging decision-maker. This novel perspective is necessary to shed light on the aging individual in cyberspace, where the range of malicious activities perpetrated by malevolent actors is regrettably wide and, in many cases, triggered by poor decision-making, with often severe personal and societal consequences. Many of these threats involve deception in online communications that take place via email and, more recently, social media messaging platforms. These new media are expanding the cyberfraud ecosystem from the more conventional phone and phone text messaging scams and can result in the distribution of malicious software (e.g., ransomware) and spam, perpetration of scams, and manipulation of people's opinions via misinformation and fake news.

DOI: 10.4324/9781003017189-4

Technology use can contribute to increasing social connectedness (e.g., keeping in touch with family and friends living away, forming new social networks; Hülür & Macdonald, 2020; Moore & Hancock, 2020) and can be crucial in today's tech-driven world (Isele & Rogoff, 2014). Older adults are relatively new to cyberspace (Anderson, 2019; Silver et al., 2019); and, even though getting larger in number and diversity of use as well as more comfortable online (Clement, 2020; Smith, 2014a, 2014b), they often still lack the experience necessary to use technology securely and are comparatively less experienced with digital devices as well as have lower confidence in their IT skills than young adults (Dyck & Smither, 1994; Marquié et al., 2002). Further, often they possess large assets accumulated over their lifetime and make consequential decisions for themselves and others. Together these factors may render them attractive targets for malevolent actors. This, combined with the wide spectrum of normal age-related declines in cognitive functions as well as changes in socioemotional capacities and neurobiological processes, may lead to poor decision-making online and may increase online victimization of seniors in the future. Surprisingly, however, older adults are still largely neglected in research on cybersecurity.

In this chapter, we argue that these emerging, fast-changing, modern world contexts require an extensive broadening of our view on the aging decision-maker. We propose that rethinking adulthood and aging in a digital era will open fascinating new opportunities to describe and study the aging individual and to equip them for successful and safe engagement with cyber-based resources. Toward this goal, this chapter presents literature on cognitive, socioemotional, and neurobiological influences on deception detection and fraud risk susceptibility; and integrates this information within a biopsychosocial model of the aging decision-maker in cyberspace. We integrate self-report, behavioral, and neurobiological research as well as lab-based and "in the wild" data collection methods to propose cyber-vulnerability profiles. We believe that this scientific knowledge integration is critically necessary to inform the design of tailored risk surveillance as well as fraud prevention solutions and support safe decision-making online for older adults.

Among older adults, losses due to fraud have reached epidemic proportions

In 2010, as many as 4% of older Americans fell victim to some form of financial fraud, with the majority of perpetrators strangers, costing older adults billions of dollars (MetLife, 2011). Despite these shockingly high estimates, these statistics likely underestimate the actual prevalence of elder financial exploitation[1] due to under-reporting, out of fear of appearing cognitively impaired or conforming to a negative aging stereotype (Federal Bureau of Investigation, 2016; Lachs & Berman, 2011; National Research Council, 2003). In fact, financial fraud represents one of the most common forms of elder maltreatment (Acierno et al., 2010; Amstadter et al., 2011; DeLiema, 2018; Peterson et al., 2014; Roberto, Teaster, & Duke, 2004; Wood & Lichtenberg, 2017). Combined with the rapidly growing proportion of older adults in many nations worldwide and the dramatic effects of adverse financial events in old age on health and independent living (Alexander et al., 2012; Button, Lewis, & Tapley, 2014; Carr, 2011; Dong & Simon, 2013a, 2013b; Karbach & Verhaeghen, 2014; Lantz, House, Mero, & Williams, 2005; Templeton & Kirkman, 2007; Weissberger et al., 2020), age-related decision-making deficits will bring devastating consequences for a large segment of the population, harming victims, the healthcare system, and the economy; rendering increased financial exploitation in the elderly a burgeoning public health crisis (Schwandt, 2014). This crisis will only worsen in the coming decades as the baby boomers, the wealthiest generation in American history, continue their march into older age and become a lucrative target population for fraud. Further exacerbating this already dire situation, an increasing number of older adults suffer from Alzheimer's disease (Matthews et al., 2019), a potent risk factor for financial exploitation (Lichtenberg, 2016; Marson, 2001; Marson et al., 2009; Sherod et al., 2009).

Modern deception and fraud increasingly occur online in the cyberspace

While undoubtedly the global digital connectedness of our modern world offers unprecedented opportunity in social, economic, and innovation spheres (Hülür & Macdonald, 2020; Moore & Hancock, 2020), these advances also come with considerable risk of cyberfraud. Online fraudsters have learned to deceive people into providing personal information, downloading malicious software, or bias their beliefs and knowledge using a host of social engineering techniques, which aim at influencing the individual, often against their best interest (Carr, 2011). The Federal Trade Commission (2020) and the Federal Bureau of Investigation (2020) warn that scammers increasingly use cyberplatforms, including email, websites, social media, and text messages, for their scams.

One such dangerous and costly type of modern cyberfraud is phishing—malicious messages distributed via diverse communication methods (e.g., email, text, phone) to influence an individual into a maladaptive action that will go against their best interests and will benefit the perpetrator. For email or text (SMS; smishing) phishing, this could entail fraudsters convincing older adults to click on a malicious link, open a malicious attachment, and/or provide personal information on fake websites. One of the classic types of phishing involves fraudsters contacting the victim and suggesting that there is something wrong with their checking account and that they need to provide their account number for resolution of the problem. Vishing (Ollmann, 2007) is phone-based phishing that often leverages advantages of new technologies (e.g., robocalls) to lure a victim into providing information that can then be used by the scammer for criminal activities such as identity theft. Typical consequences of falling for phishing for the victim include having their computer or device compromised by malware, personal information (e.g., passwords) or data stolen, and financial loss.

Phishing has become extremely popular as an attack vector because it is simple, effective, and difficult to trace, with immense costs to the individual and society. The consequences of acting on one scam phone call can result in a dramatic downward spiral of entanglement with fraudsters, sometimes over years. Similarly, a single click on just one phishing email or text message link can lead to extortion via malicious encryption of electronic information and other fraud. And despite technological solutions, such as spam filters and other automatized protections, many attacks evade detection, thus rendering these social engineering techniques extraordinarily common and dangerous.[2]

The COVID-19 pandemic has further highlighted potential risks from fraud and other cyberattacks, including among older adults (see also Han & Mosqueda, 2020 for a reflection on increased elder abuse in the COVID-19 era). In fact, there has been an alarming increase in phishing attacks impersonating the WHO and the Centers for Disease Control and Prevention (CDC) in attempts to take advantage during the COVID-19 pandemic. Also, robocalls have been one of the leading fraudulent behaviors during the COVID-19 pandemic (The United States Department of Justice, 2020). During social isolation, feelings of loneliness increase and people are turning to social media and online platforms to fulfill their social needs (Le Couteur, Anderson, & Newman, 2020) as well as perform activities of daily life (e.g., banking, submission of medical forms). This can be particularly challenging for older adults who have less digital and/or media literacy (Buckingham, 2019; Moore & Hancock, 2020), and thus are often less knowledgeable of suspicious cues in malicious messages (e.g., in phishing emails). Additionally, lower digital fluency can leave older adults more vulnerable to misinformation distributed via fake news on various social media platforms (Brashier & Schacter, 2020).

Human factors in cybersecurity research

Only recently has research on cybersecurity started to investigate human factors that contribute to greater online deception risks. This research suggests that the extent to which individuals use the internet (Moody, Galletta, & Dunn, 2017; Vishwanath, 2015; Vishwanath, Harrison, & Ng, 2018) and familiarity with the sender of deceptive messages (Benenson, Gassmann, & Landwirth, 2017; Jagatic, Johnson, Jakobsson, & Menczer, 2007) were associated with susceptibility to deception (Mohebzada, Zarka, Bhojani, & Darwish, 2012; Snyder, Reiter, & Kanich, 2016). This research has also shown that individuals are typically not aware of their susceptibility (Hong & Cha, 2013; Lin et al., 2019), which may render them even more vulnerable to fraud. In addition, greater susceptibility to phishing was associated with greater trust (Friend & Fox Hamilton, 2016; Uebelacker & Quiel, 2014), greater curiosity (Benenson et al., 2017; Moody et al., 2017), as well as higher commitment or obedience to authority (Workman, 2007). Phishing susceptibility has been shown to vary by gender (Hong & Cha, 2013; Jagatic et al., 2007; Sheng, Holbrook, Kumaraguru, Cranor, & Downs, 2010) and age, with older women constituting a particularly at-risk demographic (Lin et al., 2019). Ebner et al. (2020) further demonstrated that low cognitive functioning and low positive affect were associated with higher phishing susceptibility and lower susceptibility awareness observed among the oldest individuals in their study. However, older age so far has been largely neglected as a risk factor in research on cybersecurity.

Despite diverse and growing risks online, older adults have been largely ignored in cybersecurity research

The relative paucity of research on cyberfraud in later life is striking in light of evidence that deception detection may be particularly impaired among older adults (Carr, 2011; Stanley & Blanchard-Fields, 2008; Sweeney & Ceci, 2014). Reduced deception detection may be associated with general age-related decline across a broad range of fluid cognitive abilities, including processing speed, episodic, semantic, and working memory (Hedden & Gabrieli, 2004; Spreng & Turner, 2019; Verhaeghen & Salthouse, 1997). This decline leads to altered decision-making ability, leaving older adults vulnerable to false information (Jacoby, 1999) and deception (Boyle et al., 2012; Denburg et al., 2007; Han et al., 2016a; James, Boyle, & Bennett, 2014). Further, while sensitivity to untrustworthy information and deceptive cues declines with age (Bailey & Leon, 2019; Boyle, Yu, Schneider, Wilson, & Bennett, 2019; Castle et al., 2012;

Frazier et al., 2020; Frazier, Lighthall, Horta, Perez, & Ebner, 2019; Ruffman, Murray, Halberstadt, & Vater, 2012), this occurs in the context of increased interpersonal trust in older age (Bailey et al., 2015; Zebrowitz, Boshyan, Ward, Gutchess, & Hadjikhani, 2017; Zebrowitz, Franklin, Hillman, & Boc, 2013).

Importantly, fraud is transactional, involving decisions about potential losses and rewards, and detecting others' intentions. Thus, socioemotional changes in aging likely play a similarly important role as determinants of fraud susceptibility; however the contribution of these factors to fraud susceptibility remain largely understudied (Ebner et al., 2020; Spreng, Ebner, Levin, & Turner, in press; Spreng, Karlawish, & Marson, 2016). Finally, age-related cognitive and socioemotional changes occur in the context of changes in brain structure and function as well as neurotransmitter and hormonal changes both in normal aging and brain disease. While these neurobiological factors contribute to changes in decision-making, deception detection and trust, relatively little is known about their impact on financial exploitation risk, specifically in cyberspace.

Toward a biopsychosocial model of deception risk in aging

This idea of multifactorial influences contributing to susceptibility risk, i.e., a dynamic interplay between cognitive, socioemotional, and neurobiological influences on decision-making related to deception detection, is depicted in Figure 4.1. This *Biopsychosocial Model of Deception Risk in Aging* offers a multifaceted framework for organizing existing knowledge about influences on deception detection and can guide future work on the aging decision-maker, including in the unsafe cyberspace. Within the organization of this framework, leveraging from the broader field of deception detection research, we next reflect on interindividual differences in cognitive, socioemotional, and

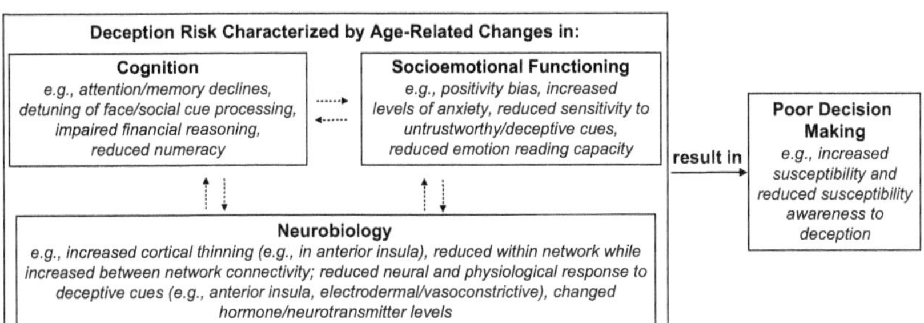

Figure 4.1 Biopsychosocial model of deception risk in aging.

neurobiological factors characterizing the human target/victim of deception. The goal is to identify risk profiles with relevance for improved surveillance and design of tailored decision-supportive solutions that counter fraud victimization in later life.

Cognitive, socioemotional, and neurobiological influences, and their interplay, on deception detection

Interindividual differences in cognition, socioemotional functioning, and neurobiology have been associated with the ability to detect deception and may impact fraud susceptibility. Current knowledge regarding these influences, and their dynamic interplay, has not yet been well integrated in research on the aging decision-maker, including in cyberspace.

Cognitive factors

One prominent model with relevance to decision-making, including in the context of deception detection, is the dual-processing model. This model proposes a quick and intuitive processing mode (called *System 1*) and a slow and deliberate processing mode (called *System 2*; Chaiken, 1987). System 1 is associated with reliance on cognitive heuristics when making decisions (i.e., mental shortcuts based on prior knowledge/beliefs; Evans, 2002, 2008; Kahneman, Slovic, & Tversky, 1982). System 2, in contrast, involves careful and systematic consideration of information. System 1 triages or streamlines decision-making, because the individual cannot permanently operate in System 2 as it is resource-intensive (Kahneman et al., 1982). The majority of everyday life decisions rely on System 1; which, however, can be flawed (Gilovich, Griffin, & Kahneman, 2002) and could lead to poor deception detection. For example, deception detection has been shown to decrease with increases in *truth bias*—the human tendency to believe that others are more likely to tell the truth than a lie (Bond & DePaulo, 2006; Kraut, 1980). Similarly, *confirmation bias* (i.e., the tendency to seek information that confirms one's views; Darley & Gross, 1983) was associated with poor deception detection.

The ability to process information at the intuitive level (System 1) remains relatively preserved, while deliberative processing (System 2) becomes less efficient with age (Drolet, Jiang, Mohammad, & Davis, 2018; Queen & Hess, 2010; Reyna & Brainerd, 2011). Relatedly, there is evidence of age-related decline in processing speed, working memory, and executive functions (Braver

& West, 2008; Lustig, Hasher, & Zacks, 2008; Verhaeghen & Salthouse, 1997) which limit information processing and decision-making associated with conscious deliberation in aging. In contrast, implicit and automatic processes (based on heuristics) remain relatively stable through later life (Peters, Hess, Västfjäll, & Auman, 2007; Zacks, Hasher, & Li, 2000). This greater reliance on System 1 over System 2 may increase susceptibility to deception in aging. Indeed, a recent study found that reduced conscious deliberation (measured via executive functioning ability) was associated with lower deception detection in older adults with the strongest associations observed in those individuals over 80 years (Calso, Besnard, & Allain, 2020).

Of note, while cognitive processes involved in financial capacities and exploitation among the elderly have been increasingly studied in more recent years (see Spreng et al., in press), the specific impact of cognitive influences on online fraud risk is still understudied (but see Ebner et al., 2020 for evidence that low memory function is associated with increased email-based phishing susceptibility among older individuals). Socioemotional influences on deception risk in aging have been the subject of even less inquiry, despite the transactional nature of deception and the likely role for these capacities in detecting, and therefore avoiding, deception.

Socioemotional factors

Various aspects of socioemotional functioning have been found to influence deception detection. Negative mood has been associated with enhanced deception detection: individuals with greater feelings of sadness and distress (dysphoric mood) compared to non-dysphoric individuals were better at lie detection (Lane & Depaulo, 1999). Similarly, negative mood increased, while positive mood decreased skepticism and deception detection (Forgas & East, 2008; Matovic, Koch, & Forgas, 2014; but see LaTour & LaTour, 2009). These results are consistent with findings that positive mood fosters reliance on System 1, while negative mood fosters reliance on System 2 (for reviews see Bless, 2001; Schwarz & Clore, 2003).

Furthermore, higher emotional intelligence, such as reflected in better perspective taking (Stewart, Wright, & Atherton, 2019), was related to enhanced deception detection (see also Riggio, Tucker, & Throckmorton, 1987; Wojciechowski, Stolarski, & Matthews, 2014), including improved lie detection (Ruffman et al., 2012). Emotional intelligence also partially mediated age-related differences in scam susceptibility, in that older participants who scored higher in emotional intelligence were more sensitive to risk and less susceptible to scams (Mueller, Wood, Hanoch, Huang, & Reed, 2020). In addition, low self-control was associated with higher likelihood of disclosing personal information, risk-taking, and responding to scam offers (Lee, 2014; Reisig, Pratt, & Holtfreter, 2009). It is possible that low self-control limits the ability to assess risk severity and personal risk vulnerability (Holtfreter, Reisig, Piquero, & Piquero, 2010).

Finally, personality factors more broadly influence deception detection. For example, individuals high on agreeableness were less proficient in deception detection in a task requiring identification of false memories (Campbell & Porter, 2002). In addition, high threat-sensitive individuals, who are generally suspicious and score low on agreeableness, were more accurate in lie detection than individuals low on threat-sensitivity (Ein-Dor & Perry, 2014).

While aging research has extensively addressed socioemotional functioning (Ebner & Fischer, 2014; Gutchess & Samanez-Larkin, 2019; Scheibe & Carstensen, 2010), comparatively little research exists on the role of these processes in financial exploitation risk in later life (Lichtenberg et al., 2016), and particularly in the realm of online fraud. Pioneering this field of research, Ebner et al. (2020) found that low positive affect was associated with increased susceptibility to phishing attacks among older individuals.

Neurobiological factors

Emerging literature suggests that neurobiological mechanisms, including psychophysiology, peripheral and brain chemistry, as well as brain structure/function play a role in deception detection.

Psychophysiology

The literature supports that interoceptive awareness—the ability to accurately read internal physiological signals (e.g., "gut feelings")—was associated with greater physiological reaction (e.g., arousal) to liars than truth-tellers, which in turn led to improved deception detection (ten Brinke, Lee, & Carney, 2019). Thus, individuals with greater interoceptive awareness may be better decision-makers, consistent with evidence in gambling paradigms showing a positive association between interoception ability and financial decision-making related to rejection of unfair offers in the Ultimatum game (Dunn, Evans, Makarova, White, & Clark, 2012; Kirk, Downar, & Montague, 2011).

Neurochemistry

Hormones can influence deception detection, possibly through their impact on risk-taking behavior (Apicella et al., 2008) and social processes (Bos, Panksepp, Bluthé, & Honk, 2012). For example, individuals with high levels of steroid hormones (specifically the sex hormones testosterone and estrogen) took greater financial risks than individuals with lower steroid hormone levels (Durante, Griskevicius, Cantú, & Simpson, 2014; Stanton, Liening, & Schultheiss, 2011; Van Honk et al., 2004; see Stanton, 2017 for a review). Increased levels of cortisol were associated with reduced risk-taking behavior (i.e., cortisol-related risk aversion; Hardy et al., 2014). This effect held for both financially disadvantageous (i.e., Iowa Gambling Task; Preston, Buchanan, Stansfield, & Bechara, 2007) and financially advantageous (i.e., Balloon Analogue Risk Task; Lighthall et al., 2012) risk-taking.

Increased levels of the neurotransmitters serotonin and dopamine reinforced impulsive and risky behavior under uncertainty (for a review see Rogers, 2011), which may impact deception detection and response to deceptive messages/scams. For example, higher serotonin levels were associated with increased preference for risky choices in gambling tasks (Heitland et al., 2012). Also, increased incidence of compulsive gambling in Parkinson's disease patients who take dopamine agonists supports dopaminergic involvement in risky decision-making (Dodd et al., 2005; Driver-Dunckley, Samanta, & Stacy, 2003).

The neuropeptide oxytocin has been associated with prosociality, including trust, and thus may play a role in deception detection. Intranasal oxytocin (compared to placebo) administration decreased the ability to correctly classify statements as truth vs. lie (Pfundmair, Erk, & Reinelt, 2017). Similarly, intranasal oxytocin reduced the ability to predict whether contestants in a TV show would cooperate or decline cooperation (Israel, Hart, & Winter, 2014). It appears that, more generally, oxytocin attenuates response to aversive social stimuli (see Ebner, Maura, MacDonald, Westberg, & Fischer, 2013; Grace, Rossell, Heinrichs, Kordsachia, & Labuschagne, 2018; Horta, Kaylor, Feifel, & Ebner, 2020; for overviews), such as angry faces (Quintana et al., 2016; Radke et al., 2017), fear (Kirsch et al., 2016), and social betrayal of trust (Baumgartner, Heinrichs, Vonlanthen, Fischbacher, & Fehr, 2008; Chen et al., 2016; de Dreu, Dussel, & Ten Velden, 2015; Frazier et al., 2020; Rilling et al., 2014; but see Chen, Gautam, Haroon, & Rilling, 2017; Nave, Camerer, & McCullough, 2015).

Role of brain structure and function. Evidence regarding neural substrates of deception detection has been derived primarily from patient case studies.

Winner, Brownell, Happé, Blum, and Pincus (1998) showed that patients with brain damage to the right hemisphere performed worse than healthy controls in distinguishing lies from jokes. Freedman and Stuss (2011) found that patients with lesions in medial frontal regions, particularly in the right ventral area, were impaired at deception detection. Right frontal regions are involved in social-cognitive abilities such as perspective taking and empathy (Happé, Brownell, & Winner, 1999)—processes relevant in deception detection. Ventral medial frontal regions may also be involved in deception detection given their strong connections with the amygdala and other limbic structures in emotion processing and emotion regulation (Motzkin, Philippi, Wolf, Baskaya, & Koenigs, 2015).

Neuroimaging studies in healthy participants further confirmed involvement of limbic and paralimbic brain regions in deception detection. The amygdala and the rostral anterior cingulate cortex, for example, were activated during judgement of deceptive intention (Grèzes, Frith, Passingham, & Grezes, 2004). Lissek et al. (2008) found that orbitofrontal and medial prefrontal regions were involved in the understanding of mental states of cartoon characters engaging in deception.

There is a very recent literature that specifically examines the role of brain structure and function on deception detection in aging. Supporting the link between age-related brain structural decline and risk for financial exploitation, older adults who had become victims of financial fraud in their real life had lower cortical volumes in insula and superior temporal regions than older adults who had successfully avoided exploitation. These exploited individuals also showed reduced connectivity within the default mode network, while they showed increased connectivity between the default mode network and the salience network (Spreng et al., 2017). These networks have been implicated in domains relevant to memory functioning (Andrews-Hanna, Smallwood, & Spreng, 2014), risky decision-making, particularly when ambiguity and doubt are high (e.g., financial decision-making; Asp et al., 2012; Denburg et al., 2007; Samanez-Larkin & Knutson, 2015), and impression formation (Cassidy, Leshikar, Shih, Aizenman, & Gutchess, 2013). Thus, structural and functional changes in brain regions implicated in these networks may be an indicator of reduced deception detection ability. Finally, there is evidence that older compared to younger adults have reduced insula activity to cues of untrustworthiness (Castle et al., 2012). This suggests that older adults may be less sensitive to deceptive cues, which could underlie poorer deception detection in aging (Frazier et al., 2020; Lin et al., 2019).

These influences of psychophysiology, brain chemistry, and brain structure/function on deception detection are likely exacerbated in pathological aging (Boyle et al., 2019; Han, Boyle, James, Yu, & Bennett, 2016b). For example, financial capacity has been associated with lower cortical volumes in the angular gyrus in amnestic mild cognitive impairment (often a precursor of Alzheimer's disease; Griffith et al., 2010) and medial and dorsal frontal cortex cortical volumes in early Alzheimer's disease (Stoeckel et al., 2013).

Challenges and frontiers for future research and practice

As evident from the breadth of literature reviewed here, perhaps the greatest challenge for future research in the area of aging and cyberfraud will be in constructing integrative, multifaceted fraud susceptibility profiles to guide early surveillance and intervention. Advances in this field will necessitate interdisciplinary collaboration spanning psychology, sociology, criminology, neuroscience, computer science, data science/machine learning, engineering, law enforcement agencies, policymakers, and other disciplines. This work will gain from integration of research on age-related changes in brain and behavior with research on decision-making in the cyber era. Ultimately these cross-disciplinary efforts will inform design of decision-supportive, real-life interventions, which are currently lacking, that adopt an age-tailored approach, as opposed to a "one-size-fits-all" solution, as different age groups might be targeted by different schemes and by different methods. The long-term goal of this emerging research agenda will be risk reduction of fraud in later life. In this spirit, we will conclude this chapter with a discussion of several lines of what we deem fruitful future avenues to promote understanding of the basic mechanisms underlying cyberfraud risk in aging and this research's practical impact.

Studying fraud susceptibility in the "wild"

There appears to be an important misconception in current research on fraud susceptibility—namely, that individuals are aware of their deception risks and would subsequently adjust their behavior in light of the anticipated risks they see themselves exposed to. This misconception emerges from previous research almost exclusively relying on self-report; which not only is based on the assumption that individuals have adequate insight/introspection but also often suffers from demand characteristics and other response tendencies. Thus, self-report can lead to artificial and static data and seems to result in lower estimates of susceptibility than behavioral (Lin et al., 2019) and in-lab (Grilli et al., 2021) assessments. Actual fraud and exploitation statistics, as noted above, as well as work on susceptibility in real life (Lin et al., 2019; Oliveira et al., 2019), depict a different situation, with high numbers of individuals falling for fraud, even repeatedly and despite training and advice; and a discrepancy between self-reported phishing susceptibility awareness and actual susceptibility behavior particularly among older adults (Lin et al., 2019). Some of this discrepancy could also be due to shame and embarrassment of admitting having become a victim as well as concern, especially among older individuals, that admitting to having been defrauded may lead to their independence being taken away. Further, emotional reaction, such as depression, might impact reporting among fraud survivors. This emphasizes the importance of anonymous as well as behavior-based examinations, and avoidance of exposing terminology (e.g., "fraud", "victim") in future research to derive at more accurate and convergent numbers.

Also, along these lines, moving forward it will be critical to thoroughly study susceptibility behavior to online fraud and deception "in the wild"; that is unobtrusive and takes place in the natural contexts of individuals' everyday lives. One challenge in this context is that while the total number of individuals who have fallen for fraud seems staggeringly high, the overall base rate is not that high. For example the most recent mass-market consumer fraud in the U.S. report showed that for the fraud with the highest prevalence (i.e., having paid for an item that was never received) only just over 7% of consumers experienced it during the year before they were surveyed (Anderson, 2019). This low base rate is making it difficult to spot and study associated naturalistic behavior, requiring very large samples of randomly chosen individuals to get useful results.

Research based on the Naturalistic Decision Making (NDM) framework (Klein, 2008; as an alternative to rational decision-making model; Kahneman et al., 1982) examined the quality of decisions made in fast-paced complex and often-dangerous situations by experts (e.g., fire fighters, military leaders) in real-world settings. Given that (online) fraud typically occurs in naturalistic, highly complex contexts and based on evidence that knowledge and expertise such as accumulated over the lifespan promotes successful decision-making (e.g., in the financial realm; Li et al., 2015), the NDM research approach may be fruitful in future study of the aging decision-making in cyberspace. This will require development of reliable and ecologically valid, openly accessible behavioral paradigms that allow the study of complex decision-making in aging, in fast-changing contexts (i.e., new threats arise or mutate continually, and before automatic detection and prevention is in place; e.g., zero-day exploits; Bilge & Dumitras, 2012; Zhang, Wang, Jajodia, Singhal, & Albanese, 2016).

Assessing intraindividual variability in fraud susceptibility

While the impact of interindividual differences on deception detection has been acknowledged, within-person variations are currently understudied. Cognitive aging research has shown that individuals vary in performance even over very short retest intervals (Hertzog, Dixon, & Hultsch, 1992; Li, Aggen, Nesselroade, & Baltes, 2001). Also, daily levels of negative affect predicted individual differences in cognitive interference among older adults, both between- and within-person (Stawski, Mogle, & Sliwinski, 2011). Thus, moving forward, the study of within-person variability on different aspects of functioning (i.e., cognitive, socioemotional, neurobiological) will advance understanding of susceptibility to online deception in aging, and will importantly inform prevention and defense solutions (e.g., closer surveillance and more frequent warning at certain times of the day).

Capturing the dynamic interplay between human targets and deceptive cues

Previous research has documented that deception detection depends on an interplay between characteristics of the human target and characteristics of the deceptive cues. For example, perceived similarity and greater familiarity between the sender and the receiver of a message improves deception detection, as found in Slessor, Phillips, Ruffman, Bailey, and Insch (2014), in that older adults were more confident in making judgments about the truthfulness of older compared to younger speakers. Certainly, any of these insights can be leveraged by fraudsters who likely adjust their practices to be the most effective (e.g., sending messages to victims from senders they are familiar with); thus requiring for successful defense practice to always be "a step ahead of the game".

Additionally, individuals who process information intuitively (i.e., low cognitive reflection) were more likely to change their attitude (Chaiken & Maheswaran, 1994) and detect deception (e.g., fake news; Pehlivanoglu et al., 2021) when information was provided from a reputable source (i.e., news article paired with a reputable source outlet such as the *Washington Post* as opposed to a non-reputable outlet such as True Pundit). Of course, in the context of fraudulent offers, it is important to keep in mind that the fraudster is attempting to appear reputable since no one will fall for the attack if they understand that it is malicious. Therefore, techniques such as impersonation, where the fraudster engages in an act of pretending to be somebody else (e.g., a reputable business or a bank), are frequently used for the purpose of fraud; or utilizing reputable outlets for distribution of misinformation (e.g., politically misleading newspaper fliers in the *Miami Herald* during the 2020 presidential election). These techniques that leverage human target and deceptive cue characteristics and their interplay need to be specifically targeted in successful warning and defense solutions moving forward.

In the context of aging, older adults have been shown to prioritize positive over negative information ("positivity bias"; Carstensen, Mikels, & Mather, 2006; Reed, Chan, & Mikels, 2014), while young adults prioritize negative over positive information (Baumeister, Bratslavsky, Finkenauer, & Vohs, 2001; Rozin & Royzman, 2001). Thus, it is possible that older adults are more likely to fall for particularly positively-framed deceptive messages (i.e., gains) but are less vulnerable to negatively-framed messages (i.e., loss); a hypothesis that future research will be able to test. We propose that future research on online fraud susceptibility that considers this dynamic interplay between human and deceptive cues characteristics will be crucial to advance effectiveness of warning and training solutions.

Tailored training and design of decision-supportive tools

Automated detection (e.g., spam filters) alone has proven insufficient in mitigating exploitation (e.g., phishing), as they are never perfect (Dada et al., 2019) and also because new, undetected threats reach the human target before defense solutions can be implemented (Bilge & Dumitras, 2012; Zhang et al., 2016). Rather effective defense solutions need to involve human decision-making capacity. Typical current trainings for the human Internet user include educational games (Arachchilage & Cole, 2016; Sheng et al., 2007), simulated phishing attacks (Caputo, Pfleeger, Freeman, & Johnson, 2014), embedded techniques (such as short trainings immediately following successful simulated phishing attacks; Kumaraguru, Cranor, & Mather, 2009; Kumaraguru et al., 2007; Mohebzada et al., 2012), and provision of training literature/warning examples (Zielinska et al., 2014). Habituation (Egelman, Cranor, & Hong, 2008; Richards, 2020), overconfidence (Kumaraguru et al., 2007), and/or forgetfulness (Caputo et al., 2014), or even just the ability to reach older adults (and other vulnerable target populations), however, limit effectiveness of these trainings, and longer-term risk reduction has not yet been achieved.

We argue that a better matching between trainee characteristics and training content/scheme is warranted. For example, evidence from cognitive training research, that supports older adults' benefit from spaced and multi-session training (Baltes & Baltes, 1993), should inform the scheduling scheme of phishing training programs for older adults. It is even possible that novel training techniques using brain stimulation and neurofeedback, which directly change brain–behavior connections (Sitaram et al., 2016) and have recently been implemented among older adults (Rana et al., 2016), are fruitful in protecting against online risks. Certainly, any such future training approaches need to consider the lack of cues commonly present in interpersonal interactions such as voice / intonation, body language, and microexpressions (DePaulo et al., 2003; Zuckerman, Kernis, Driver, & Koestner, 1984), which further challenge deception detection in cyberspace.

Finally, one of the most important tasks for future research is to generate reliable fraud susceptibility profiles that can inform who is at particular risk and needs to be targeted in interventions. These approaches could benefit from leveraging our proposed biopsychosocial model of the aging decision-maker to assure multifaceted nature of the profiling. Moving forward, clinical tools (e.g., interviews and questionnaires that are intended to assess susceptibility to various scams and underlying cognitive / socioemotional mechanisms; see Spreng et al., in press) as well as rigorous statistical and novel machine-learning methodology will be crucial in this effort toward comprehensive risk profiling, effective risk surveillance, and design of decision-supportive tools for older adults to counter online fraud.

For example, age-tailored defense solutions could be developed to offer on-the-spot warning about potentially deceptive online messages (in SMS, email, social media platforms) using natural-language and image-based machine-learning algorithms. These applications should apply user-friendly, age-tailored designs and could be specifically based on individual risk profiles (e.g., more frequent and explicit warnings for users at higher risk). Such personalized automated cueing has tremendous potential to assist in the decision-making process, reducing the burden of detecting deception for the individual.

Conclusions

Cyberfraud risk continues to grow as individuals navigate through a complex computerized, connected world. Though evidence is still mixed, older adults may be a particular target of deception online with risks for this population likely further increasing in the future. They have (often large) assets accumulated over a lifetime that they increasingly manage online, while being lower in computer literacy, decision-making capacity, sensitivity to deception cues, as well as experiencing various socioemotional and neurobiological changes (e.g., positivity bias). But although older adults constitute a fast-growing segment of the population in many nations worldwide, older adults, and those among them with age-related pathology, are currently neglected in cybersecurity research. With this chapter, we have offered a reflection and integration of the multifactorial influences on online fraud susceptibility, introducing a biopsychosocial framework within which the aging decision-maker in a fast-developing digital era can be better understood.

Acknowledgements

Research reported in this publication was supported by the NIH grant 1R01AG057764, McKnight Brain Research Foundation AGR DTD 04-11-2018, NIA grant T32AG020499, and NSF grant SBE-1450624.

Notes

1 Elder financial exploitation (i.e., committed by individuals in positions of trust) and elder fraud (i.e., committed by predatory strangers) constitute two forms of financial victimization in older adults (DeLiema, 2018) that are used interchangeably for the purpose of this chapter.

2 Also highly prevalent, but not separately addressed in this chapter, are mass-market consumer frauds, where consumers are deceived into purchasing deceptively promoted goods and services (e.g., see Anderson, 2019). This fraud also quite frequently occurs online, with 62% of fraudulent goods purchased through the internet (Anderson, 2019). While mass-market consumer fraud is distinct from phishing, for the purpose of this chapter a differentiation between these two concepts is not necessary.

References

Acierno, R., Hernandez, M. A., Amstadter, A. B., Resnick, H. S., Steve, K., Muzzy, W., & Kilpatrick, D. G. (2010). Prevalence and correlates of emotional, physical, sexual, and financial abuse and potential neglect in the United States: The National Elder Mistreatment Study. *American Journal of Public Health, 100*(2), 292–297. https://doi.org/10.2105/AJPH.2009.163089

Alexander, G. E., Ryan, L., Bowers, D., Foster, T. C., Bizon, J. L., Geldmacher, D. S., & Glisky, E. L. (2012). Characterizing cognitive aging in humans with links to animal models. *Frontiers in Aging Neuroscience, 4*(21), 1–18. https://doi.org/10.3389/fnagi.2012.00021

Amstadter, A. B., Zajac, K., Strachan, M., Hernandez, M. A., Kilpatrick, D. G., & Acierno, R. (2011). Prevalence and correlates of elder mistreatment in South Carolina:

The South Carolina elder mistreatment study. *Journal of Interpersonal Violence*, *26*(15), 2947–2972. https://doi.org/10.1177/0886260510390959

Anderson, K. B. (2019). Mass-market consumer fraud in the United States: A 2017 update. Federa; Trade Commission. Retrieved from https://www.ftc.gov/system/files/documents/reports/mass-market-consumer-fraud-united-states-2017-update/p105502massmarketconsumerfraud2017report.pdf

Andrews-Hanna, J. R., Smallwood, J., & Spreng, R. N. (2014). The default network and self-generated thought: Component processes, dynamic control, and clinical relevance. *Annals of the New York Academy of Sciences*, *1316*(1), 29–52. https://doi.org/10.1111/nyas.12360

Apicella, C. L., Dreber, A., Campbell, B., Gray, P. B., Hoffman, M., & Little, A. C. (2008). Testosterone and financial risk preferences. *Evolution and Human Behavior*, *29*(6), 384–390. https://doi.org/10.1016/j.evolhumbehav.2008.07.001

Arachchilage, N. A. G., & Cole, M. (2016). Designing a mobile game for home computer users to protect against phishing attacks. *International Journal for E-Learning Security*, *1*(1), 19–26. Retrieved from http://arxiv.org/abs/1602.03929

Asp, E., Manzel, K., Koestner, B., Cole, C. A., Denburg, N. L., & Tranel, D. (2012). A neuropsychological test of belief and doubt: Damage to ventromedial prefrontal cortex increases credulity for misleading advertising. *Frontiers in Neuroscience*, (July). https://doi.org/10.3389/fnins.2012.00100

Bailey, P. E., & Leon, T. (2019). A systematic review and meta-analysis of age-related differences in trust. *Psychology and Aging*, *34*(5), 674–685. https://doi.org/10.1037/PAG0000368

Bailey, P. E., Slessor, G., Rieger, M., Rendell, P. G., Moustafa, A. A., & Ruffman, T. (2015). Trust and trustworthiness in young and older adults. *Psychology and Aging*, *30*(4), 977–986. https://doi.org/10.1037/a0039736

Baltes, P. B., Baltes, M. M. (Eds.). (1993). *Successful aging: Perspectives from the behavioral sciences* (Vol. 4). Cambridge University Press, Cambridge.

Baumeister, R. F., Bratslavsky, E., Finkenauer, C., & Vohs, K. D. (2001). Bad is stronger than good. *Review of General Psychology*, *5*(4), 323–370. https://doi.org/10.1037/1089-2680.5.4.323

Baumgartner, T., Heinrichs, M., Vonlanthen, A., Fischbacher, U., & Fehr, E. (2008). Oxytocin shapes the neural circuitry of trust and trust adaptation in humans. *Neuron*, *58*(4), 639–650. https://doi.org/10.1016/j.neuron.2008.04.009

Benenson, Z., Gassmann, F., & Landwirth, R. (2017). Unpacking spear phishing susceptibility. In *International Conference on Financial Cryptography and Data Security* (pp. 610–627). https://doi.org/10.1007/978-3-319-70278-0_39

Bilge, L., & Dumitras, T. (2012). Before we knew it: An empirical study of zero-day attacks in the real world. In *Proceedings of the ACM Conference on Computer and Communications Security* (pp. 833–844). New York: ACM Press. https://doi.org/10.1145/2382196.2382284

Bless, H. (2001). Mood and the use of general knowledge structures. In L. L. Martin & G. L. Clore (Eds.). *Theories of mood and cognition: A user's guidebook* (pp. 9–26). Lawrence Erlbaum Associates Publishers.

Bond, C. F. J., & DePaulo, B. M. (2006). Accuracy of deception judgments. *Personality and Social Psychology Review*, *10*(3), 214–234. https://doi.org/10.1207/s15327957pspr1003_2

Bos, P. A., Panksepp, J., Bluthé, R. M., & Honk, J. v. (January 2012). Acute effects of steroid hormones and neuropeptides on human social-emotional behavior: A review of single administration studies. *Frontiers in Neuroendocrinology*. https://doi.org/10.1016/j.yfrne.2011.01.002

Boyle, P. A., Yu, L., Schneider, J. A., Wilson, R. S., & Bennett, D. A. (2019). Scam awareness related to incident Alzheimer dementia and mild cognitive impairment. *Annals of Internal Medicine*, *170*(10), 702–709. https://doi.org/10.7326/M18-2711

Boyle, P. A., Yu, L., Wilson, R. S., Gamble, K., Buchman, A. S., & Bennett, D. A. (2012). Poor decision making is a consequence of cognitive decline among older persons without Alzheimer's disease or mild cognitive impairment. *PloS One*, *7*(8), e43647. https://doi.org/10.1371/journal.pone.0043647

Brashier, N. M., & Schacter, D. L. (2020). Aging in an era of fake news. *Current Directions in Psychological Science*, *29*(3), 316–323. https://doi.org/10.1177/0963721420915872

Braver, T. S., & West, R. (2008). Working memory, executive control, and aging. In Craik, F. I., & Salthouse, T. (Eds.), *The handbook of aging and cognition* (3rd ed., pp. 311–372). New York: Psychology Press.

ten Brinke, L., Lee, J. J., & Carney, D. R. (2019). Different physiological reactions when observing lies versus truths: Initial evidence and an intervention to enhance accuracy. *Journal of Personality and Social Psychology*. https://doi.org/10.1037/pspi0000175

Buckingham, D. (2019). Teaching media in a "post-truth" age: Fake news, media bias and the challenge for media/digital literacy education. *Cultura y Educacion*, *31*(2), 213–231. https://doi.org/10.1080/11356405.2019.1603814

Button, M., Lewis, C., & Tapley, J. (2014). Not a victimless crime: The impact of fraud on individual victims and their families. *Security Journal*, *27*(1), 36–54. https://doi.org/10.1057/sj.2012.11

Calso, C., Besnard, J., & Allain, P. (2020). Study of the theory of mind in normal aging: Focus on the deception detection and its links with other cognitive functions. *Aging, Neuropsychology, and Cognition*, *27*(3), 430–452. https://doi.org/10.1080/13825585.2019.1628176

Campbell, M. A., & Porter, S. (2002). Pinpointing reality: How well can people judge true and mistaken emotional childhood memories? *Canadian Journal of Behavioural Science*, *34*(4), 217–229. https://doi.org/10.1037/h0087174

Caputo, D. D., Pfleeger, S. L., Freeman, J. D., & Johnson, M. E. (2014). Going spear phishing: Exploring embedded training and awareness. *IEEE Security & Privacy*, *12*(1), 28–38. https://doi.org/10.1109/MSP.2013.106

Carr, J. (2011). In Loukides, M. (Ed.), *Inside cyber warfare* (2nd ed.). Sebastopol: O'Reilly Media. https://doi.org/10.1080/19393555.2013.828804

Carstensen, L. L., Mikels, J. A., & Mather, M. (2006). Aging and the intersection of cognition, motivation, and emotion. In *Handbook of the psychology of aging* (pp. 343–362). Elsevier Inc. https://doi.org/10.1016/B978-012101264-9/50018-5

Cassidy, B. S., Leshikar, E. D., Shih, J. Y., Aizenman, A., & Gutchess, A. H. (2013). Valence-based age differences in medial prefrontal activity during impression formation. *Social Neuroscience*, *8*(5), 462–473. https://doi.org/10.1080/17470919.2013.832373

Castle, E., Eisenberger, N. I., Seeman, T. E., Moons, W. G., Boggero, I. A., Grinblatt, M. S., & Taylor, S. E. (2012). Neural and behavioral bases of age differences in perceptions of trust. *Proceedings of the National Academy of Sciences*, *109*(51), 20848–20852. https://doi.org/10.1073/pnas.1218518109/-/DCSupplemental.www.pnas.org/cgi/doi/10.1073/pnas.1218518109

Chaiken, S. (1987). The heuristic model of persuasion. In M. P. Zanna, J. M. Olson, & C. P. Herman (Eds.), *Social influence: The Ontario symposium*, Vol. 5, pp. 3–39). Lawrence Erlbaum Associates, Inc.

Chaiken, S., & Maheswaran, D. (1994). Heuristic processing can bias systematic processing: Effects of source credibility, argument ambiguity, and task importance on attitude judgment. *Journal of Personality and Social Psychology*, *66*(3), 460–473. https://doi.org/10.1037/0022-3514.66.3.460

Chen, X., Gautam, P., Haroon, E., & Rilling, J. K. (2017). Within vs. between-subject effects of intranasal oxytocin on the neural response to cooperative and non-cooperative social interactions. *Psychoneuroendocrinology*, *78*, 22–30. https://doi.org/10.1016/j.psyneuen.2017.01.006

Chen, X., Hackett, P. D., DeMarco, A. C., Feng, C., Stair, S., Haroon, E., … Rilling, J. K. (2016). Effects of oxytocin and vasopressin on the neural response to unreciprocated cooperation within brain regions involved in stress and anxiety in men and women. *Brain Imaging and Behavior*, *10*(2), 581–593. https://doi.org/10.1007/s11682-015-9411-7

Clement, J. (2020). U.S. internet usage penetration 2019, by age group. *Pew Research Center*. Retrieved from https://www.statista.com/statistics/266587/percentage-of-internet-users-by-age-groups-in-the-us/

Dada, E. G., Bassi, J. S., Chiroma, H., Abdulhamid, S. M., Adetunmbi, A. O., & Ajibuwa, O. E. (2019). Machine learning for email spam filtering: Review, approaches and open research problems. *Heliyon*, *5*(6), e01802. https://doi.org/10.1016/j.heliyon.2019.e01802

Darley, J. M., & Gross, P. H. (1983). A hypothesis-confirming bias in labeling effects. *Journal of Personality and Social Psychology*, *44*(1), 20–33. https://doi.org/10.1037/0022-3514.44.1.20.

DeLiema, M. (2018). Elder fraud and financial exploitation: Application of routine activity theory. *The Gerontologist*, *58*(4), 706–718. https://doi.org/10.1093/geront/gnw258

Denburg, N. L., Cole, C. A., Hernandez, M., Yamada, T. H., Tranel, D., Bechara, A., & Wallace, R. B. (2007). The orbitofrontal cortex, real-world decision making, and normal aging. In *Annals of the New York Academy of Sciences* (Vol. 1121, pp. 480–498). Blackwell Publishing Inc. https://doi.org/10.1196/annals.1401.031

DePaulo, B. M., Malone, B. E., Lindsay, J. J., Muhlenbruck, L., Charlton, K., Cooper, H., … Cooper, H. (2003). Cues to deception. *Psychological Bulletin*, *129*(1), 74–118. https://doi.org/10.1037/0033-2909.129.1.74

Dodd, M. L., Klos, K. J., Bower, J. H., Geda, Y. E., Josephs, K. A., & Ahlskog, J. E. (2005). Pathological gambling caused by drugs used to treat Parkinson disease. *Archives of Neurology*, *62*(9), 1377–1381. https://doi.org/10.1001/archneur.62.9.noc50009

Dong, X., & Simon, M. A. (2013a). Association between reported elder abuse and rates of admission to the skilled nursing facilities: Findings from a longitudinal population-based cohort study. *Gerontology*, *59*(5), 464–472. https://doi.org/10.1038/jid.2014.371

Dong, X., & Simon, M. A. (2013b). Elder abuse as a risk factor for hospitalization in older persons. *JAMA Internal Medicine*, *173*(10), 911–917. https://doi.org/10.1001/jamainternmed.2013.238

de Dreu, C. K. W., Dussel, D. B., & Ten Velden, F. S. (2015). In intergroup conflict, self-sacrifice is stronger among pro-social individuals, and parochial altruism emerges especially among cognitively taxed individuals. *Frontiers in Psychology*, *6*(May). https://doi.org/10.3389/fpsyg.2015.00572

Driver-Dunckley, E., Samanta, J., & Stacy, M. (2003). Pathological gambling associated with dopamine agonist therapy in Parkinson's disease. *Neurology*, *61*(3), 422–423. https://doi.org/10.1212/01.wnl.0000076478.45005.ec

Drolet, A., Jiang, L., Pour Mohammad, A., & Davis, C. (2018). The influence of aging on consumer decision-making. *Consumer Psychology Review*, *2*(1), arcp.1046. https://doi.org/10.1002/arcp.1046

Dunn, B. D., Evans, D., Makarova, D., White, J., & Clark, L. (2012). Gut feelings and the reaction to perceived inequity: The interplay between bodily responses, regulation, and perception shapes the rejection of unfair offers on the ultimatum game. *Cognitive, Affective and Behavioral Neuroscience*, *12*(3), 419–429. https://doi.org/10.3758/s13415-012-0092-z

Durante, K. M., Griskevicius, V., Cantú, S. M., & Simpson, J. A. (2014). Money, status, and the ovulatory cycle. *Journal of Marketing Research*, *51*(1), 27–39. https://doi.org/10.1509/jmr.11.0327

Dyck, J. L., & Smither, J. A. (1994). Age differences in computer anxiety: The role of computer experience, gender and education. *Journal of Education and Computer Research*, 10, 238–248.

Ebner, N C, & Fischer, H. (2014). Studying the various facets of emotional aging. *Frontiers in Psychology*, *5*, 1007.

Ebner, N. C., Maura, G. M., MacDonald, K., Westberg, L., & Fischer, H. (2013). Oxytocin and socioemotional aging: Current knowledge and future trends. *Frontiers in Human Neuroscience*, *7*, 487. https://doi.org/10.3389/fnhum.2013.00487

Ebner, Natalie C., Ellis, D. M., Lin, T., Rocha, H. A., Yang, H., Dommaraju, S., … Oliveira, D. S. (2020). Uncovering susceptibility risk to online deception in aging. *Journals of Gerontology - Series B Psychological Sciences and Social Sciences*, *75*(3), 522–533. https://doi.org/10.1093/geronb/gby036

Egelman, S., Cranor, L. F., & Hong, J. (2008). You've been warned: An empirical study of the effectiveness of web browser phishing warnings. In *Conference on Human Factors in Computing Systems - Proceedings* (pp. 1065–1074). New York: ACM Press. https://doi.org/10.1145/1357054.1357219

Ein-Dor, T., & Perry, A. (2014). Full house of fears: Evidence that people high in attachment anxiety are more accurate in detecting deceit. *Journal of Personality*, *82*(2), 83–92. https://doi.org/10.1111/jopy.12035

Evans, J. S. B. T. (2002). Logic and human reasoning: An assessment of the deduction paradigm. *Psychological Bulletin*, *128*(6), 978–996. https://doi.org/10.1037/0033-2909.128.6.978

Evans, J. S. B. T. (2008). Dual-processing accounts of reasoning, judgment, and social cognition. *Annual Review of Psychology*, *59*(1), 255–278. https://doi.org/10.1146/annurev.psych.59.103006.093629

Federal Bureau of Investigation. (2016). *Fraud against seniors*. Retrieved from https://www.fbi.gov/scams-and-safety/common-fraud-schemes/seniors

Federal Bureau of Investigation. (2020). *Scams and Safety: Spoofing and Phishing*. Retrieved from https://www.fbi.gov/scams-and-safety/common-scams-and-crimes/spoofing-and-phishing

Federal Trade Commission. (2020). *Consumer Protection Data Spotlight*. Retrieved from https://www.ftc.gov/news-events/blogs/data-spotlight/2020/10/scams-starting-social-media-proliferate-early-2020

Forgas, J. P., & East, R. (2008). On being happy and gullible: Mood effects on skepticism and the detection of deception. *Journal of Experimental Social Psychology*, *44*(5), 1362–1367. https://doi.org/10.1016/j.jesp.2008.04.010

Frazier, I., Lighthall, N. R., Horta, M., Perez, E., & Ebner, N. C. (2019). CISDA: Changes in integration for social decisions in aging. *Wiley Interdisciplinary Reviews: Cognitive Science*, e1490. https://doi.org/10.1002/wcs.1490

Frazier, I., Lin, T., Liu, P., Skarsten, S., Feifel, D., & Ebner, N. C. (2020). Age and intranasal oxytocin effects on trust-related decisions: Behavioral and brain evidence. *Psychology and Aging*, *36*(1), 10–21. http://dx.doi.org/10.1037/pag0000545

Freedman, M., & Stuss, D. T. (2011). Theory of mind in Parkinson's disease. *Journal of the Neurological Sciences*, *310*(1–2), 225–227. https://doi.org/10.1016/j.jns.2011.06.004

Friend, C., & Fox Hamilton, N. (2016). Deception detection: The relationship of levels of trust and perspective taking in real-time online and offline communication environments. *Cyberpsychology, Behavior, and Social Networking*, *19*(9), 532–537. https://doi.org/10.1089/cyber.2015.0643

Gilovich, T., Griffin, D., & Kahneman, D. (2002). *Heuristics and biases: The psychology of intuitive judgment*. Cambridge University Press.

Grace, S. A., Rossell, S. L., Heinrichs, M., Kordsachia, C., & Labuschagne, I. (2018). Oxytocin and brain activity in humans: A systematic review and coordinate-based meta-analysis of functional MRI studies. *Psychoneuroendocrinology*, *96*, 6–24. https://doi.org/10.1016/j.psyneuen.2018.05.031

Grèzes, J., Frith, C., Passingham, R. E., & Grezes, J. (2004). Brain mechanisms for inferring deceit in the actions of others. *The Journal of Neuroscience*, *24*(24), 5500–5505. https://doi.org/10.1523/JNEUROSCI.0219-04.2004

Griffith, H. R., Stewart, C. C., Stoeckel, L. E., Okonkwo, O. C., Den Hollander, J. A., Martin, R. C., … Marson, D. C. (2010). Magnetic resonance imaging volume of the angular gyri predicts financial skill deficits in people with amnestic mild cognitive impairment. *Journal of the American Geriatrics Society*, *58*(2), 265–274. https://doi.org/10.1111/j.1532-5415.2009.02679.x

Grilli, M. D., McVeigh, K. S., Hakim, Z. M., Wank, A. A., Getz, S. J., Levin, B. E., … Wilson, R. C. (2021). Is this phishing? Older age is associated with greater difficulty discriminating between safe and malicious emails. *The Journals of Gerontology: Series B*, *76*(9), 1711–1715.

Gutchess, A., & Samanez-Larkin, G. R. (2019). Social function and motivation in the aging brain. In *The aging brain: Functional adaptation across adulthood* (pp. 165–184). American Psychological Association. https://doi.org/10.1037/0000143-007

Han, S. D., Boyle, P. A., James, B. D., Yu, L., Barnes, L. L., & Bennett, D. A. (2016a). Discrepancies between cognition and decision making in older adults. *Aging Clinical and Experimental Research*, *28*(1), 99–108. https://doi.org/10.1007/s40520-015-0375-7

Han, S. D., Boyle, P. A., James, B. D., Yu, L., & Bennett, D. A. (2016b). Mild cognitive impairment and susceptibility to scams in old age. *Journal of Alzheimer's Disease*, *49*(3), 845–851. https://doi.org/10.3233/JAD-150442

Han, S. D., & Mosqueda, L. (2020). Elder abuse in the COVID-19 era. *Journal of the American Geriatrics Society*. https://doi.org/10.1111/jgs.16496

Happé, F., Brownell, H., & Winner, E. (1999). Acquired "theory of mind" impairments following stroke. *Cognition*, *70*(3), 211–240. https://doi.org/10.1016/S0010-0277(99)00005-0.

Hardy, B., Page, L., Schaffner, M., Graggaber, J., Powlson, A. S., Fletcher, P. C., … Coates, J. (2014). Cortisol shifts financial risk preferences Narayanan Kandasamy1. *Proceedings of the National Academy of Sciences of the United States of America, 111*(9), 3608–3613. https://doi.org/10.1073/pnas.1317908111

Hedden, T., & Gabrieli, J. D. E. (2004). Insights into the ageing mind: A view from cognitive neuroscience. *Nature Reviews. Neuroscience.* https://doi.org/10.1038/nrn1323

Heitland, I., Oosting, R. S., Baas, J. M. P., Massar, S. A. A., Kenemans, J. L., & Böcker, K. B. E. (2012). Genetic polymorphisms of the dopamine and serotonin systems modulate the neurophysiological response to feedback and risk taking in healthy humans. *Cognitive, Affective and Behavioral Neuroscience, 12*(4), 678–691. https://doi.org/10.3758/s13415-012-0108-8

Hertzog, C., Dixon, R. A., & Hultsch, D. F. (1992). Intraindividual change in text recall of the elderly. *Brain and Language, 42*(3), 248–269. https://doi.org/10.1016/0093-934X(92)90100-S.

Holtfreter, K., Reisig, M. D., Piquero, N. L., & Piquero, A. R. (2010). Low self-control and fraud: Offending, victimization, and their overlap. *Criminal Justice and Behavior, 37*(2), 188–203. https://doi.org/10.1177/0093854809354977

Hong, I. B., & Cha, H. S. (2013). The mediating role of consumer trust in an online merchant in predicting purchase intention. *International Journal of Information Management, 33*(6), 927–939. https://doi.org/10.1016/j.ijinfomgt.2013.08.007

Horta, M., Kaylor, K., Feifel, D., & Ebner, N. C. (2020). Chronic oxytocin administration as a tool for investigation and treatment: A cross-disciplinary, systematic review. *Neuroscience and Biobehavioral Reviews, 108*, 1–23. https://doi.org/10.1016/j.neubiorev.2019.10.012

Hülür, G., & Macdonald, B. (2020). Rethinking social relationships in old age: Digitalization and the social lives of older adults. *American Psychologist, 75*(4), 554–566. https://doi.org/10.1037/amp0000604

Isele, E., & Rogoff, E. G. (2014). Senior entrepreneurship: The new normal. *Public Policy & Aging Report, 24*(4), 141–147. https://doi.org/10.1093/ppar/pru043

Israel, S., Hart, E., & Winter, E. (2014). Oxytocin decreases accuracy in the perception of social deception. *Psychological Science, 25*(1), 293–295. https://doi.org/10.1177/0956797613500794

Jacoby, L. (1999). Deceiving the elderly: Effects of accessibility bias in cued-recall performance. *Cognitive Neuropsychology, 16*(3–5), 417–436.

Jagatic, T. N., Johnson, N. A., Jakobsson, M., & Menczer, F. (2007). Social phishing. *Communications of the ACM, 50*(10), 94–100. https://doi.org/10.1145/1290958.1290968

James, B. D., Boyle, P. A., & Bennett, D. A. (2014). Correlates of susceptibility to scams in older adults without dementia. *Journal of Elder Abuse & Neglect, 26*(2), 107–122. https://doi.org/10.1080/08946566.2013.821809

Kahneman, D., Slovic, S. P., & Tversky, A. (1982). *Judgment under uncertainty: Heuristics and biases*. Cambridge: Cambridge University Press.

Karbach, J., & Verhaeghen, P. (2014). Making working memory work: A meta-analysis of executive-control and working memory training in older adults. *Psychological Science, 25*(11), 2027–2037. https://doi.org/10.1177/0956797614548725

Kirk, U., Downar, J., & Montague, P. R. (2011). Interoception drives increased rational decision-making in meditators playing the ultimatum game. *Frontiers in Neuroscience, 5*(APR), 49. https://doi.org/10.3389/fnins.2011.00049

Kirsch, P., Meyer-Lindenberg, A., Kirsch, P., Esslinger, C., Chen, Q., Mier, D., … Meyer-Lindenberg, A. (2016). Oxytocin modulates neural circuitry for social cognition and fear in humans, November. https://doi.org/10.1523/JNEUROSCI.3984-05.2005

Klein, G. (2008). Naturalistic decision making. *Human Factors: The Journal of the Human Factors and Ergonomics Society*, *50*(3), 456–460.

Kraut, R. (1980). Humans as lie detectors. *Journal of Communication*, *30*(4), 209–218. https://doi.org/10.1111/j.1460-2466.1980.tb02030.x

Kumaraguru, P., Cranor, L. F., & Mather, L. (2009). Anti-phishing landing page: Turning a 404 into a teachable moment for end users. *Sixth Conference on Email and AntiSpam*. https://doi.org/10.1.1.165.1417

Kumaraguru, P., Rhee, Y., Acquisti, A., Cranor, L. F., Hong, J., & Nunge, E. (2007). Protecting people from phishing: The design and evaluation of an embedded training email system. In *Conference on Human Factors in Computing Systems - Proceedings* (pp. 905–914). New York: ACM Press. https://doi.org/10.1145/1240624.1240760

Lachs, M., & Berman, J. (2011). Under the radar: New York State elder abuse prevalence study. *Lifespan of Greater Rochester Inc., Weill Cornell Medical Center of Cornell University, New York City Department for the Aging*. Retrieved from https://www.ncjrs.gov/App/Publications/abstract.aspx?ID=258421

Lane, J. D., & Depaulo, B. M. (1999). Completing Coyne's cycle: Dysphorics' ability to detect deception. *Journal of Research in Personality*, *33*(3), 311–329. https://doi.org/10.1006/jrpe.1999.2253

Lantz, P. M., House, J. S., Mero, R. P., & Williams, D. R. (2005). Stress, life events, and socioeconomic disparities in health: Results from the Americans' changing lives study. *Journal of Health and Social Behavior*, *46*(3), 274–288. https://doi.org/10.1177/002214650504600305

LaTour, K. A., & LaTour, M. S. (2009). Positive mood and susceptibility to false advertising. *Journal of Advertising*, *38*(3), 127–142. https://doi.org/10.2753/JOA0091-3367380309

Le Couteur, D. G., Anderson, R. M., & Newman, A. B. (2020). COVID-19 is a disease of older people. *The Journals of Gerontology. Series A, Biological Sciences and Medical Sciences*, *XX*, 1–2. https://doi.org/10.1093/gerona/glaa077

Lee, Y.-K. (2014). Gender stereotypes as a double-edged sword in political advertising: Persuasion effects of campaign theme and advertising style. *International Journal of Advertising: The Quarterly Review of Marketing Communications*, *33*(2), 203–234. https://doi.org/10.2501/IJA-33-2-203-234

Li, S.-C., Aggen, S. H., Nesselroade, J. R., & Baltes, P. B. (2001). Short-term fluctuations in elderly people's sensorimotor functioning predict text and spatial memory performance: The MacArthur successful aging studies. *Gerontology*, *47*(2), 100–116. https://doi.org/10.1159/000052782

Li, Y., Gao, J., Enkavi, A. Z., Zaval, L., Weber, E. U., & Johnson, E. J. (2015). Sound credit scores and financial decisions despite cognitive aging. *Proceedings of the National Academy of Sciences of the United States of America*, *112*(1), 65–69. https://doi.org/10.1073/pnas.1413570112

Lichtenberg, P. A. (2016). Financial exploitation, financial capacity, and Alzheimer's disease. *American Psychologist*, *71*(4), 312–320. https://doi.org/10.1037/a0040192

Lichtenberg, P. A., Howard, H., Simaskp, P., Mall, S., Speir, J., Farrell, C., … Ficker, L. J. (2016). The lichtenberg financial decision screening scale (LFDSS): A new tool for assessing financial decision making and preventing financial exploitation. *Journal of Elder Abuse & Neglect*, *28*(3), 134–151. https://doi.org/10.1080/08946566.2016.1168333

Lighthall, N. R., Sakaki, M., Vasunilashorn, S., Nga, L., Somayajula, S., Chen, E. Y., … Mather, M. (2012). Gender differences in reward-related decision processing under stress. *Social Cognitive and Affective Neuroscience*, *7*(4), 476–484. https://doi.org/10.1093/scan/nsr026

Lin, T., Capecci, D. E., Ellis, D. M., Rocha, H. A., Dommaraju, S., Oliveira, D. S., & Ebner, N. C. (2019). Susceptibility to spear-phishing emails: Effects of internet user demographics and email content. *ACM Transactions on Computer-Human Interaction*, *26*(5), 1–28. https://doi.org/10.1145/3336141

Lissek, S., Peters, S., Fuchs, N., Witthaus, H., Nicolas, V., Tegenthoff, M., … Brüne, M. (2008). Cooperation and deception recruit different subsets of the theory-of-mind network. *PLoS ONE*, *3*(4). https://doi.org/10.1371/journal.pone.0002023

Lustig, C., Hasher, L., & Zacks, R. T. (2008). Inhibitory deficit theory: Recent developments in a "new view." In *Inhibition in cognition* (pp. 145–162). American Psychological Association. https://doi.org/10.1037/11587-008

Marquié, J. C., Jourdan-Boddaert, L., & Huet, N. (2002). Do older adults underestimate their actual computer knowledge? *Behaviour and Information Technology*. 21, 273–280.

Marson, D. C. (2001). Loss of financial competency in dementia: Conceptual and empirical approaches. *Aging, Neuropsychology, and Cognition*, *8*(3), 164–181. https://doi.org/10.1076/anec.8.3.164.827

Marson, D. C., Martin, R. C., Wadley, V., Griffith, H. R., Snyder, S., Goode, P. S., … Harrell, L. E. (2009). Clinical interview assessment of financial capacity in older adults with mild cognitive impairment and Alzheimer's disease. *Journal of the American Geriatrics Society*, *57*(5), 806–814. https://doi.org/10.1111/j.1532-5415.2009.02202.x

Matovic, D., Koch, A. S., & Forgas, J. P. (2014). Can negative mood improve language understanding? Affective influences on the ability to detect ambiguous communication. *Journal of Experimental Social Psychology*, *52*, 44–49. https://doi.org/10.1016/j.jesp.2013.12.003

Matthews, K. A., Xu, W., Gaglioti, A. H., Holt, J. B., Croft, J. B., Mack, D., & McGuire, L. C. (2019). Racial and ethnic estimates of Alzheimer's disease and related dementias in the United States (2015–2060) in adults aged ≥65 years. *Alzheimer's and Dementia*, *15*(1), 17–24. https://doi.org/10.1016/j.jalz.2018.06.3063

MetLife. (2011). *The MetLife study of elder financial abuse: Crimes of occasion, desperation, and predation against America's elders*. Retrieved from https://ltcombudsman.org/uploads/files/issues/mmi-elder-financial-abuse.pdf

Mohebzada, J. G., Zarka, A. E., Bhojani, A. H., & Darwish, A. (2012). Phishing in a university community: Two large scale phishing experiments. In *2012 International Conference on Innovations in Information Technology, IIT 2012*. https://doi.org/10.1109/INNOVATIONS.2012.6207742

Moody, G. D., Galletta, D. F., & Dunn, B. K. (2017). Which phish get caught An exploratory study of individuals' susceptibility to phishing. *European Journal of Information Systems*, *26*(6), 564–584. https://doi.org/10.1057/s41303-017-0058-x

Moore, R. C., & Hancock, J. T. (2020). Older adults, social technologies, and the coronavirus pandemic: Challenges, strengths, and strategies for support. *Social Media + Society*, *6*(3), 205630512094816. https://doi.org/10.1177/2056305120948162

Motzkin, J. C., Philippi, C. L., Wolf, R. C., Baskaya, M. K., & Koenigs, M. (2015). Ventromedial prefrontal cortex is critical for the regulation of amygdala activity in humans. *Biological Psychiatry*, *77*(3), 276–284. https://doi.org/10.1016/j.biopsych.2014.02.014

Mueller, E. A., Wood, S. A., Hanoch, Y., Huang, Y., & Reed, C. L. (2020). Older and wiser: Age differences in susceptibility to investment fraud: The protective role of emotional intelligence. *Journal of Elder Abuse and Neglect*, *32*(2), 152–172. https://doi.org/10.1080/08946566.2020.1736704

National Research Council. (2003). *Elder mistreatment: Abuse, neglect, and exploitation in an aging America*. Washington, DC: The National Academy Press.

Nave, G., Camerer, C., & McCullough, M. (2015). Does oxytocin increase trust in humans? A critical review of research. *Perspectives on Psychological Science*, *10*(6), 772–789. https://doi.org/10.1177/1745691615600138

Oliveira, D. S., Lin, T., Rocha, H., Ellis, D., Dommaraju, S., Yang, H., … Ebner, N. C. (2019). Empirical analysis of weapons of influence, life domains, and demographic-targeting in modern spam: An age-comparative perspective. *Crime Science*, *8*(1), 3. https://doi.org/10.1186/s40163-019-0098-8

Ollmann, G. (2007). *The vishing guide*. IBM Global Technologies. Retrieved from http://www.gupiaoya.com/tools/Miscellaneous/IBM_ISS_vishing_guide.pdf

Pehlivanoglu, D., Lin, T., Deceus, F., Heemskerk, A., Ebner, N. C., & Cahill, B. S. (2021). The role of analytical reasoning and source credibility on the evaluation of real and fake full-length news articles. *Cognitive Research: Principles and Implications*, *6*(1), 1–12.

Peters, E., Hess, T. M., Västfjäll, D., & Auman, C. (2007). Adult age differences in dual information processes: Implications for the role of affective and deliberative processes in older adults' decision making. *Perspectives on Psychological Science: A Journal of the Association for Psychological Science*, *2*(1), 1–23. https://doi.org/10.1111/j.1745-6916.2007.00025.x

Peterson, J. C., Burnes, D. P. R., Caccamise, P. L., Mason, A., Henderson, C. R., Wells, M. T., … Lachs, M. S. (2014). Financial exploitation of older adults: A population-based prevalence study. *Journal of General Internal Medicine*, *29*(12), 1615–1623. https://doi.org/10.1007/s11606-014-2946-2

Pfundmair, M., Erk, W., & Reinelt, A. (2017). "Lie to me"—Oxytocin impairs lie detection between sexes. *Psychoneuroendocrinology*, *84*, 135–138. https://doi.org/10.1016/j.psyneuen.2017.07.001

Preston, S. D., Buchanan, T. W., Stansfield, R. B., & Bechara, A. (2007). Effects of anticipatory stress on decision making in a gambling task. *Behavioral Neuroscience*, *121*(2), 257–263. https://doi.org/10.1037/0735-7044.121.2.257

Queen, T. L., & Hess, T. M. (2010). Age differences in the effects of conscious and unconscious thought in decision making. *Psychology and Aging*, *25*(2), 251–261. https://doi.org/10.1037/a0018856

Quintana, D. S., Westlye, L. T., Alnæs, D., Rustan, Ø. G., Kaufmann, T., Smerud, K. T., … Andreassen, O. A. (2016). Low dose intranasal oxytocin delivered with breath powered device dampens amygdala response to emotional stimuli: A peripheral effect-controlled within-subjects randomized dose-response fMRI trial. *Psychoneuroendocrinology*, *69*, 180–188. https://doi.org/10.1016/j.psyneuen.2016.04.010

Radke, S., Volman, I., Kokal, I., Roelofs, K., de Bruijn, E. R. A., & Toni, I. (2017). Oxytocin reduces amygdala responses during threat approach. *Psychoneuroendocrinology*, *79*, 160–166. https://doi.org/10.1016/j.psyneuen.2017.02.028

Rana, M., Varan, A. Q., Davoudi, A., Cohen, R. A., Sitaram, R., & Ebner, N. C. (2016). Real-time fMRI in neuroscience research and its use in studying the aging brain. *Frontiers in Aging Neuroscience*. https://doi.org/10.3389/fnagi.2016.00239

Reed, A. E., Chan, L., & Mikels, J. A. (2014). Meta-analysis of the age-related positivity effect: Age differences in preferences for positive over negative information. *Psychology and Aging*, *29*(1), 1–15. https://doi.org/10.1037/a0035194

Reisig, M. D., Pratt, T. C., & Holtfreter, K. (2009). Perceived risk of internet theft victimization: Examining the effects of social vulnerability and financial impulsivity. *Criminal Justice and Behavior*, *36*(4), 369–384. https://doi.org/10.1177/0093854808329405

Reyna, V. F., & Brainerd, C. J. (2011). Dual processes in decision making and developmental neuroscience: A fuzzy-trace model. *Developmental Review*. https://doi.org/10.1016/j.dr.2011.07.004

Richards, K. E. (2020). Habituation: A possible mitigation of a wicked problem. In *Advances in intelligent systems and computing* (Vol. 1219 AISC, pp. 95–101). Springer. https://doi.org/10.1007/978-3-030-52581-1_13

Riggio, R. E., Tucker, J., & Throckmorton, B. (1987). Social skills and deception ability. *Personality and Social Psychology Bulletin*, *13*(4), 568–577. https://doi.org/10.1177/0146167287134013.

Rilling, J. K., DeMarco, A. C., Hackett, P. D., Chen, X., Gautam, P., Stair, S., … Pagnoni, G. (2014). Sex differences in the neural and behavioral response to intranasal oxytocin and vasopressin during human social interaction. *Psychoneuroendocrinology*, *39*(1), 237–248. https://doi.org/10.1016/j.psyneuen.2013.09.022

Roberto, K. A., Teaster, P. B., & Duke, J. O. (2004). Older women who experience mistreatment: Circumstances and outcomes. *Journal of Women & Aging*, *16*(1–2), 3–16. https://doi.org/10.1300/J074v16n01_02

Rogers, R. D. (January 2011). The roles of dopamine and serotonin in decision making: Evidence from pharmacological experiments in humans. *Neuropsychopharmacology*. https://doi.org/10.1038/npp.2010.165

Rozin, P., & Royzman, E. B. (2001). Negativity bias, negativity dominance, and contagion. *Personality and Social Psychology Review*, *5*(4), 296–320. https://doi.org/10.1207/S15327957PSPR0504_2

Ruffman, T., Murray, J., Halberstadt, J., & Vater, T. (2012). Age-related differences in deception. *Psychology and Aging*, *27*(3), 543–549. https://doi.org/10.1037/a0023380

Samanez-Larkin, G. R., & Knutson, B. (April 2015). Decision making in the ageing brain: Changes in affective and motivational circuits. *Nature Reviews Neuroscience*. https://doi.org/10.1038/nrn3917

Scheibe, S., & Carstensen, L. L. (2010). Emotional aging: Recent findings and future trends. *The Journals of Gerontology Series B: Psychological Sciences and Social Sciences*, *65B*(2), 135–144. https://doi.org/10.1093/geronb/gbp132

Schwandt, H. (2014). Wealth shocks and health outcomes: Evidence from stock market fluctuations. *American Economic Journal: Applied Economics*, *10*(4), 349–377. https://doi.org/10.1257/APP.20140499

Schwarz, N., & Clore, G. (2003). Mood as information: 20 years later. *Psychological Inquiry*. https://doi.org/10.1207/S15327965PLI1403&4_20

Sheng, S., Holbrook, M., Kumaraguru, P., Cranor, L. F., & Downs, J. (2010). Who falls for phish? A demographic analysis of phishing susceptibility and effectiveness of interventions. In *Conference on Human Factors in Computing Systems - Proceedings* (Vol. 1, pp. 373–382). New York: ACM Press. https://doi.org/10.1145/1753326.1753383

Sheng, S., Magnien, B., Kumaraguru, P., Acquisti, A., Cranor, L. F., Hong, J., & Nunge, E. (2007). Anti-Phishing Phil: the design and evaluation of a game that teaches people not to fall for phish. In *Proceedings of the 3rd symposium on Usable privacy and security (SOUPS '07)* (pp. 88–99). Association for Computing Machinery, New York, NY. https://doi.org/10.1145/1280680.1280692

Sherod, M. G., Griffith, H. R., Copeland, J., Belue, K., Krzynwanski, S., Zamrini, E. Y., ... Marson, D. C. (2009). Neurocognitive predictors of financial capacity across the dementia spectrum: Normal aging, mild cognitive impairment, and Alzheimer's disease. *Journal of the International Neuropsychological Society, 15*(2), 258–267. https://doi.org/10.1017/S1355617709090365

Silver, L., Smith, A., Johnson, C., Taylor, K., Jiang, J., Monica, A., & Rainie, L. (2019). Use of smartphones and social media is common across most emerging economies. Retrieved from https://www.pewInternet.org/2019/03/07/use-of-smartphones-and-social-media-is-common-across-most-emerging-economies/

Sitaram, R., Ros, T., Stoeckel, L. E., Haller, S., Scharnowski, F., Lewis-Peacock, J., ... Sulzer, J. (2016). Closed-loop brain training: The science of neurofeedback. *Nature Neuroscience, 18*(2), 86–100. https://doi.org/10.1038/nrn.2016.164

Slessor, G., Phillips, L. H., Ruffman, T., Bailey, P. E., & Insch, P. (2014). Exploring own-age biases in deception detection. *Cognition and Emotion, 28*(3), 493–506. https://doi.org/10.1080/02699931.2013.839438

Smith, A. (2014a). Older adults and technology use. *Pew Research Center*. Retrieved from http://www.pewinternet.org/2014/04/03/older-adults-and-technology-use/

Smith, A. (2014b). Older adults and technology use. *Pew Research Center*. Retrieved from http://www.pewinternet.org/2014/04/03/older-adults-and-technology-use/

Snyder, M. K. Reiter, and C. Kanich. (2016). The effect of repeated login prompts on phishing susceptibility. In *The {LASER} Workshop: Learning from Authoritative Security Experiment Results ({LASER} 2016)* (pp. 13–19). San Jose, CA, USA.

Spreng, R. N., Cassidy, B. N., Darboh, B. S., Dupre, E., Lockrow, A. W., Setton, R., & Turner, G. R. (2017). Financial exploitation is associated with structural and functional brain differences in healthy older adults. *Journals of Gerontology - Series A Biological Sciences and Medical Sciences, 72*(10), 1365–1368. https://doi.org/10.1093/gerona/glx051

Spreng, R. N., Ebner, N. C., Levin, B. E., & Turner, G. R. (in press) Aging and financial exploitation risk. In Factora, R. (Ed.), *Aging and money* (2nd ed.). New York: Springer Press. https://doi.org/10.31219/osf.io/w2bfz

Spreng, R. N., Karlawish, J., & Marson, D. C. (2016). Cognitive, social, and neural determinants of diminished decision-making and financial exploitation risk in aging and dementia: A review and new model. *Journal of Elder Abuse and Neglect, 28*(4–5), 320–344. https://doi.org/10.1080/08946566.2016.1237918

Spreng, R. N., & Turner, G. R. (2019). The shifting architecture of cognition and brain function in older adulthood. *Perspectives on Psychological Science, 14*(4), 523–542. https://doi.org/10.1177/1745691619827511

Stanley, J. T., & Blanchard-Fields, F. (2008). Challenges older adults face in detecting deceit: The role of emotion recognition. *Psychology and Aging, 23*(1), 24–32. https://doi.org/10.1037/0882-7974.23.1.24

Stanton, S. J. (June 2017). The role of testosterone and estrogen in consumer behavior and social & economic decision making: A review. *Hormones and Behavior*. https://doi.org/10.1016/j.yhbeh.2016.11.006

Stanton, S. J., Liening, S. H., & Schultheiss, O. C. (2011). Testosterone is positively associated with risk taking in the Iowa Gambling Task. *Hormones and Behavior, 59*(2), 252–256. https://doi.org/10.1016/j.yhbeh.2010.12.003

Stawski, R. S., Mogle, J., & Sliwinski, M. J. (2011). Intraindividual coupling of daily stressors and cognitive interference in old age. *The Journals of Gerontology. Series B, Psychological Sciences and Social Sciences, 66*(1), 121–129. https://doi.org/10.1093/geronb/gbr012

Stewart, S. L. K., Wright, C., & Atherton, C. (2019). Deception detection and truth detection are dependent on different cognitive and emotional traits: An investigation of emotional intelligence, theory of mind, and attention. *Personality and Social Psychology Bulletin, 45*(5), 794–807. https://doi.org/10.1177/0146167218796795

Stoeckel, L. E., Stewart, C. C., Griffith, H. R., Triebel, K., Okonkwo, O. C., den Hollander, J. A., ... Marson, D. C. (2013). MRI volume of the medial frontal cortex predicts financial capacity in patients with mild Alzheimer's disease. *Brain Imaging and Behavior, 7*(3), 282–292. https://doi.org/10.1007/s11682-013-9226-3

Sweeney, C. D., & Ceci, S. J. (2014). Deception detection, transmission, and modality in age and sex. *Frontiers in Psychology, 5*(590), 1–10. https://doi.org/10.3389/fpsyg.2014.00590

Templeton, V. H., & Kirkman, D. N. (July 2007). Fraud, vulnerability, and aging: Case studies. *Alzheimer's Care Today*. https://doi.org/10.1097/01.ALCAT.0000281875.55721.0f

The United States Department of Justice. (2020). Coronavirus (COVID-19). Retrieved from https://www.justice.gov/coronavirus

Uebelacker, S., & Quiel, S. (2014). The social engineering personality framework. In *2014 Workshop on Socio-Technical Aspects in Security and Trust* (pp. 24–30). IEEE.

Van Honk, J., Schutter, D. J. L. G., Hermans, E. J., Putman, P., Tuiten, A., & Koppeschaar, H. (2004). Testosterone shifts the balance between sensitivity for punishment and reward in healthy young women. *Psychoneuroendocrinology, 29*(7), 937–943. https://doi.org/10.1016/j.psyneuen.2003.08.007

Verhaeghen, P., & Salthouse, T. A. (1997). Meta-analyses of age-cognition relations in adulthood: Estimates of linear and nonlinear age effects and structural models. *Psychological Bulletin, 122*(3), 231–249.

Vishwanath, A. (2015). Habitual Facebook use and its impact on getting deceived on social media. *Journal of Computer-Mediated Communication, 20*(1), 83–98. https://doi.org/10.1111/jcc4.12100

Vishwanath, A., Harrison, B., & Ng, Y. J. (2018). Suspicion, cognition, and automaticity model of phishing susceptibility. *Communication Research, 45*(8), 1146–1166. https://doi.org/10.1177/0093650215627483

Weissberger, G. H., Mosqueda, L., Nguyen, A. L., Samek, A., Boyle, P. A., Nguyen, C. P., & Han, S. D. (2020). Physical and mental health correlates of perceived financial exploitation in older adults: Preliminary findings from the Finance, Cognition, and Health in Elders Study (FINCHES). *Aging and Mental Health, 24*(5), 740–746. https://doi.org/10.1080/13607863.2019.1571020

Winner, E., Brownell, H., Happé, F., Blum, A., & Pincus, D. (1998). Distinguishing lies from jokes: Theory of mind deficits and discourse interpretation in right hemisphere brain-damaged patients. *Brain and Language, 62*(1), 89–106. https://doi.org/10.1006/brln.1997.1889

Wojciechowski, J., Stolarski, M., & Matthews, G. (2014). Emotional intelligence and mismatching expressive and verbal messages: A contribution to detection of deception. *PLoS ONE*, *9*(3). https://doi.org/10.1371/journal.pone.0092570

Wood, S., & Lichtenberg, P. A. (2017). Financial capacity and financial exploitation of older adults: Research findings, policy recommendations and clinical implications. *Clinical Gerontologist*, *40*(1), 3–13. https://doi.org/10.1080/07317115.2016.1203382

Workman, M. (2007). Gaining access with social engineering: An empirical study of the threat. *Information Systems Security*, *16*(6), 315–331. https://doi.org/10.1080/10658980701788165.

Zacks, R. T., Hasher, L., & Li, K. Z. H. (2000). Human memory. In F. I. M. Craik, & T. A. Salthouse (Eds.), *The handbook of aging and cognition* (2nd ed., pp. 293–357). Mahwah, NJ: Erlbaum.

Zebrowitz, L. A., Boshyan, J., Ward, N., Gutchess, A., & Hadjikhani, N. (2017). The older adult positivity effect in evaluations of trustworthiness: Emotion regulation or cognitive capacity? *PLoS ONE*, *12*(1), e0169823. https://doi.org/10.1371/journal.pone.0169823

Zebrowitz, L. A., Franklin, R. G., Hillman, S., & Boc, H. (2013). Older and younger adults' first impressions from faces: Similar in agreement but different in positivity. *Psychology and Aging*, *28*(1), 202–212. https://doi.org/10.1037/a0030927

Zhang, M., Wang, L., Jajodia, S., Singhal, A., & Albanese, M. (2016). Network diversity: A security metric for evaluating the resilience of networks against zero-day attacks. *IEEE Transactions on Information Forensics and Security*, *11*(5), 1071–1086. https://doi.org/10.1109/TIFS.2016.2516916

Zielinska, O. A., Tembe, R., Hong, K. W., Ge, X., Murphy-Hill, E., & Mayhorn, C. B. (2014). One phish, two phish, how to avoid the internet phish. *Proceedings of the Human Factors and Ergonomics Society Annual Meeting*, *58*(1), 1466–1470. https://doi.org/10.1177/1541931214581306

Zuckerman, M., Kernis, M. R., Driver, R., & Koestner, R. (1984). Segmentation of behavior: Effects of actual deception and expected deception. *Journal of Personality and Social Psychology*, *46*(5), 1173–1182. https://doi.org/10.1037/0022-3514.46.5.1173

5

Psychological Aspects of Elder Financial Exploitation: Risk Factors, Intervention Approaches, and Case Studies

Peter A. Lichtenberg, Rebecca Campbell, and Latoya Hall

Introduction

While the financial exploitation of older adults appears to be skyrocketing overall, one of the most rapidly increasing forms is theft and scams by strangers (Conrad, Iris, Ridings, Langley, & Wilber, 2010). In their review of media-based stories of fraud and financial exploitation (FE) of older adults, MetLife researchers found that 51% of fraud cases are perpetrated by strangers (2009, 2011). Burnes et al. (2017) conducted a meta-analysis to measure the prevalence of a specific form of FE—fraud—and demonstrated that there is great variability in how fraud is measured and how that variability is related to prevalence rates. Overall, a prevalence rate of 5.6% for fraud victimization per year was reported.

DOI: 10.4324/9781003017189-5

Conrad et al. (2010) advanced the conceptual framework of FE by identifying six clusters: (a) theft and scams, (b) abuse of trust, (c) financial entitlement, (d) coercion, (e) signs of possible FE, and (f) money-management difficulties. Specifically, they defined FE of older adults as the illegal or improper use of an older adult's funds or property for another person's profit or advantage, and ordered their clusters by severity of the problem. Thefts and scams, which were considered the most severe forms of FE, are defined as taking an older adult's monies without their permission, either by outright stealing or by committing fraudulent activities (i.e., perpetrating a scam). FE types such as "abuse of trust" and "financial entitlement," in contrast, imply an ongoing relationship between the parties.

The focus of this chapter is on our evolving research at the intersection of fraud, financial decision-making, and contextual factors, which include the psychological aspects of how older adults relate to their finances and financial transactions. Fraud is defined more narrowly than financial exploitation and is used in this chapter as the wrongful or criminal deception intended to result in financial gain by the person perpetrating the fraud. In addition, our intervention research (financial coaching for fraud victims) delineates the multiple dimensions of vulnerability many fraud victims experience.

National Studies on Financial Exploitation and Fraud Prevalence and Predictors in Older Adults

In 2010, the prevalence of FE and its correlates began to be examined in population-based samples. That year, Acierno et al. (2010) reported that 5.2% of all older adults in their sample had experienced FE during the previous year, and 60% of the instances involved misappropriation of money by a family member. Laumann, Leitsch, and Waite (2008) reported that 3.5% of their sample had been victims of FE during the previous year; younger older adults (those aged 55–65) and African Americans were more likely to report FE, and participants with a romantic partner were less likely to do so. Beach, Schulz, Castle, and Rosen (2010) found that 3.5% of their sample reported having experienced FE during the six months prior to the interview, and almost 10% had at some point since turning 60. The most common experience was signing documents the participant did not understand. In their sample, African Americans were more likely to report FE than Non-Hispanic Caucasians. Risk for depression and having any deficits in Activities of Daily Living were additional correlates of FE in this sample.

Using newly available data from a sub-study of the Health and Retirement Survey, we published the first population-based study based on the use of prospective data to predict FE of any kind (Lichtenberg, Stickney, & Paulson, 2013). Participants were asked to report whether they had been a victim of FE during a defined time frame in the past (6 months, 12 months, or any time since turning 60), and all of the correlates were obtained concurrent with the participant's report of mistreatment. Our study design advanced the field in three ways. First, we used baseline data on demographic, depression, physical-health, and function variables to predict later reports of having been a victim of financial fraud. Second, we obtained interview data on unique variables not used in other studies (e.g., financial satisfaction and social needs) concurrent with data on reported victimization. And third, we examined the impact of fraud on those most likely to need mental health services; these are the most psychosocially vulnerable older adults. This allowed us to investigate whether these new and unique variables would aid in the prediction of fraud, and whether clinicians should be alerted to their older patients' increased vulnerability to financial fraud.

To evaluate the most psychologically vulnerable, the experience of fraud by those scoring in the highest 10% in the depressive symptoms category (CES-D scores $\geq$ 5 out of 8); those scoring in the bottom 10% of the social needs fulfillment category; and those scoring in the most vulnerable category—the highest 10% reporting depressive symptoms and the lowest 10% in social needs fulfillment—were compared with the rest of the group.

The sample contained 4,440 respondents. The mean age was 65.8 years ($SD = 8.5$ years) and the average respondent had 12.7 years of education ($SD= 2.9$). The sample was 61.9% female and predominantly White (85.4%). Most respondents (70.6%) reported that they had a romantic partner—i.e., a spouse or similar relationship. The incidence of financial fraud was low in the sample (4.5%), and more than half of the sample (52.7%) reported being either "very satisfied" or "completely satisfied" with their finances.

Fraud was significantly predicted by greater educational attainment ($\beta = 0.09$, Wald $\chi^2 = 8.67$, $p = 0.003$, Exp(B) = 1.09); more depression symptoms ($\beta = 0.09$, Wald $\chi^2= 4.54$, $p = 0.03$, Exp(B) = 1.09); less financial satisfaction ($\beta = -0.27$, Wald $\chi^2 = 13.67$, $p < 0.001$, Exp(B) = 0.764); and less fulfillment of status needs ($\beta = -0.07$, Wald $\chi^2 = 4.99$, $p = 0.03$, Exp(B) = 0.932). Nagelkerke's R^2 for the total model was 0.03. The strongest finding, however, was for fraud prevalence in those with the highest depression and the lowest social needs fulfillment (14%), compared with the rest of the sample (4.1%; $\chi^2 = 20.49$; $p < 0.001$). This finding regarding the importance of social needs is consistent with the work of Liu et al. (2017), who found that daily negative interactions within one's social network was a unique and significant predictor of being financially exploited.

Our follow-up longitudinal study using the sub-study sample of 4,661 participants of the Health and Retirement Study (Lichtenberg, Sugarman, Paulson, Ficker, & Rahaman-Filipiak, 2016) found that fraud prevalence increased to 6.1% between 2008 and 2012—a more than 20% increase—which likely reflected both an actual increase and also a greater willingness to report being defrauded. In this sample, we excluded anyone who had reported fraud in the 2008 sample.

Our findings were remarkably similar to those of the first study. We conducted analyses of the most psychologically vulnerable and found that of those who had the highest 10% of depression scores on the CES-D at baseline (≥ 5), 7.2% later experienced fraud compared with 4.0% for the rest of the sample. This 81% increased risk was statistically significant ($\chi^2 = 9.01$, $p = 0.003$). However, fraud prevalence among those who were in both the highest 10% of depression scores and the lowest 10% in social-needs fulfillment was 10.5%, compared with 4.2% for the rest of the sample ($\chi^2 = 9.13$, $p = 0.003$). These studies expanded our knowledge of risk factors, but we were left wondering why people choose to engage with fraudsters. We suspected that at least part of the answer lay in the realm of financial decision-making.

The Intersection of Financial Decision-Making and Financial Exploitation

Hsu and Willis (2013) examined financial decision-making in their 10-year study of couples in the Health and Retirement Survey and were able to assess real-world decision-making in areas such as how participants managed their retirement funds. In general, those with declining cognition were no longer the primary financial respondent for their household. Even so, a surprisingly high number of cognitively impaired individuals continued in this role.

Financial decision-making may well be a construct that is related to, but separate from, cognition. Boyle, Wilson, Yu, Buchman, and Bennett (2012; see also Han et al., 2015) examined financial decision-making and cognition longitudinally and found, in a sample of more than 400 older adults in the Rush University Memory and Aging Project, that even modest global cognitive decline (i.e., >1 SD and <1.5 SD—outside the range of actual cognitive impairment) is related to a decline in financial decision-making ability. Further, they speculated that decision-making and cognition are related but independent constructs.

In a subsequent study, Boyle, Wilson, Yu, Buchman, and Bennett (2013) found that older persons without dementia—but with medical and/or financial decision-making deficits—experienced a fourfold increase in mortality across a 4-year follow-up. Han et al. (2015) tested the discrepancy between cognition and financial decision-making in a sample of 689 older adults and found that in 13% of cases, decision-making scores were more than one z-score below cognition; in 11% of cases, cognition scores were lower than decision-making scores. A chief concern regarding a decline in financial decision-making skills is whether this leads to increased vulnerability to FE; declines in cognitive abilities and decision-making have been linked to increased risk of FE (Lichtenberg et al., 2018), and Boyle et al. (2012) found that reduced decision-making is related to increased susceptibility to scams.

Lichtenberg, Stoltman, Ficker, Iris, and Mast (2015) proposed—and Lichtenberg et al. (2017) later validated—a new conceptual model and related assessment instrument to understand financial decision-making and for use in the assessment of financial capacity: a conceptual model of financial decision-making and the Lichtenberg Financial Decision-making Rating Scale (LFDRS). The conceptual frameworks used in creating the LFDRS were the Whole Person Dementia Assessment model (Mast, 2011) and the decision-making model of Appelbaum and Grisso (1988), which elaborates on what Lichtenberg et al. (2015) term the *intellectual factors* involved in capacity assessment: choice, understanding, appreciation, and reasoning. The Whole Person Assessment model is described in some depth in Lichtenberg et al. (2015) and applies person-centered principles of respect for individuality and personhood to the standardized psychological assessment process. This includes focusing on contextual issues and actual decisions instead of hypothetical vignettes.

These intellectual factors have been established as fundamental aspects of decisional abilities (ABA/APA, 2008). Although originally articulated for medical decision-making, they also apply to financial decisions. That is, the older adult must be capable of clearly communicating his or her choice. Understanding is the ability to comprehend the nature of the proposed decision and provide some explanation or demonstrate awareness of its risks and benefits. Appreciation refers to the situation and its consequences, and often involves their impact on both the older adult and others.

Regarding the fourth intellectual factor, reasoning, Appelbaum and Grisso (1988) contend that the most common causes of impairment in appreciation are due to lack of awareness of deficits and/or delusions or distortions. Reasoning includes the ability to compare options—for instance, treatment alternatives in the case of healthcare—and to provide a rationale for the decision or explain the communicated choice. The LFDRS incorporates contextual variables (i.e., financial situational awareness, psychological vulnerability, and susceptibility to undue influence and to FE) in Appelbaum and Grisso's (1988) decision-making model.

The scale developed is an attempt to quantify financial decision-making risk—that is, risk for meeting the legal standards for financial incapacity and risk for vulnerability to FE. The scale, which is multiple choice, was adapted from the original 66-item scale. Through confirmatory factor analyses, a 34-item short form (LFDRS-SF) was developed (Lichtenberg et al., 2018). The 34-item scale serves as the Financial Vulnerability Assessment (FVA) tool on the https://olderadultnestegg.com website. We examined the intersection of FE and financial decision-making using the scale in a sample of 200 community-dwelling older adults.

Similar to the procedures employed to diagnose Alzheimer's disease, we used a consensus conference to determine whether decisional ability deficits were present in individual participants. While all three coauthors had access to the LFDRS-SF answers, no risk scores were calculated before the consensus conference had yielded a decision on each case. The decision-making process was based on instructions for the LFDRS-SF, which state:

> For the intellectual factor items, were there any discrepancies between the rater's choice and the older adult's response? Any discrepancies should raise concerns about the older adult's decisional abilities. Did there appear to be a lot of psychological vulnerability and susceptibility or a high level of financial strain? These factors influence a final rating as well.

A final dichotomous rating of some/major concerns or no concerns was assigned (1 = decisional ability impairment, 2 = intact decisional abilities). The consensus conference increased the test's value by ensuring that cases in which discrepancies were more likely due to not understanding the question, or were so minor that decision-making was probably intact, were acknowledged as such.

We used Conrad et al.'s (2010) definition of FE—the illegal or improper use of an elder's funds, property, or assets by either someone known to the victim or a stranger—and included theft and scams. A number of questions on the LFDRS-SF can trigger responses that suggest FE. These include items such as whether the person had recently made a financial decision they regretted or worried about, whether they were currently helping someone regularly with finances, and how they felt about the situation.

Other items include whether they had noticed money missing from a bank account and whether they had ever lost money as a result of a financial decision. We used follow-up questions to learn the details of any concerns about suspected FE and a consensus conference method to identify suspected FE. Examples of such cases included paying someone in advance for work that was never performed and giving a family member access to a bank account to withdraw $400, who instead withdrew $5,000 and kept the money.

Coauthors met and reviewed each item and the description of any money loss that might be related to suspected FE. An example of what was not considered FE was purchasing a home during an auction and having to pay recording or other fees they had not realized would be added to the base price. We then rated each person as having or not having experienced FE within the previous 18 months (1 = suspected FE, 2 = no FE).

The consensus conference helped ensure that only serious matters of exploitation (those that would qualify for reporting to APS) were used in assigning exploitation to a case. In none of the cases was the suspected exploitation current or ongoing, and thus no reports to APS were made. Overall area under the curve analyses found good ratings (above 0.80 in each case) for both decisional ability scores and FE scores, which demonstrates the intersection of financial decision-making deficits and risk for FE.

How Much Does Context Matter in Cases of Fraud?

In their review of the literature, Shao, Zhang, Ren, Li, and Lin (2019) focused on what renders older adults vulnerable to fraud. While there is considerable debate about whether older adults are more susceptible to fraud than other age groups, Shao et al. considered six phenomena that had been related to fraud in some studies or conceptualizations: (1) cognitive functioning and cognitive decline (James et al., 2014); (2) emotional regulation and the positivity effect—i.e., the tendency of older adults to have reduced arousal response to negative circumstances surrounding a financial decision and to have positive expectations around decision-making (Spreng, Karlawish, & Marson, 2016); (3) the interplay between personal competencies and the environment (Pinkser, McFarland, & Pachana 2009); (4) social isolation (Alves & Wilson, 2008); (5) risk taking (Samanez-Larkin et al., 2007); and (6) psychological vulnerability (Lichtenberg, et al., 2016).

DeLiema (2018) investigated routine activity theory, which requires the convergence of three factors—an offender, a target, and the absence of others to protect the target—as a context for fraud susceptibility, and found that isolation and a lack of trustworthy friends or family best distinguished those who had been defrauded from those who had not. Other recent research has focused on social contexts that influence exploitation. Quinn, Nerenberg, Navarro, and Wilber (2017) highlight diverse ways in which vulnerabilities of all adults impact the risk of being unduly influenced, and Ruffman, Murray, Halberstadt, and Vater (2012) find that older adults are less able than younger adults to detect lies, due to changes in emotion recognition.

Context Matters: Psychosocial and Financial Vulnerability in Financial Exploitation

Although the LFDRS was developed to assess financial decision-making, the scale contains three subscales that query the psychosocial and financial contexts in which an older adult is making a financial decision: Financial Awareness, Psychological Vulnerability, and Susceptibility. The Financial Awareness subscale assesses the person's understanding and experience of their financial situation. The Psychological Vulnerability subscale assesses common psychological factors, such as anxiety and depression, and their impact on the person's financial world. Finally, the Susceptibility subscale queries the nature and severity of the conflict and strain the person's relationships have undergone with respect to finances.

In a recent study (Lichtenberg, Campbell, Hall and Gross, 2020), we sought to determine which of the 34 LFDRS items that make up these contextual subscales would differentiate people who had been financially exploited from those who had not. In order to examine the context of financial decision-making, we deliberately removed items that directly asked about FE experiences, such as, "Has anyone used or taken your money without your permission?" Each of the items is scored on a 0–2 or 0–3 scale, with higher scores reflecting greater contextual risk for problematic financial decision-making. The participant sample consisted of 200 older adult volunteers from the community, and 43 other participants were recruited after they had experienced FE through a scam or identity theft and were seeking financial coaching services. Of the full sample, 164 participants were judged through our consensus conference not to have experienced any recent FE, and 79 had. Details on sample demographics are reported in Table 5.1.

We found that 17 of these contextual items successfully discriminated between participants who had experienced FE and those who had not (see Table 5.2). Further, this scale had psychometric properties and clinical utility for detecting exploitation superior to demographic factors such as gender,

Table 5.1 Sample Demographics, Neuropsychological Testing, and Total LFDRS

	No Financial Exploitation (n = 164)	*Financial Exploitation (n = 79)*	*Overall Sample (n = 243)*	
Age Years M (SD)	71.5 (7.4)	70.1 (7.8)	71.1 (7.6)	t(233) = 1.29, p = 0.20
Education Years M (SD)	15.4 (2.6)	14.3 (2.3)	15.1 (2.6)	t(234) = 3.25, d = 0.46**
Gender Female N (%)	117 (71.3%)	59 (74.7%)	176 (72.4%)	$\chi^2(1) = 1.86$, p = 0.172
Race Black N (%)	81 (49.4%)	49 (68.1%)	130 (55.1%)	$\chi^2(1) = 7.05$, φ = 0.17*
LFDRS Total M (SD)	17.6 (6.9)	24.6 (10.7)	19.6 (8.8)	t(233) = −5.97, d = −0.85**
WRAT-IV Word Reading Raw Score M (SD)	58.0 (7.5)	54.9 (10.7)	57.0 (8.7)	t(236) = 2.52, d = 0.35*
MMSE Raw Score M (SD)	28.7 (1.9)	27.8 (2.5)	28.3 (2.2)	t(236) = 2.85, d = 0.40*
TMT-B Seconds M (SD)	100.0 (46.2)	153.1 (76.9)	117.4 (62.8)	t(232) = −6.55, d = −0.92**

Note: *p < 0.05; **p < 0.001.

Table 5.2 Independent Samples T-Test Contextual Items Analysis between Exploitation Groups

	No Financial Exploitation (n = 164)	*Financial Exploitation (n = 78)*	
Contextual Factors Total Scale	*4.14 (3.88)*	*9.77 (4.90)*	*t(236) = −9.53, d = −1.33***
1. How worried are you about having enough money to pay for things?	0.60 (0.61)	1.11 (0.70)	t(241) = −5.81**
Not at all worried	76 (46.3%)	15 (19.0%)	
Somewhat worried	77 (47.0%)	40 (50.6%)	
Very worried	11 (6.7%)	24 (30.4%)	
Don't know	0 (0%)	0 (0%)	
2. Overall, how satisfied are you with your finances?	0.49 (0.68)	1.19 (0.91)	t(241) = −6.69**
Satisfied	100 (61.0%)	24 (30.4%)	
Neither satisfied nor dissatisfied	47 (28.7%)	18 (22.8%)	
Dissatisfied	17 (10.4%)	35 (44.3%)	
Don't know	0 (0%)	2 (2.5%)	
3. Who manages your money day to day?	0.02 (0.15)	0.13 (0.40)	t(241) = −22.84*
I do, without any help	160 (97.6%)	71 (89.9%)	
I get help from someone	4 (2.4%)	6 (7.6%)	

	No Financial Exploitation (n = 164)	*Financial Exploitation (n = 78)*	
Contextual Factors Total Scale	*4.14 (3.88)*	*9.77 (4.90)*	*t(236) = −9.53, d = −1.33***
Someone else manages all my money	0 (0%)	2 (2.5%)	
Don't know	0 (0%)	0 (0%)	
4. Dow satisfied are you with this (money management) arrangement?	0.08 (0.311)	0.37 (0.66)	t(241) = −4.60**
Satisfied	153 (93.3%)	58 (73.4%)	
Neither satisfied nor dissatisfied	9 (5.5%)	13 (16.5%)	
Dissatisfied	2 (1.2%)	8 (10.1%)	
Don't know	0 (0%)	0 (0%)	
5. How confident are you in making big financial decisions?	0.29 (0.56)	0.65 (0.79)	t(241) = −4.08**
Confident	125 (76.2%)	42 (53.2%)	
Unsure	32 (19.5%)	24 (30.4%)	
Not confident	6 (3.7%)	12 (15.2%)	
Don't know	1 (0.6%)	1 (1.3%)	
6. How often do you worry about financial decisions you've recently made?	0.30 (0.61)	0.85 (0.80)	t(241) = −5.85**
No worries	127 (77.4%)	32 (40.5%)	
Sometimes	24 (14.6%)	27 (34.2%)	
Often	13 (7.9%)	20 (25.3%)	
Don't know	0 (0%)	0 (0%)	
7. Have you noticed any money taken from your bank account without your permission?	0.10 (0.30)	0.25 (0.44)	t(241) = −3.25**
No	148 (90.2%)	59 (74.7%)	
Yes	16 (9.8%)	20 (25.3%)	
Don't know	0 (0%)	0 (0%)	
8. How often do your monthly expenses exceed your regular monthly income?	0.30 (0.61)	0.82 (0.87)	t(241) = −5.43**
marely or never	128 (78.0%)	38 (48.1%)	
Some of the time	23 (14.0%)	17 (21.5%)	
Most of the time	13 (7.9%)	24 (30.4%)	
Don't know	0 (0%)	0 (0%)	
9. How often do you talk with to visit others on a regular basis?	0.01 (0.16)	0.09 (0.33)	t(241) = −2.46*
Daily or weekly	163 (99.4%)	73 (92.4%)	
Monthly	0 (0%)	5 (6.3%)	
Less than monthly	1 (0.6%)	1 (1.3%)	
Don't know	0 (0%)	0 (0%)	
10. How often do you wish you had someone to talk to about financial decisions, transactions, or plans?	0.44 (0.64)	0.78 (0.76)	t(241) = −3.71**
None of the time	105 (64.0%)	33 (41.8%)	

	No Financial Exploitation (n = 164)	*Financial Exploitation (n = 78)*	
Contextual Factors Total Scale	*4.14 (3.88)*	*9.77 (4.90)*	*t(236) = −9.53, d = −1.33***
Some of the time	46 (28.0%)	30 (38.0%)	
A lot of the time	13 (7.9%)	16 (20.3%)	
Don't know	0 (0%)	0 (0%)	
11. How often do you feel anxious about your financial decisions and/or transactions?	0.42 (0.64)	0.87 (0.74)	t(241) = −4.92**
Never or rarely	108 (65.9%)	27 (34.2%)	
Sometimes	43 (26.2%)	35 (44.3%)	
Often	13 (7.9%)	17 (21.5%)	
Don't know	0 (0%)	0 (0%)	
12. Do you have a confidante with whom you can discuss anything, including your financial situations and decisions?	0.16 (0.37)	0.30 (0.46)	t(241) = −2.52*
Yes	137 (83.5%)	55 (69.6%)	
No	27 (16.5%)	24 (30.4%)	
Don't know	0 (0%)	0 (0%)	
13. How often do you feel downhearted or blue about your financial situation or decisions?	0.41 (0.57)	0.78 (0.65)	t(241) = −4.57**
None of the time	104 (63.4%)	27 (34.2%)	
Some of the time	53 (32.3%)	42 (53.2%)	
A lot of the time	7 (4.3%)	10 (12.7%)	
Don't know	0 (0%)	0 (0%)	
14. Are your memory, thinking skills, or ability to reason with regard to financial decisions or financial transactions worse than a year ago?	0.13 (0.34)	0.24 (0.43)	t(241) = −2.23*
No	143 (87.2%)	60 (75.9%)	
Yes	21 (12.8%)	19 (24.1%)	
Don't know	0 (0%)	0 (0%)	
15. Has a relationship with a family member or friend become strained due to finances as you have gotten older?	0.25 (0.45)	0.54 (0.58)	t(238) = −4.24**
No	124 (75.6%)	38 (48.1%)	
Yes	39 (23.8%)	35 (44.3%)	
Don't know	1 (0.6%)	3 (3.8%)	
16. Did anyone ever tell you that someone else you know wants to take your money?	0.02 (0.13)	0.21 (0.52)	t(239) = −4.36**
No	161 (98.2%)	65 (82.3%)	
Yes	3 (1.8%)	8 (10.1%)	
Don't know	0 (0%)	4 (5.1%)	

	No Financial Exploitation (n = 164)	*Financial Exploitation (n = 78)*	
Contextual Factors Total Scale	*4.14 (3.88)*	*9.77 (4.90)*	*$t(236) = -9.53$, $d = -1.33$***
17. How likely is it that anyone now wants to take or use your money without your permission?	0.11 (0.43)	0.49 (0.99)	$t(238) = -4.13$**
Unlikely	153 (93.3%)	58 (73.4%)	
Somewhat likely	4 (2.4%)	7 (8.9%)	
Very likely	7 (4.3%)	3 (3.8%)	
Don't know	0 (0%)	8 (10.1%)	

Note: Means and standard deviations are provided for each item. Frequency and percentage are provided for each of the response options. *$p < 0.05$; **$p < 0.001$.

race, and years of education, as well as for estimating global cognitive abilities; see Lichtenberg, Campbell, Hall and Gross (2020) for further details about the study and statistical analyses.

These 17 contextual items were used to construct a new scale, the Financial Exploitation Vulnerability Scale (FEVS), to detect the contextual psychosocial and financial risk of FE in older adults. Items on the FEVS are based on all three of the LFDRS contextual subscales, and assess factors such as the person's experience of their financial situation (e.g., "Who manages your money day to day?"); psychological factors related to finances (e.g., "How often do you feel downhearted or blue about your financial situation or decision?"; and the social context of the person's financial world (e.g., "How often do you wish you had someone to talk to about financial decisions, transactions, or plans?"). All scale items are listed in Table 5.3.

Discrepancies in the endorsement of FEVS items between exploitation groups suggest that the financial and psychosocial contexts in which decisions are being made differ meaningfully between people who have been exploited and those who have not. Broadly, people who have been financially exploited were more likely to report feelings of dissatisfaction and a lack of control over their finances, psychological distress due to finances, and social isolation or strain due to finances. Interestingly, on items that asked about social conflict and the trustworthiness of people in their lives with regard to finances, those who had been exploited were more likely to report that their relationships were strained and that they viewed others as untrustworthy. Perceived lack of mastery or control regarding one's financial world yielded the highest scores on the FEVS. Thus financial strain, lack of financial decision-making confidence and disappointment in helping others financially were examples of items related to financial control and mastery. Scoring for responses to FEVS

Table 5.3 Financial Exploitation Vulnerability Scale Items and Response Options

1. How worried are you about having enough money to pay for things?
   Not at all worried (0)
   Somewhat worried (1)
   Very worried (2)
   Don't know (3)
2. Overall, how satisfied are you with your finances?
   Satisfied (0)
   Neither satisfied nor dissatisfied (1)
   Dissatisfied (2)
   Don't know (3)
3. Who manages your money day to day?
   I do, without any help (0)
   I get help from someone (1)
   Someone else manages all my money (2)
   Don't know (3)
4. How satisfied are you with this (money management) arrangement?
   Satisfied (0)
   Neither satisfied nor dissatisfied (1)
   Dissatisfied (2)
   Don't know (3)
5. How confident are you in making big financial decisions?
   Confident (0)
   Unsure (1)
   Not confident (2)
   Don't know (3)
6. How often do you worry about financial decisions you've recently made?
   No worries (0)
   Sometimes (1)
   Often (2)
   Don't know (3)
7. Have you noticed any money taken from your bank account without your permission?
   No (0)
   Yes (1)
   Don't know (2)
8. How often do your monthly expenses exceed your regular monthly income?
   Rarely or never (0)
   Some of the time (1)
   Most of the time (2)
   Don't know (3)
9. How often do you talk with to visit others on a regular basis?
   Daily or weekly (0)
   Monthly (1)
   Less than monthly (2)
   Don't know (3)
10. How often do you wish you had someone to talk to about financial decisions, transactions, or plans?
    None of the time (0)
    Some of the time (1)
    A lot of the time (2)
    Don't know (3)

11. How often do you feel anxious about your financial decisions and/or transactions?
    Never or rarely (0)
    Sometimes (1)
    Often (2)
    Don't know (3)
12. Do you have a confidante with whom you can discuss anything, including your financial situations and decisions?
    Yes (0)
    No (1)
    Don't know (2)
13. How often do you feel downhearted or blue about your financial situation or decisions?
    None of the time (0)
    Some of the time (1)
    A lot of the time (2)
    Don't know (3)
14. Are your memory, thinking skills, or ability to reason with regard to financial decisions or financial transactions worse than a year ago?
    No (0)
    Yes (1)
    Don't know (2)
15. Has a relationship with a family member or friend become strained due to finances as you have gotten older?
    No (0)
    Yes (1)
    Don't know (2)
16. Did anyone ever tell you that someone else you know wants to take your money?
    No (0)
    Yes (1)
    Don't know (2)
17. How likely is it that anyone now wants to take or use your money without your permission?
    Unlikely (0)
    Somewhat likely (1)
    Very likely (2)
    Don't know (3)

---

items can be found in Table 5.3. Total scores for the FEVS range from 0 to 46, with higher scores reflecting greater risk for FE.

Independent samples t-test analyses were used to examine group differences between participants who had been financially exploited and those who had not. Chi-square analyses were used for dichotomously-coded variables (gender and race). Financial exploitation status was related to fewer years of formal education, as well as poorer performance on measures of word reading, estimated global cognition, and a measure of executive functioning. Black participants were more likely to have experienced exploitation than white participants. Effect sizes for these differences were small, except for the LFDRS and executive functioning, which had a large effect sizes ($d = 0.85$–0.92—see Table 5.1 for details).

In Lichtenberg et al. (2020), we presented an ROC curve analysis for FEVS total scores and found that the scale had good indicators of clinical utility for differentiating those with previous FE from those who did not experience FE (AUC = 0.814, CI95%: 0.757–0.871). A cut score that balances adequate sensitivity and specificity would be 7 or greater (sensitivity = 0.737; specificity = 0.756), and is the score we recommend for broad use by professionals who use the FEVS to screen for FE vulnerability or risk. We did not have data to determine the predictive validity of FEVS at this time. However, if the examiner would like to use the scale in a manner that detects almost everyone who may be at risk for experiencing FE, then a cut score of 2 or greater could be used (sensitivity = 0.974). On the other hand, if the professional's resources are limited and they want to reduce the chance of a false positive risk result, then a cut score of 13 or greater may be ideal (specificity = 0.957). See Table 5.4 for the ranges of sensitivity and specificity values for each potential cut score.

Other measures that assess aspects of financial decision-making and vulnerability for exploitation often employ hypothetical scenarios or rely heavily on the assessment of cognitive skills (Boyle et al., 2012; James et al., 2014; Marson, 2001). Although these are important areas of assessment, they are not accessible for many professionals who interact with older adults, such as APS workers, financial professionals, and healthcare providers. Also, these measures often take more time to administer than is feasible in those settings and require extensive, specialized training to administer accurately. In contrast, the FEVS is a brief, standardized measure that allows professionals who work with older adults to quickly screen for contextual risk factors for FE. They can then follow up with the appropriate standard of care, such as

Table 5.4 Financial Exploitation Vulnerability Scale (FEVS) Sensitivity, Specificity, and Negative and Positive Predictive Power for Each Cutoff Score

Cutoff	*Sensitivity*	*Specificity*	*PPP*	*NPP*
1 or greater	0.987	0.177	0.361	0.967
2 or greater	0.974	0.329	0.406	0.964
3 or greater	0.908	0.445	0.435	0.911
4 or greater	0.868	0.518	0.459	0.893
5 or greater	0.842	0.616	0.508	0.892
6 or greater	0.803	0.683	0.544	0.880
7 or greater	0.737	0.756	0.587	0.859
8 or greater	0.658	0.823	0.636	0.836
9 or greater	0.553	0.866	0.660	0.805
10 or greater	0.500	0.896	0.693	0.792
11 or greater	0.395	0.927	0.718	0.765
12 or greater	0.329	0.933	0.698	0.747
13 or greater	0.263	0.957	0.744	0.734

additional screening, connecting the older adult to resources and support, and other interventions.

We are pleased to present the FEVS for use in screening for contextual vulnerability for FE and abuse. In Lichtenberg et al. (2020), we demonstrated that the FEVS has good psychometric properties and clinical utility for detecting exploitation through identity theft, scams, and financial abuse by trusted others. Although the initial sample of participants was robust (N = 243), this novel scale will require further investigation and cross-validation with additional participants. Exploratory and confirmatory factor analyses will also be used in subsequent research to determine the factor structure of the scale and, potentially, reduce the number of items. Longitudinal research will be required to determine whether the FEVS can predict the occurrence of FE.

Providing Services and Learning from Older Adults Experiencing Exploitation

The Successful Aging through Financial Empowerment (SAFE) program was created in 2017 at Wayne State University's Institute of Gerontology. The SAFE program offers extensive community education on detecting and protecting against FE in the form of scams and identity theft, as well as free financial coaching support for older adult victims of FE. The community education presentations are offered to older adults, their caregivers, and professionals who provide services to older adults. The goal is to raise awareness of older adults' vulnerability to scams and identity theft and share information on identifying risks and avoiding victimization.

Financial coaching services are offered to scam and identity theft victims 55 and older to support their financial and emotional recovery. SAFE's financial coaching clients are referred to the program by professionals who work with older adults or community education participants who self-refer after attending a presentation. The SAFE financial coach assists scam and identity theft clients in reporting their cases to the proper agencies, accessing and reviewing credit reports, and completing fraud affidavit processes, as well as with any other matters clients feel they need one-on-one support to address.

To date, the program has delivered community education to more than 11,000 older adults, professionals working with older adults, and caregivers, provided one-on-one financial coaching services to 70 older adults, and saved or recovered approximately $70,000 in funds for its clients. The following are examples of SAFE clients and their outcomes after working with the program's financial coach. This will be followed by a summary of our cross-sectional and longitudinal research findings.

Identity Theft

Mr. X, a 68-year-old male client, contacted the SAFE program when he began to receive notices about a student loan that was going into collections. Mr. X had recently been diagnosed with cancer and planned to retire within the year. He told the financial coach that he was under a lot of stress, given his recent diagnosis and treatment, preparing for a major life transition (retirement), and now having his financial security in retirement threatened by a debt that was not his. Mr. X also informed the financial coach that he had never attended college, so he knew that the student loan debt could not be his. Mr. X and the SAFE financial coach began working together, with the goal of having the debt discharged and repairing his credit report.

Mr. X and the financial coach completed the steps involved in the identity theft restoration process. Mr. X received support in contacting the creditor, filing the necessary reports (local police report, identity theft affidavit, fraud alerts, etc.), and following the loan servicer's instructions to resolve the fraudulent debt. Mr. X and the financial coach also contacted the Department of Education to cancel the master promissory note that had been forged using Mr. X's information to ensure that no future loans would be given to the identity thief. All of the necessary documentation was collected and submitted to the loan servicer to remove the debt from Mr. X's credit report.

Mr. X received financial coaching services for 2 months to assist in addressing the identity theft. At the time of his 6-month follow-up appointment, Mr. X had completed his cancer treatment and was in his first month of retirement. Mr. X informed the coordinator that the $27,000 in student loan debt had been deleted and removed from his credit report at the time of his follow-up interview. Mr. X's follow-up assessment revealed a higher social support measure (he had recently remarried) and a lower depression score.

Suspected Fraud

Mrs. A contacted the SAFE program because she believed she was the victim of a stolen check. Her daughter had recently died and Mrs. A was the beneficiary of a substantial retirement fund. She received an unearned income form from the State of Michigan that listed the receipt of two checks totaling

$130,000. Mrs. A believed the second check had been stolen, because she stated that she had not received it and the Teacher's Insurance and Annuity Association of America (TIAA, formerly known as TIAA Cref) told her they had dispersed all funds. Mrs. A was anxious about finding the money, because her daughter had two small children and Mrs. A wanted to make sure that she saved a portion of the money for them.

Mrs. A and the financial coach began working together to locate the missing funds. TIAA verified that there had been two checks, as Mrs. A stated previously. However, further conversation with a customer service employee revealed that no information on the check was available to that department, as it had been issued more than 2 years ago. The agent filled out a ticket and submitted the claim to the payments issued department. An employee in that department called Mrs. A 2 weeks later and confirmed that two checks had been issued for the amounts on the state's unearned income form. However, Mrs. A had requested that the payouts be pre-taxed. The payments were heavily taxed, but she never received the 1099 form explaining the payments and taxes. Because she was unaware of the pre-taxed amounts, she assumed the $95,454 payment was only the first payment and that the second payment had never arrived. However, both payments had in fact been received, and the tax amounts withheld by the IRS and state rendered the total amount, $95,454, significantly less than the $130,000 she had expected. The financial coach referred Mrs. A to a trusted accounting professional, who could amend her prior year's tax returns to reflect the taxes paid on the daughter's retirement fund.

Sweepstakes Scam

Ms. S contacted the SAFE financial coach because she believed she had been the victim of a sweepstakes scam. Ms. S said she had been contacted by phone 4 months earlier and told that she had won $375,000 in a sweepstake. Ms. S says she was given a bank account number and instructed to deposit $1,200 into the account to cover the taxes and fees on her winnings. Ms. S said she complied and deposited the money because she was no longer working and only receiving Social Security, and believed that the money would render her more financially secure and allow her to help support her children and grandchildren. However, when she had not received any new information or a payout on the winnings in a couple of weeks, Ms. S says she contacted the person she had spoken to previously and was informed that she needed to send another $200 through Western Union before she would be able to receive the winnings. Ms. S said this went on for a few weeks, and in the end she had sent an additional $1,000 to the scammers.

Ms. S and the SAFE financial coach reported the scam to the local police, Federal Trade Commission, FBI, and Consumer Financial Protection Bureau (since the scammers had used a bank to carry out the scam). A few months after she reported the scam, the FTC offered a remittance payment to anyone who had been financially scammed by individuals using Western Union. Ms. S and the SAFE financial coach completed the FTC/Western Union claim process, and Ms. S was able to recover $974 of the $2,200 she had lost. At the 6-month follow-up, Ms. S had higher scores on social support measures and lower depression and anxiety scores.

SAFE Evaluation Research

A major goal of SAFE's financial coaching component is to aid older adults in their financial and emotional recovery after being victims of FE (Lichtenberg, Hall, Gross & Campbell, 2019). To assess the program's impact, participants complete baseline assessments at intake and again at follow-up, 6 months after completion of the financial coaching services. SAFE assessments include multiple measures of physical, cognitive, and emotional health. Assessment data are used to gauge changes in the participant's cognitive, emotional, and physical health from intake to follow-up, and to understand the cognitive, emotional, and physical differences between those who seek services to resolve exploitation and a matched group with no history of FE.

Lichtenberg et al. (2019) describe the program's methodology and provide case examples and preliminary findings regarding the vulnerability of older adult victims of FE compared with peers with no history of FE. Forty-two community-dwelling, older, urban adults participated in the study: 21 SAFE program clients and 21 matched comparison group participants with no history of FE. Comparison group participants were drawn from the Lichtenberg Financial Decision-Making Rating Scale (LFDRS) validation study sample (see Lichtenberg et al., 2017). The main purpose of the study was to determine whether those who sought services for scam and identity theft assistance were more psychologically or cognitively vulnerable than those who did not.

Study results demonstrated that SAFE clients were among the most vulnerable of the older adult population, and had significantly less education, more health problems, and worse self-rated health than the comparison group. Older adults seeking services to address scams and identity theft had significantly higher financial decision-making risk scores (as gauged by the LFDRS) than the comparison group ($t = 3.40$, $p < 0.01$). Older adult FE victims seeking services also fared worse on three of the four measures used to assess neurocognitive functioning. In addition, SAFE clients' emotional health measures provided evidence that they had higher levels of depression ($t = 4.19$, $p < 0.001$) and anxiety ($t = 3.84$, $p < 0.001$) than the comparison group.

SAFE Longitudinal Study

Using longitudinal data, Hall, Campbell, Gross, and Lichtenberg (in press) examined the ability of the SAFE program's financial coaching component to serve as a protective factor for the neurocognitive mental and emotional health of its clients. Forty community-dwelling older adults participated in the study: 20 SAFE clients and 20 older adults with no history of FE. As with the baseline study, the longitudinal study drew comparison group participants from the Lichtenberg Financial Decision-Making Rating Scale (LFDRS) validation study sample (see Lichtenberg et al., 2017). SAFE financial coaching clients and comparison group participants completed identical baseline and follow-up measures. The study's main purpose was to investigate the impact of SAFE's financial coaching services on the wellbeing of its clients.

Study results provide evidence that the program has served as a protective factor in negating many of the adverse outcomes associated with FE; they also support financial coaching programs as an appropriate intervention. The comparison of SAFE clients' baseline scores versus follow-up assessments revealed that SAFE clients experienced no further decline in cognitive, emotional, or physical health measures; instead, they showed significant trends toward improved executive functioning on the Stroop color-word task and self-report instrumental activities of daily living (IADLs). SAFE clients also had significantly lower anxiety scores at the time of follow-up ($t = 1.83$, $p < 0.01$). Comparison group participants did not demonstrate any trends or significant changes in IADLs, executive functioning, or anxiety—and thus the changes do not appear to be related to practice effects, but rather reflect actual improvements. These data are exciting, because they demonstrate that not only does financial coaching for fraud victims impact their financial health, but it also impacts mental and neurocognitive health and functional abilities.

Future Directions

The psychological aspects of both fraud vulnerability and fraud consequences demand increased attention in both research and clinical practice. The linkage between financial health and physical and mental health in older age is well documented (GSA, 2020) and is especially significant when it comes to fraud. Health and mental health practitioners who work with older adults need to perform fraud and other FE screening as necessary, become more aware of the effects older adults experience as victims of fraud, and respond to these accordingly.

The field of older adult fraud research increasingly requires the use of conceptual frameworks to guide empirical studies. Given the ample evidence of fraud prevalence and predictors, delineating how psychologically vulnerable adults can be protected from fraud is now vital. While general models of gerontology are clearly useful in this regard (e.g., socioemotional selectivity theory) they lack the specificity of conceptual models that are geared to financial decision-making when faced with the conditions (both within the environment and the scammer and within the person) that render an older adult at high risk for fraud.

The field of elder abuse is historically geared to what Jackson (2012) termed hybrid FE—that is, the case in which an older adult is living with or highly dependent on the abuser and when FE is coupled with other forms of abuse. Clearly, however, incorporating fraud in the elder abuse field is necessary; these financial crimes typically impact wealth, the ability to be financially solvent, and psychological vulnerability. Fraud is a form of elder abuse—and yet, understandably, traditional multidisciplinary teams are likely to have much less experience in this area. As a result, teams and other professionals who provide services for older victims of abuse will need to expand their expertise to include fraud victimization and its impacts.

References

Acierno, R., Hernandez, M. A., Amastader, A. B., Resnick, H. S., Steve, K., Muzzy, W., & Kilpatrick, D. G. (2010). Prevalence and correlates of emotional, physical, sexual and financial abuse and potential neglect in the United States: The national elder abuse mistreatment study. *American Journal of Public Health, 100*(2), 292–297.

American Bar Association Commission on Law and Aging and American Psychological Association. (2008). *Assessment of Older Adults with Diminished Capacity: A Handbook for Psychologists*. Washington, DC: American Bar Association.

Alves, L. M., & Wilson, S. R. (2008). The effects of loneliness on telemarketing fraud vulnerability among older adults. *Journal of Elder Abuse & Neglect, 20*(1), 63–85. doi: 10.1300/J084v20n01_04.

Appelbaum, P. S., & Grisso, T. (1988). Assessing patients' capacities to consent to treatment. *New England Journal of Medicine, 319*, 1635–1638. doi: 10.1056/NEJM198812223192504.

Beach, S. R., Schulz, R., Castle, N. G., & Rosen, J. (2010). Financial exploitation and psychological mistreatment among older adults: Differences between African Americans and non-African Americans in a population based survey. *Gerontologist, 50*, 744–757.

Boyle, P. A., Wilson, R. S., Yu, L. Y., Buchman, A. S., & Bennett, D. A. (2012). Poor decision making is a consequence of cognitive decline among older persons without Alzheimer's disease or mild cognitive impairment. *PLOS One, 7*(8), 1–5. doi: 10.1371/journal.pone.0043647.

Boyle, P. A., Wilson, R. S., Yu, L. Y., Buchman, A. S., & Bennett, D. A. (2013). Poor decision making is associated with an increased risk of mortality among community-dwelling older persons without dementia. *Neuroepidemiology, 40*(4), 247–252. doi: 10.1159/000342781.

Burnes, D., Henderson, C. R., Sheppard, C., Zhao, R., Pillemer, K., & Lachs, M. (2017). Prevalence of financial fraud and scams among older adults in the United States: A systematic review and meta-analysis. *American Journal of Public Health, 107*, e13–e21. doi: 10.2105/AJPH.2017.303821.

Conrad, K. J., Iris, M., Ridings, J. W., Langley, K., & Wilber, K. H. (2010). Self-report measure of financial exploitation of older adults. *Gerontologist, 50*, 758–773. doi: 10.1080/08946566.2011.584045.

DeLiema, M. (2018). Elder fraud and financial exploitation: Application of routine activity theory. *Gerontologist, 58*, 706–718. doi: 10.1093/geront/gnw258.

Hall, L., Campbell, R., Gross, E. & Lichtenberg, P.A. (in press) The Impact of Financial Coaching on Older Adult Victims of Financial Exploitation: A Quasi-Experimental Research Study. *Journal of Financial Counseling and Planning*.

Han, S. D., Boyle, P. A., James, B. D., Yu, L. Y., Barnes, L. L., & Bennett, D. A. (2015). Discrepancies between cognition and decision making in older adults. *Aging—Clinical and Experimental Research, 28*, 99–108. doi: 10.1007/s40520-015-0375-7.

Hsu, J. W., & Willis, R. (2013). Dementia risk and financial decision making by older households: The impact of information. *Journal of Human Capitol, University of Chicago, 17*, 340–377. http://www.journals.uchicago.edu/doi/pdfplus/10.1086/674105

Jackson, S. L. (2012). Pure financial exploitation vs. hybrid financial exploitation co-occurring with physical abuse and/or neglect of elderly persons. *Psychology of Violence, 2*, 285–296.

James, B. D., Boyle, P. A., & Bennett, D. A. (2014). Correlates of susceptibility to scams in older adults without dementia. *Journal of Elder Abuse and Neglect, 26*(2), 107–122.

Laumann, E. O., Leitsch, S. A., & Waite, L. J. (2008). Elder mistreatment in the United States: Prevalence estimates from a nationally representative study. *Journals of Gerontology Series B: Psychological Sciences and Social Sciences, 63*(4), S248–S254. Retrieved from http://psychsocgerontology.oxfordjournals.org/

Lichtenberg, P. A., Gross, E., & Campbell, R. (2018). A short form of the lichtenberg financial decision-making rating scale. *Clinical Gerontologist*. doi: 10.1080/07317115.2018.1527424.

Lichtenberg, P. A., Hall, L., Gross, E., & Campbell, R. (2019). Providing assistance to older adult financial exploitation victims: Implications for clinical gerontologists. *Clinical Gerontologist*. doi: 10.1080/07317115.2019.1569190.

Lichtenberg, P. A., Ocepek-Welikson, K., Ficker, L. J., Gross, E., Rahman-Filipak, A., & Teresi, J. A. (2017). Conceptual and empirical approaches to financial decision-making by older adults: Results from a financial decision-making rating scale. *Clinical Gerontologist, 48*(1). doi: 10.1080/07317115.2017.1367748.

Lichtenberg, P. A., Stickney, L., & Paulson, D. (2013). Is psychological vulnerability related to the experience of fraud in older adults? *Clinical Gerontologist, 36*, 132–146. doi: 10.1080/07317115.2012.749323.

Lichtenberg, P. A., Stoltman, J., Ficker, L. J., Iris, M., & Mast, B. T. (2015). A person-centered approach to financial capacity assessment: Preliminary development of a new rating scale. *Clinical Gerontologist, 38*, 49–67. doi: 10.1080/07317115.2014.970318.

Lichtenberg, P. A., Sugarman, M. A., Paulson, D., Ficker, L. J., & Rahaman-Filipiak, A. (2016). Psychological and functional vulnerability predicts fraud cases in older adults: Results of a longitudinal study. *Clinical Gerontologist, 39*(1), 48–63.

Lichtenberg, P. A., Campbell, R., Hall, L., & Gross, E. Z. (2020) Context matters: Financial, psychological and relationship insecurities around personal finance is related to financial exploitation. *The Gerontologist, XX*, XX1–10. doi: 10.1093/geront/gnaa020.

Liu, M. W., Berger, D., & Wilbur, K. (2017). Examining the role of social support in elder financial exploitation using a community sample. *Innovation in Aging, 1*(1), igx016, https://doi.org/10.1093/geroni/igx016

Marson, D. C. (2001). Loss of financial competency in dementia: Conceptual and empirical approaches. *Aging, Neuropsychology, and Cognition, 8*, 164–181.

Mast, B. T. (2011). *Whole Person Dementia Assessment*. Baltimore, MD: Health Professions Press, Inc.

MetLife. (2009). *Broken Trust: Elders, Family and Finances*. New York: MetLife Mature Market Institute.

MetLife. (2011). *The MetLife Study of Elder Financial Abuse: Crimes of Occasion, Desperation and Predation against America's Elders*. New York: MetLife Mature Market Institute.

Pinkser, D. M., McFarland, K., & Pachana, N. A. (2009). Exploitation in older adults: Social vulnerability and personal competence factors. *Journal of Applied Gerontology, 29*, 740–761. doi: 10.1177/0733464809346559.

Quinn, M. J., Nerenberg, L., Navarro, A. E., & Wilber, K. H. (2017). Developing an undue influence screening tool for Adult Protective Services. *Journal of Elder Abuse and Neglect, 29*, 157–185. doi: 10.1080/089466566.2017.1314844.

Ruffman, T., Murray, J., Halberstadt, J., & Vater, T. (2012). Age-related differences in deception. *Psychology and Aging, 27*, 543–549. doi: 10.1037/a0023380.

Samanez-Larkin, G. R., Gibbs, S. E., Khanna, K., Nielsen, L., Carstensen, L. L., & Knutson, B. (2007). Anticipation of monetary gain but not loss in healthy older adults. *Nature Neuroscience, 10*(6), 787–791. doi: 10.1038/nn1894.

Shao, J., Zhang, Q., Ren, Y., Li, X., & Lin, T. (2019) Why are older adults victims of fraud? Current knowledge and prospects regarding older adults' vulnerability to fraud. *Journal of Elder Abuse & Neglect, 31*(3), 225–243. doi: 10.1080/08946566.2019.1625842.

Spreng, R. N., Karlawish, J., & Marson, D. C. (2016). Cognitive, social and neural determinants of diminished decision-making and financial exploitation risk in aging and dementia: A review and new model. *Journal of Elder Abuse and Neglect, 28*, 320–344. doi: 10.1080/o8946566.2016.1237918.

6 Cognitive and Metacognitive Predictors of Financial Exploitation: Understanding Fraud Susceptibility in Adulthood

Laura C. Walzak and Wendy Loken Thornton

Cognitive and Metacognitive Predictors of Financial Exploitation: Understanding Fraud Susceptibility in Adulthood

As technology continues to influence our everyday lives, the digital age has yielded an entirely new medium of sophisticated fraudulent schemes. Exercising discretion as a consumer becomes an increasingly risky or difficult endeavor because we are bombarded by ever-evolving, persuasive attempts to solicit products and services across multiple mediums. If you have an email address, you get spam. The incoming phone call from an unregistered number is more likely than not a telemarketing scheme. Our mailboxes fill with junk offers and our internet pages are rife with pop-up advertisements of miracle products, wild promises, and time-limited deals. Many of us

DOI: 10.4324/9781003017189-6

correctly assume that these solicitations are likely scams. However, according to the Better Business Bureau (BBB) 2019 Annual Report, scams are not only increasing in frequency, but their victims are too. Further, according to a 2019 US Federal Trade Commission report, $1.90 *billion* dollars was lost to fraud in 2019, up 23% since 2018.

Context and Scope

To date, findings related to the prevalence of financial exploitation have been primarily limited to financial abuse, in which exploitation occurs within a trusting relationship (e.g., family members). In contrast, comparatively little is known regarding frauds and scams, which are perpetrated by strangers (Burnes et al., 2017). In this chapter we focus specifically on *fraud* to describe situations with deception perpetrated by strangers for the purpose of financial gain. Consider the following example:

> Your 68-year-old neighbour is hurriedly on his way to the gas station. He received an email earlier that day that instructed him to express ship $5,000 worth of preloaded Visa gift cards to his nephew, vacationing in Thailand, who had apparently been in a scooter accident and required urgent medical care. Wasting no time, your neighbour immediately purchased the cards and mailed them directly from the store. A few days later, he received a call from his credit card company inquiring about the fraudulent charges and he realized that he had been scammed.

While some fraudulent solicitations are gaining wider awareness amongst the general public for their reputation in targeting older adults, there is little reason to believe that younger adults are not also susceptible to such schemes. For example, this variant of the infamous "grandparent scheme" described above where an imposter poses as a close friend/relative for financial gain is a type of Relationship and Trust Fraud, a category of fraud victimization that appears to affect all ages (Stanford Centre on Longevity, 2015). Further, other sophisticated consumer scams (e.g., investment schemes, sweepstakes draws) can be less easily recognisable as fraudulent. To illustrate this point, please consider the following example:

> This time, your 23-year-old neighbor is on his way to the bank in a hurry. He received an email earlier that day that instructed him to wire $5,000 cash to his uncle, vacationing in Thailand, who had apparently

> been in a scooter accident and required urgent medical care. Wasting no time, he immediately made an appointment with a financial advisor since the monetary amount was higher than what he could transfer himself. The advisor sat down and sympathetically listened to his request. He was well under the 'age of suspicion' and therefore was not flagged for a financial exploitation screening. She turned away from her cabinet of standardized questions and got to work on the transaction.

As illustrated with the examples above, determining actual prevalence rates of fraud across adulthood presents a difficult challenge, as "fraud" may be not easily identified by those being scammed, and fraud victims may be reluctant to come forward once aware. Of the 71,000 mass marketing fraud complaints received in 2017 in Canada—with an estimated dollar loss of over $110 million—fewer than 5% of victims actually filed a fraud report with the Canadian Anti-Fraud Centre (CAFC), citing reasons including embarrassment and worry that they were accountable.

Aside from significant financial losses and stigma, falling victim to fraud is associated with an array of other devastating consequences (Alves & Wilson, 2008; Button, Lewis, & Tapley, 2014; Burnes et al., 2017; Wood & Lichtenberg, 2017; Shao et al., 2019), making the identification of vulnerable groups a priority for government and policymakers. While there is little doubt that senior fraud is a pressing social problem as the proportion of older adults continues to rise (and they have less means to recover from financial losses than their younger counterparts), the question as to whether older adults are uniquely *susceptible* to fraud remains hotly debated (see Ross, Grossmann, & Schryer, 2014; Norris, Brookes, & Dowell, 2019). Current data at least suggest that older adults appear disproportionately *targeted* as victims of fraud, but incidence of scam victimization is on the rise across the lifespan (Competition Bureau, 2019).

In response to this evolving social issue, laws were enacted in several U.S. states to safeguard the elderly against consumer fraud (Cauchi; National Conference of State Legislatures, 2013), allowing bank employees to intervene in the event of a suspicious request from an elderly client. However, the development of such laws with well-intended emphasis on elder fraud are based upon the commonly held belief that older adults are particularly vulnerable to scams (Ross et al., 2014). In addition, a sole focus on elder fraud campaigns prematurely limits our understanding of vulnerabilities to fraud in other age groups and populations (e.g., non-native English speakers, immigrants), not to mention reinforcing damaging old-age stereotypes of frailty and cognitive impairment that may lower rates of reporting fraud due to stigma (Ross et al., 2014). As illustrated in the vignettes above, public policy measures need to be research-informed in order to develop a successful screening tool for fraud risk. Many scams target specific age groups (e.g., Vishwanath et al., 2018) and hence, one risk screening tool may not be relevant to all groups and will likely need to attune to the nature of the scam itself. Thus, developing a coherent understanding of the true function of age in fraud susceptibility is essential before one can develop accurate predictions regarding fraud risk, and before effective strategies to protect vulnerable individuals from fraud can be developed.

Age as a Predictor of Fraud

A key principle that has shaped much of the extant literature to date holds that older adults are uniquely susceptible to fraud (James, Boyle, & Bennett, 2014). A recent meta-analysis by Burnes et al. (2017) estimated that the prevalence for fraud in cognitively intact, community dwelling older adults was 5.6%, a particularly sobering figure considering that the scope of this problem is expected to increase along with the growth of the older adult population and given the plethora of serious consequences associated with fraud victimization in later life. Nonetheless, current literature regarding age differences is inconclusive; competing models argue that vulnerability to fraud should *increase* in later life (e.g., Asp et al., 2012; James et al., 2014; Burnes et al., 2017), *decrease* in later life (e.g., Ross et al., 2014), or that *middle-aged* adults are most robust in resisting fraud compared with both younger and older adults (Agarwal, Athey, & Yang, 2009).

A guiding assumption that underlies the study of age differences in fraud susceptibility is that older adults should demonstrate increased fraud susceptibility as a result of age-related cognitive declines (Asp et al., 2012). Indeed, Burnes et al. (2017) posited that older adults have distinct age-associated characteristics that make them more vulnerable to fraud and scams, underscoring the notion that avoiding or resisting scams and fraudulent activities requires complex, higher-order cognitive functions that are more likely to decline in older adults.

Still other research groups have argued that fraud susceptibility should *decline* in later life, given that older adults tend to display more aversion to risk (Modic & Anderson, 2014) and prioritize minimizing losses/maximizing gains (e.g., Ebner et al., 2006; Ross et al., 2014). Interestingly, demographic-based studies on self-reported fraud prevalence suggest that "young old" (average age = late 60s) and more highly educated respondents endorsed higher rates of fraud than older age groups (Laumann, Leitsch, & Waite,

2008; Lichtenberg et al., 2016). Furthermore, middle-aged adults outperform both younger and older adults on financial decision-making tasks, mirroring the economic phenomena of the inverted U-shaped curve for maximizing optimal performance (Agarwal et al., 2009). These findings are consistent with previous reports from our lab and others, in which mid-life capitalizes on the relative maintenance of cognitive capacity along with the cumulative benefits of decision-making experience (Denney & Pearce, 1989; Thornton & Dumke, 2005; Thornton et al., 2013). The relationship between age and fraud susceptibility appears complex and, regrettably, the prospective study of age differences in this area has been largely limited to younger vs. older adult comparisons with little emphasis on middle age. Thus, the question as to whether and when age differences emerge on critical dimensions of fraud susceptibility across adulthood remains unresolved.

The Search for Predictors of Fraud Susceptibility

It is important to note that our understanding of the relationship between fraud susceptibility and a plethora of proposed predictors is somewhat limited as the majority of studies to date are based on retrospective reports and consumer complaints from older adults, and thus reflect features of the sampled populations (James et al., 2014). Although such studies offer valuable insights into what might make people good targets for fraud, findings have a higher likelihood of reporting errors or biases and research suggests that relative to victims of violent crime, fraud victims are unwilling to report their experience to the authorities (Van Wyk & Mason, 2001). Further, many individuals lack awareness that they have been defrauded and there is a lack of commonly accepted measures to assess fraud experiences (Shao et al., 2019). Researchers have also raised concerns about the operationalization of the concept "susceptibility to fraud" in empirical work thus far due to the absence of closely approximated laboratory-based tasks that mimic real-world social decision experiences (Shao et al., 2019). Finally, the field lacks a unifying classification system regarding types of fraud, if differentiated at all (e.g., financial vs. romantic fraud; Stanford Center on Longevity, 2015), and lacks an appreciation for how these scams appeal to different age groups.

Balancing these limitations in consideration, several broad risk factors are well established in their association to fraud susceptibility in the present collection of population-based studies; for example, in studies with older adults, demographic variables, including older age, non-Caucasian background, and lower socioeconomic class (Beach et al., 2010), may increase susceptibility to fraud. Low social engagement (Lichtenberg, Ficker, & Rahman-Filipiak, 2015), psychological vulnerability (Lichtenberg et al., 2016), and depressive symptoms (James et al., 2014; Lichtenberg et al., 2016) are also consistent predictors of financial exploitation among older adults.

Cognitive Predictors

With the caveat that older populations garner much of the focus of this research relative to younger counterparts, recent research on financial decision-making has shaped a theoretical framework to capture the various contextual and intellectual factors that influence decisions, ultimately determining likelihood of financial exploitation. Lichtenberg et al. (2015) proposed that cognitive abilities (*intellectual* factors) related to financial management and decision-making are crucial components directly impacted by *contextual* factors, including excessive persuasion or undue influence. Since it is proposed that cognitive skills underlie sound financial management, and declines in these abilities compromise good decision-making, it is reasonable to assume that global cognitive declines would result in increased susceptibility to financial exploitation.

Lichtenberg et al.'s (2015) initial theoretical model was extended to incorporate neuropsychological findings by Wood, Hanoch, and Woods (2016a), acknowledging a number of cognitive abilities that are proposed to underpin successful decision-making at any age. Specifically, numeracy (a distinct construct integrating calculation abilities, engagement, comprehension, and use of numeric reasoning; Schwartz et al., 1997) has been identified as an integral component of decision-making and predictive of financial exploitation, even in the presence of other risk factors (Wood et al., 2016b). Numeracy tends to decline with age, resulting in lower comprehension and worse decision-making when unfamiliar numerical information is present (Hibbard et al., 2001; Wood et al., 2016b). Numeracy is also related to financial literacy (e.g., the ability to correctly answer financial questions, make financial decisions about retirement savings, propensity for paying off loans and credit cards; Lusardi & Mitchell, 2011) and given that older adults tend to perform poorer on numeracy than their younger counterparts (Jenkins, Akerman, Frumkin, Salter, & Vorhaus, 2011), it is likely that they may be at higher risk for financial exploitation due to deterioration of this skill. Findings indicate that numeracy is related to deliberative reasoning and that those with lower numeracy abilities appear to be influenced by competing irrelevant affective factors (Reyna et al., 2009), suggesting that emotion-based appeals may be more effective in the absence of strong cognitive/numeracy skills. Interestingly, older adults with lower numeracy demonstrate higher susceptibility to persuasion tactics that are emotional in nature, and some evidence suggests that older adults can be better protected from fraudulent exploitation by strengthening their financial familiarity (Gamble et al., 2014).

A study on substantiated fraud victims conducted by Wood et al. (2016b) revealed that older adults who had been successfully scammed were also more likely to demonstrate poorer verbal memory, calculation abilities, and executive functioning skills (including working memory). Slowed processing speed has also been implicated as a key cognitive predictor for impaired financial decisions (Denburg et al., 2007; Shao et al., 2019), though its mechanisms remain unclear. A parallel line of research investigating the relationship between cognitive abilities and *financial capacity* suggests that arithmetic/calculation skills, semantic memory, and executive functioning are predictive of financial incapacity and lead to worse financial decisions (Griffith et al., 2003; Martin et al., 2008).

Aside from numeracy and other cognitive predictors, cognitive functioning is also thought to impact financial decision-making more broadly. For example, research has shown that among healthy older adults, stronger global cognitive skills are associated with an increased likelihood to participate in financial decisions (Cole & Shastry, 2009). Bolstering these findings, other researchers have identified significant positive associations between decision-making abilities and global neurocognitive status (as measured by the Mini Mental State Exam; Lichtenberg et al., 2015). Recent research on non-demented older adults suggests that susceptibility to telemarketing scams is significantly associated with decreased gray matter volume in the frontal and temporal regions (Han et al., 2016), further supporting age-driven hypotheses that fraud vulnerability is related to normative cognitive declines.

The handful of studies on cognitive predictors of fraud indicate that cognitive impairment (meeting criteria for "mild cognitive impairment" in most studies; Stiegel, 2012) serves as a significant risk factor for financial exploitation, and age-related declines in cognitive abilities can hold real-world implications with regards to fraud susceptibility. For example, Stiegel (2012) proposed that age-related cognitive decline amongst residence-dwelling older adults can result in two-fold vulnerabilities: (1) loss of financial skills and judgment; and (2) the inability to detect, and therefore prevent, financial exploitation. However, the majority findings do not address whether these relationships are necessarily *specific* to older adults, or if individual differences in ability levels and risks may underlie fraud susceptibility *across* adulthood. It is also critically important to note that several previous studies have either been focused on or included older adults with serious age-related cognitive impairments, such as dementia (e.g., Wood et al., 2014), and are generally limited in specifying the cognitive attributes of their samples. Thus, while certain cognitive predictors have been associated with fraud susceptibility in older adults, the universality of these relationships in healthy community-dwelling adults across the lifespan is yet to be determined.

Theory of Mind & Decision-Making

Decoding the complex decision-making process into integral components, researchers have emphasized the importance of cognitive and emotional appraisals (including the evaluation of other's mental states and emotions) in order to arrive at an accurate decision. As such, the capacity for monitoring and understanding mental state and affective information (i.e., Theory of Mind; ToM) is likely an important prerequisite in making appropriate decisions in the context of fraud (Brabec, Gfeller, & Ross, 2012; Seo & Lee, 2012). Poor performance on so-called "risky" or ambiguous decision-making is documented in healthy, cognitively intact, community-dwelling older adults (Rogalsky, Vidal, Li, & Damasio, 2012), with stronger performance when asked to make decisions in explicit, transparent scenarios (Bauer et al., 2013; see also Thornton & Dumke, 2005 and Thornton, et al., 2013).

Some authors have suggested that ToM declines in aging may underlie deficits in decision-making and may relate to increased willingness to tolerate risky financial or medical decisions in real-world settings (Rogalsky et al., 2012). Indeed, research on phishing scams suggests that people who rely on rational (i.e., sometimes referred to as "cold", cognitive-based) processing strategies tend to report lower trust in the legitimacy of a fraudulent email; conversely, those who employ more intuitive (i.e., aka "hot", affective-based) decision-making strategies tend to make less accurate judgments and rate their trust in the legitimacy as higher (Vishwanath, Harrison, & Ng, 2018). Context is also important; older adults tend to make less optimal decisions during risk-seeking, but not risk-avoidant financial decisions (Samanez-Larkin et al., 2007). Further, when older adults are faced with situations that involve risk, they tend to exercise more caution than younger counterparts (Rolison, Hanoch, & Wood, 2012) and demonstrate either *suppressed confidence* (Hansson et al., 2008) or *inflated confidence* (Gamble et al., 2014) in their decision irrespective to actual performance. These compelling findings indicate that a disruption in the deception-detection system as well as the more general decision-making process may underpin fraud susceptibility mechanisms.

Supporting these findings, a study on deceptive advertising by Denburg et al. (2007) found that older adults who exhibited risky decisions on the Iowa Gambling Task (IGT) were more susceptible to false advertisements relative to less risky decision-makers; over one-third of older adults failed to identify the misleading aspect of ads and continued to make high-risk decisions despite cumulative consequences. Interestingly, these participants also failed to show anticipatory physiological arousal during risky choices. However, in a study on IGT performance across the lifespan, Wood et al. (2005) found no age differences in performance between younger and older adult groups, though the age groups utilized different strategies that were proposed to mirror their relative biases and strengths (e.g., older adults tended to weigh gains and losses equally, dependent on recent outcomes, while younger adults weighed losses more heavily, demonstrating a negativity bias). Such studies provide a foundation of evidence to suggest that older adults are adaptive decision-makers in social contexts who may demonstrate unique patterns of decision-making relative to younger counterparts; further, it is possible that a subgroup within the older adult population is more at risk to fraud due to a combination of shared individual differences which puts them at disproportionately higher risk (see Wood et al., 2018; Norris et al., 2019).

Neuroanatomical support for the potential link between ToM and decision-making in the context of fraud is emerging. The ventromedial prefrontal cortex (vmPFC) is one of the primary neural regions that has been implicated in decision-making under uncertainty (Xie & Boush, 2011), with additional recruitment of the amygdala, insula, ventral striatum, and dorsolateral prefrontal cortex as decisions become more transparent (Lawrence et al., 2009). Interestingly, individuals with damage to the vmPFC have also demonstrated high intention to purchase products from misleading advertisements and were particularly credulous to misleading ads, relative to patients with other areas of brain damage and healthy controls (Asp et al., 2012). Notably, these findings suggest a region of functional overlap between areas supporting risky decision-making and those supporting ToM (Xie & Boush, 2011); ToM relies upon the prefrontal cortex, with suggested dissociations between ventromedial regions supporting affective ToM (the ability to reason about another's emotions) and dorsolateral regions supporting cognitive ToM (the ability to reason about another's mental state) (Sebastian et al., 2012; Shamay-Tsoory, 2011). Brain regions supporting risky decision-making show the greatest overlap with those supporting affective ToM (ventromedial prefrontal cortex), and potential overlap with cognitive ToM regions (dorsolateral prefrontal cortex) as decisions are more explicit, or when greater cognitive support is required to make a decision (i.e., as in older age; Rogalsky et al., 2012; Wang

& Su, 2013). Though no published studies to date have specifically examined overlap between ToM and fraud susceptibility in aging, one study found that individuals' engagement in a financial decision-making paradigm activated neural circuitry associated with ToM more closely than classical reward circuitry (Evans et al., 2011). Parallel lines of work on other meta-cognitive skills such as counterfactual thinking have suggested a link between imagining mental states and ability to detect deception (see Briazu et al., 2017).

Successful navigation of our social world relies on ToM, and reduced ToM may impair an individual's capacity to accurately assess the motivations of others and make sound judgments, thus heightening fraud susceptibility in the social world. Declines in this social/affective cognitive skillset in later life have been widely reported by our lab and others (Bernstein, Thornton, & Sommerville, 2011; Bernstein et al., 2017; Moran, 2013; Henry et al., 2013; Fischer et al., 2014; Fischer et al., 2017), and poorer ToM in both younger and older adults is associated with reductions in other aspects of cognition (i.e., executive functions, working memory, processing speed, semantic/episodic memory; de Belvis et al., 2008; Fischer et al., 2014, 2017) and health (Walzak & Thornton, 2018). A multitude of outcomes are theorized to relate to poor ToM (e.g., impaired social functioning, poor decision-making; Baksh et al., 2018), yet to our knowledge no published studies have yet directly investigated these associations in healthy adulthood using validated measures (e.g. Calso, Besnard, & Allain, 2019).

Cognition Applied in the Decision-Making Context: A Pilot Study from the Cognitive Aging Laboratory

Background

Fraud susceptibility is currently assessed in laboratory settings using a variety of self-report and interview-style measures, the majority of which have demonstrated poor ecological validity to date (Spreng, Karlawish, & Marson, 2016; Shao et al., 2019), underscoring the need to develop more real-world laboratory-based measures. To that end, several critical dimensions of fraud susceptibility have been identified within deceptive-advertising paradigms as they relate to judgment and decision-making (see Denburg et al., 2007).

In these paradigms, *purchase intention* refers to the "buy-in," or likelihood that an individual will purchase a product or participate in an offer and *deceit detection* (sometimes referred to as credulity) describes a person's ability to accurately discern misleading advertisements from genuine ones (Asp et al.,

2012). *Decision confidence* (a subjective rating of how certain an individual is in their decision) is another key factor for inclusion in models of fraud susceptibility given that amongst individuals with decision-making impairments, confidence ratings tend to deviate from actual performance (Denburg et al., 2007). For example, Gamble et al. (2014) used longitudinal comparisons to demonstrate that while a decrease in cognition was predictive of declining financial literacy in older adults, it did not predict a decline in *financial confidence* (specifically, an individual's thoughts about their ability to manage their own finances). While these dimensions of purchase intention, deceit detection and decision confidence have not yet been modelled across the entire adult lifespan, they have been utilized in a number of studies to investigate judgment, decision-making, and credulity within deceptive-advertising paradigms.

Task Development

Guided by theoretical rationale supporting the dimensional relationship between ToM, decision-making, and fraud susceptibility, we developed the Everyday Social Decisions (ESD) task modelled after other paradigms where participants were asked to evaluate real-world advertisements (Denburg et al., 2007; Asp et al., 2012; Shao et al., 2019). Despite past research identifying potential predictors of fraud susceptibility at the population level, it is unclear how reduced performance on laboratory tasks may translate into impaired decision-making abilities within the context of fraud. Further, no studies to date have investigated whether reliable age-related declines in a variety of cognitive and ToM skills extend to fraud susceptibility as well, and whether age differences emerge across the adult lifespan.

We designed the ESD task to integrate the dimensions of *purchase intention, deceit detection*, and *decision confidence* across potentially misleading scenarios to assess fraud susceptibility. The scenarios include emails, television commercials, and voice messages which were derived from real public advertisements (or replicated from documented fraud cases) with content commonly targeted toward adults (i.e., health products, internet services, investment opportunities, goods and services). Each scenario was judged for inclusion according to criteria developed by the Federal Trade Commission (FTC Decisions, 2002) in determining whether it met classification as false advertising (i.e., using deceptive claims to create a discrepancy between the product's factual performance and what the consumer is led to believe). Thus, we designed this measure to maximize external validity considerations.

Half of the 10 scenarios on the ESD reflect genuine advertising and half of the scenarios reflect false advertising where the authors' intent is to mislead consumers. *Purchase intention* was assessed by asking participants to decide whether or not they would participate in or purchase each offer/item (7-point Likert scale where *1 = not at all likely to participate* and *7 = very likely to participate*). *Deceit detection* and *confidence* were measured by asking participants to respond to two questions rating their perception about the advertisement's intent on a 7-point Likert scale ("Based on your evaluation, how likely is the [author's] intent to mislead?"; "How confident are you in your judgment about this [author's] intent?")

Pilot Study

The primary goals of this research program are twofold: (1) develop a comprehensive model of predictors of fraud susceptibility in adulthood, and (2) determine whether potential predictors of fraud susceptibility are age-group-specific, representing an important first step in decomposing the mechanisms that underlie this complex social decision-making skill. We are interested in whether age-related cognitive and social cognitive declines are associated with one's ability to discern genuine from fraudulent social information.

Using a contemporary model of ToM emphasizing both cognitive and affective components, we piloted our ESD task with a sample of both younger ($N = 38$; $M = 23$ years) and older ($N = 35$; $M = 72$ years) adults to examine links between fraud susceptibility and age, ToM, and a number of cognitive predictors. Participants completed a series of psychosocial questionnaires and standardized measures of neurocognition, cognitive ToM (Strange Stories; Happé, 1994), affective ToM (Reading the Eyes in the Mind; Baron-Cohen et al., 2001), and fraud susceptibility (ESD). We applied correlational analyses and hierarchical regression to identify predictors of fraud susceptibility in both age groups.

In terms of age differences, preliminary data from our lab using this task (Walzak et al., 2020) revealed that while the likelihood of participating in a fraudulent offer did not significantly differ between younger and older adults (*purchase intention*; $t_{71} = -0.56$, $p = 0.58$), older adults were significantly more accurate in discerning genuine from fraudulent advertisements (*deceit detection*; $t_{71} = -2.95$, $p = 0.00$) and were also more confident in their decision than younger adults ($t_{71} = -4.30$, $p = 0.00$). Purchase intention and deceit detection were strongly correlated in both age groups ($r = 0.59$, $p = 0.000$), and stronger deceit detection was associated with higher decision confidence ($r = 0.24$,

$p = 0.05$). In terms of predictors, cognitive ToM was associated with better discernment of the advertisements in both age groups ($r = 0.35$, $p = 0.05$), while affective ToM showed emerging associations with purchase intention ($r = 0.23$, $p = 0.06$). In a series of hierarchical regressions, poorer affective ToM increased participants' likelihood to participate in a scam ($\beta = 0.28$, 95% CI = [0.13, 1.18], $p = 0.02$) after controlling for age. With the exception of semantic memory, no cognitive variables were reliably associated with performance on the ESD task in either age group.

Pilot results from this ongoing study are consistent with theories predicting that cognitive and affective ToM may differentially impact aspects of deception detection (see Stewart, Wright, & Atherton, 2019). Specifically, it appears that affective ToM may be more closely associated with initial "buy-in" and salience for products/advertisements, whereas strong cognitive ToM skills may be prerequisite for the sophisticated decision-making process of separating genuine information from fraudulent. These preliminary findings highlight the potential importance of social cognition in predicting crucial everyday outcomes such as fraud susceptibility. In light of well-established findings that older adults are at increased risk for social deficits and are over-represented in fraud victimization cases, the initial results suggesting a potential older age advantage in decision-making are paradoxical and underscore the need for studying ToM in tandem with real-world functioning outcomes. In addition to understanding the role of age in fraud susceptibility, we are continuing to model the effects of demographic, psychosocial, and social cognitive measures that have been overlooked to date in order to more accurately map out these novel relationships across the adult lifespan.

Summary and Conclusions

In an ever-social world, fraud susceptibility has emerged as an important construct in the 21st century with mounting societal and clinical relevance. While the National Council on Aging (2018) has stated that "Financial scams targeting seniors have become so prevalent that they're now considered the crime of the 21st century," preliminary data from our lab support the notion that younger adults may be at just as much risk for impaired decision-making when it comes to fraudulent information than their older counterparts. The idea that older adults are more susceptible to fraud bolsters the harmful old-age stereotype of cognitive loss and frailty, and also cements societal stigma by suppressing reporting of victimization and obscuring true prevalence rates (Ross et al., 2014; Norris et al., 2019). Since the current literature on age differences and fraud susceptibility maintains competing models, either predicting that fraud susceptibility should *increase* in later life, *decrease* in later life, or be minimized in middle age, it is an exciting time for researchers to be addressing these major knowledge gaps.

Although decision-making represents a diverse and well-studied interdisciplinary area, questions remain as to whether deficits observed in the laboratory or clinic translate to real-world scenarios, such as in susceptibility to financial exploitation or loss of capacity to make one's own decisions. Further, there is a significant gap between laboratory measures and real-world decision-making, specifically in the aging context, where external pressures such as health and finances may be the primary drivers of decisions related to risk. Bridging this gap between the laboratory and real life is critically important; as the population of older adults continues to grow, fuelling concerns about the maintenance of independence, it has become a public priority to understand factors that can contribute to the preservation of autonomy (particularly as it concerns financial decisions; Spreng et al., 2016). More work needs to be done across the lifespan, in controlled settings with controlled exposure, thus expanding variables of interest beyond cognition to better understand the depth of factors underpinning fraud susceptibility mechanisms that exist in the real world (e.g., social variables, decision confidence). The development of more ecologically and theoretically valid measures of fraud susceptibility will not only aid in validating existing screening tools and self-report measures, but also ultimately helps us to better identifying both vulnerabilities and resilience to fraud.

As advances in our understanding of the neural, cognitive, affective, and social determinants of fraud susceptibility form a necessary foundation to develop more targeted decision-making aids, such progress may also open new avenues for identifying individual predictors of exploitation risk. Our research program hopes to resolve existing controversies in the cognitive aging and fraud literatures by clarifying the magnitude and extent of age differences in fraud susceptibility and identifying important predictors. Findings will lead to better integration of social cognitive and neurocognitive models of aging and enhance theoretical development in this burgeoning area of research, hopefully extending to targeted initiatives that ultimately minimize fraud risk.

Acknowledgement

This work was supported in part by Social Sciences and Humanities Research Council grants (SSHRC-410-2010-0407; 425-2020-0183) awarded to Dr. Wendy

Loken Thornton. Laura C. Walzak was supported by a Social Sciences and Humanities Research Council Doctoral Fellowship. The authors extend their gratitude to members of the SFU Cognitive Aging Lab for assistance with data collection and to the participants who very generously provided their time and effort.

References

Agarwal, N., Athey, S., & Yang, D. (2009). Skewed bidding in pay-per-action auctions for online advertising. *American Economic Review, 99*(2), 441–447.

Alves, L. M., & Wilson, S. R. (2008). The effects of loneliness on telemarketing fraud vulnerability among older adults. *Journal of Elder Abuse & Neglect, 20*(1), 63–85.

Asp, E., Manzel, K., Koestner, B., Cole, C., Denburg, N. L., & Tranel, D. (2012). A neuropsychological test of belief and doubt: damage to ventromedial prefrontal cortex increases credulity for misleading advertising. *Frontiers in Neuroscience, 6*, 100.

Baksh, R. A., Abrahams, S., Auyeung, B., & MacPherson, S. E. (2018). The Edinburgh Social Cognition Test (ESCoT): Examining the effects of age on a new measure of theory of mind and social norm understanding. *PloS One, 13*(4), e0195818.

Baron-Cohen, S., Wheelright, S., Hill, J., Raste, Y., & Plumb, I. (2001). The "Reading the Mind in the Eyes" Test revised version: A study with normal adults, and adults with Asperger syndrome or high-functioning autism. *Journal of Child Psychology and Psychiatry, 42*, 241–251. doi:10.1111/1469-7610.00715.

Bauer, A. S., Timpe, J. C., Edmonds, E. C., Bechara, A., Tranel, D., & Denburg, N. L. (2013). Myopia for the future or hypersensitivity to reward? Age-related changes in decision making on the Iowa Gambling Task. *Emotion, 13*(1), 19.

Beach, S. R., Schulz, R., Castle, N. G., & Rosen, J. (2010). Financial exploitation and psychological mistreatment among older adults: Differences between African Americans and Non-African Americans in a population-based survey. *The Gerontologist, 50*, 744–757. doi:10.1093/geront/gnq053.

Bernstein, D. M., Thornton, W. J. L., & Sommerville, J. A. (2011). Theory of mind through the ages: Older and middle-aged adults exhibit more errors than do younger adults on a continuous false belief task. *Experimental Aging Research, 37*(5), 481–502.

Bernstein, D. M., Coolin, A., Fischer, A. L., Thornton, W. L., & Sommerville, J. A. (2017). False-belief reasoning from 3 to 92 years of age. *PloS One, 12*(9), e0185345.

Brabec, C. M., Gfeller, J. D., & Ross, M. J. (2012). An exploration of relationships among measures of social cognition, decision making, and emotional intelligence. *Journal of Clinical and Experimental Neuropsychology, 34*, 887–894.

Briazu, R. A., Walsh, C. R., Deeprose, C., & Ganis, G. (2017). Undoing the past in order to lie in the present: Counterfactual thinking and deceptive communication. *Cognition.*

Burnes, D., Henderson Jr, C. R., Sheppard, C., Zhao, R., Pillemer, K., & Lachs, M. S. (2017). Prevalence of financial fraud and scams among older adults in the United States: A systematic review and meta-analysis. *American Journal of Public Health, 107*(8), e13–e21.

Button, M., Lewis, C., & Tapley, J. (2014). Not a victimless crime: The impact of fraud on individual victims and their families. *Security Journal, 27*(1), 36–54.

Calso, C., Besnard, J., & Allain, P. (2019). Study of the theory of mind in normal aging: Focus on the deception detection and its links with other cognitive functions. *Aging, Neuropsychology, and Cognition*, 1–23.

Canadian Anti-Fraud Centre (2017). *Annual Report: Facts & Figures*. Retrieved from https://www.antifraudcentre-centreantifraude.ca/index-eng.htm

Cauchi, R. (2013). National Conference of State Legislatures. Retrieved April, 7, 2015.

Competition Bureau of Canada. Competition Bureau Insights 2019: Resisting Scams in the 21st Century. (March 22, 2019). Retrieved from https://www.competitionbureau.gc.ca/eic/site/cb-bc.nsf/eng/04333.html

Cole, S. A., & Shastry, G. K. (2009). *Smart Money: The Effect of Education, Cognitive Ability, and Financial Literacy on Financial Market Participation* (pp. 09–071). Boston, MA: Harvard Business School.

de Belvis, A. G., Avolio, M., Spagnolo, A., Damiani, G., Sicuro, L., Cicchetti, A., Ricciardi, W., & Rosano, A. (2008). Factors associated with health-related quality of life: The role of social relationships among the elderly in an Italian region. *Public Health*, *122*, 784–793. doi:10.1016/j.puhe.2007.08.018.

Denburg, N. L., Cole, C. A., Hernandez, M., Yamada, T. H., Tranel, D., Bechara, A., & Wallace, R. B. (2007). The orbitofrontal cortex, real-world decision making, and normal aging. *Annals of the New York Academy of Sciences*, *1121*, 480–498.

Denney, N. W., & Pearce, K. A. (1989). A developmental study of practical problem solving in adults. *Psychology & Aging*, *4*, 438–442.

Ebner, N. C., Freund, A. M., & Baltes, P. B. (2006). Developmental changes in personal goal orientation from young to late adulthood: From striving for gains to maintenance and prevention of losses. *Psychology and Aging*, *21*, 664–678. doi:10.1037/0882-7974.21.4.664.

Evans, S., Fleming, S. M., Dolan, R. J., & Averbeck, B. B. (2011). Effects of emotional preferences on value-based decision-making are mediated by mentalizing and not reward networks. *Journal of Cognitive Neuroscience*, *23*(9), 2197–2210.

Fischer, A. L., Bernstein, D. M., & Thornton, W. L. (2014). Vascular health modifies theory of mind performance in older adults. *Journals of Gerontology Series B: Psychological Sciences and Social Sciences*, *69*, 219–227. doi:10.1093/geronb/gbs120.

Fischer, A. L., O'Rourke, N., & Thornton, W. L. (2017). Age differences in cognitive and affective theory of mind: Concurrent contributions of neurocognitive performance, sex, and pulse pressure. *The Journals of Gerontology Series B:Psychological Sciences and Social Science. Special Issue: 50 Years of Cognitive Aging*, *72*(1), 71–81. doi:10.1093/geronbgbw088.

Federal Trade Commission Advisory Board. Federal Trade Commission (FTC) Decisions: Findings, Opinions, and Orders. (June 30, 2002). Retrieved from https://www.ftc.gov/sites/default/files/documents/commission_decision_volumes/volume-133/volume133.pdf

Federal Trade Commission Advisory Board. Federal Trade Commission (FTC) Annual Report 2019. (2019). Retreived from https://public.tableau.com/profile/federal.trade.commission#!/

Gamble, K. J., Boyle, P. A., Yu, L., & Bennett, D. A. (2014). Aging and financial decision making. *Management Science*, *61*(11), 2603–2610.

Griffith, H. R., Belue, K., Sicola, A., Krzywanski, S., Zamrini, E., Harrell, L., & Marson, D. C. (2003). Impaired financial abilities in mild cognitive impairment: A direct assessment approach. *Neurology*, *60*(3), 449–457.

Han, S. D., Boyle, P. A., Yu, L., Arfanakis, K., James, B. D., Fleischman, D. A., & Bennett, D. A. (2016). Grey matter correlates of susceptibility to scams in community-dwelling older adults. *Brain Imaging and Behavior*, 10(2), 524–532.

Hansson, P., Rönnlund, M., Juslin, P., & Nilsson, L. G. (2008). Adult age differences in the realism of confidence judgments: Overconfidence, format dependence, and cognitive predictors. *Psychology and Aging, 23*(3), 531.

Happé, F. G. (1994). An advanced test of theory of mind: Understanding of story characters' thoughts and feelings by able autistic, mentally handicapped, and normal children and adults. *Journal of Autism and Developmental Disorders, 24*(2), 129–154.

Henry, J. D., Phillips, L. H., Ruffman, T., & Bailey, P. E. (2013). A meta-analytic review of age differences in theory of mind. *Psychology and Aging, 28*, 826–839. doi:10.1037/a0030677.

Hibbard, J. H., Slovic, P., Peters, E., Finucane, M. L., & Tusler, M. (2001). Is the informed-choice policy approach appropriate for Medicare beneficiaries? *Health Affairs, 20*(3), 199–203.

James, B. D., Boyle, P. A., & Bennett, D. A. (2014). Correlates of susceptibility to scams in older adults without dementia. *Journal of Elder Abuse & Neglect, 26*(2), 107–122.

Jenkins, A., Akerman, R., Frumkin, L., Salter, E., & Vorhaus, J. (2011). Literacy, numeracy and disadvantage among older adults in England. *Discovery UK Annals*.

Laumann, E. O., Leitsch, S. A., & Waite, L. J. (2008). Elder mistreatment in the United States: Prevalence estimates from a nationally representative study. *The Journals of Gerontology Series B: Psychological Sciences and Social Sciences, 63*(4), S248–S254.

Lawrence, N. S., Jollant, F., O'Daly, O., Zelaya, F., & Phillips, M. L. (2009). Distinct roles of prefrontal cortical subregions in the Iowa Gambling Task. *Cerebral Cortex, 19*(5), 1134–1143.

Lichtenberg, P. A., Ficker, L. J., & Rahman-Filipiak, A. (2015). Financial decision-making abilities and exploitation in older African Americans: Preliminary validity evidence for the Lichtenberg financial decision rating scale (LFDRS). *Journal of Elder Abuse & Neglect*, 150818092716004. doi:10.1080/08946566.2015.1078760.

Lichtenberg, P. A., Sugarman, M. A., Paulson, D., Ficker, L. J., & Rahman-Filipiak, A. (2016). Psychological and functional vulnerability predicts fraud cases in older adults: Results of a longitudinal study. *Clinical Gerontologist, 39*(1), 48–63.

Lusardi, A., & Mitchell, O. S. (2011). *Financial Literacy around the World: An Overview (No. w17107)*. National Bureau of Economic Research.

Martin, R., Griffith, H. R., Belue, K., Harrell, L., Zamrini, E., Anderson, B., ... & Marson, D. (2008). Declining financial capacity in patients with mild Alzheimer disease: A one-year longitudinal study. *The American Journal of Geriatric Psychiatry, 16*(3), 209–219.

Modic, D., & Anderson, R. (2014). Reading this may harm your computer: The psychology of malware warnings. *Computers in Human Behavior, 41*, 71–79.

Moran, J. M. (2013). Lifespan development: The effects of typical aging on theory of mind. *Behavioural Brain Research, 237*, 32–40. doi:10.1016/j.bbr.2012.09.020.

Norris, G., Brookes, A., & Dowell, D. (2019). The psychology of internet fraud victimisation: A systematic review. *Journal of Police and Criminal Psychology, 34*(3), 231–245.

Reyna, V. F., Nelson, W. L., Han, P. K., & Dieckmann, N. F. (2009). How numeracy influences risk comprehension and medical decision making. *Psychological Bulletin, 135*(6), 943.

Rogalsky, C., Vidal, C., Li, X., & Damasio, H. (2012). Risky decision-making in older adults without cognitive deficits: An fMRI study of VMPFC using the Iowa Gambling Task. *Social Neuroscience, 7*(2), 178–190.

Rolison, J. J., Hanoch, Y., & Wood, S. (2012). Risky decision making in younger and older adults: the role of learning. *Psychology and Aging, 27*(1), 129.

Ross, M., Grossmann, I., & Schryer, E. (2014). Contrary to psychological and popular opinion, there is no compelling evidence that older adults are disproportionately victimized by consumer fraud. *Perspectives on Psychological Science, 9*(4), 427–442.

Samanez-Larkin, G. R., Gibbs, S. E., Khanna, K., Nielsen, L., Carstensen, L. L., & Knutson, B. (2007). Anticipation of monetary gain but not loss in healthy older adults. *Nature Neuroscience, 10*(6), 787–791.

Schwartz, L. M., Woloshin, S., Black, W. C., & Welch, H. G. (1997). The role of numeracy in understanding the benefit of screenings. *Annals of Internal Medicine, 127*(11), 966–972.

Sebastian, C. L., Fontaine, N. M., Bird, G., Blakemore, S. J., De Brito, S. A., McCrory, E. J., & Viding, E. (2012). Neural processing associated with cognitive and affective theory of mind in adolescents and adults. *Social Cognitive and Affective Neuroscience, 7*(1), 53–63.

Seo, H. & Lee, D. (2012). Neural basis of learning and preference during social decision-making. *Current Opinion in Neurobiology, 22*, 1–6.

Shamay-Tsoory, S. G. (2011). The neural bases for empathy. *The Neuroscientist, 17*(1), 18–24.

Shao, J., Du, W., Lin, T., Li, X., Li, J., & Lei, H. (2019). Credulity rather than general trust may increase vulnerability to fraud in older adults: A moderated mediation model. *Journal of Elder Abuse & Neglect, 31*(2), 146–162.

Spreng, R. N., Karlawish, J., & Marson, D. C. (2016). Cognitive, social, and neural determinants of diminished decision-making and financial exploitation risk in aging and dementia: A review and new model. *Journal of Elder Abuse & Neglect, 28*(4–5), 320–344.

Stanford Centre on Longevity. (2015). Annual Report: The Scope of the Problem. Accessed from http://longevity.stanford.edu/financial-fraud-research-center/

Stiegel, L. (2012). An overview of elder financial exploitation. *Generations, 36*(2), 73–80.

Stewart, S. L., Wright, C., & Atherton, C. (2019). Deception detection and truth detection are dependent on different cognitive and emotional traits: An investigation of emotional intelligence, theory of mind, and attention. *Personality and Social Psychology Bulletin, 45*(5), 794–807.

Thornton, W. L., & Dumke, A. H. (2005). Age differences in every problem-solving and decision-making effectiveness: A meta-analytic review. *Psychology and Aging, 20*, 85–99.

Thornton, W. J. L., Paterson, T., & Yeung, S. (2013). Age differences in everyday problem solving: The roles of problem context. *International Journal of Behavioral Development, 37*(1), 13–20.

Thornton, W. J. L., Shapiro, R. J., Deria, S., Gelb, S., & Hill, A. (2007). Differential impact of age on verbal memory and executive functioning in chronic kidney disease. *Journal of the Neuropsychological Society*, 344–353.

Van Wyk, J., & Mason, K. A. (2001). Investigating vulnerability and reporting behavior for consumer fraud victimization: Opportunity as a social aspect of age. *Journal of Contemporary Criminal Justice, 17*(4), 328–345.

Vishwanath, A., Harrison, B., & Ng, Y. J. (2018). Suspicion, cognition, and automaticity model of phishing susceptibility. *Communication Research, 45*(8), 1146–1166.

Walzak, L., Thornton, W. J. L., Weerasinghe, R., & Braley, M. (2020). Social cognition in older adults: Age differences & underlying mechanisms associated with fraud susceptibility. *Poster presentated at the 2020 Canadian Psychological Association (CPA) Virtual Conference in Montreal, QC.*

Walzak, L., & Thornton, W. J. L. (2018). The role of chronic illness in theory of mind performance among older adults. *Experimental Aging Research, 44*(5), 427–442. doi:10.1080/0361073X.2018.1521494.

Wang, Z., & Su, Y. (2013). Age-related differences in the performance of theory of mind in older adults: A dissociation of cognitive and affective components. *Psychology and Aging, 28*, 284–291. doi:10.1037/a0030876.

Wood, S., Busemeyer, J., Koling, A., Cox, C., & Davis, H. (2005). Older adults as adaptive decision makers. *Psychology and Aging, 20*(2), 220–225. doi:10.1037/0882-7974.20.2.220.

Wood, S., Rakela, B., Liu, P.-J., Navarro, A. E., Bernatz, S., Wilber, K. H., & Homier, D. (2014). Neuropsychological profiles of victims of financial elder exploitation at the LA County elder abuse forensic center. *Journal of Elder Abuse & Neglect, 26*(4), 414–423. doi:10.1080/ 08946566.2014.881270.

Wood, S., Hanoch, Y., & Woods, G. W. (2016a). Cognitive factors to financial crime victimization. In M. Dion, D. Weisstub, & J.-L. Richet (Eds.), *Financial Crimes: Psychological, Technological, and Ethical Issues* (pp. 129–139). Cham, Switzerland: Springer International Publishing.

Wood, S. A., Liu, P. J., Hanoch, Y., & Estevez-Cores, S. (2016b). Importance of numeracy as a risk factor for elder financial exploitation in a community sample. *Journals of Gerontology Series B: Psychological Sciences and Social Sciences, 71*(6), 978–986.

Wood, S., & Lichtenberg, P. A. (2017). Financial capacity and financial exploitation of older adults: Research findings, policy recommendations and clinical implications. *Clinical Gerontologist, 40*(1), 3–13.

Wood, S., Liu, P. J., Hanoch, Y., Xi, P. M., & Klapatch, L. (2018). Call to claim your Prize: Perceived benefits and risk drive intention to comply in a mass marketing scam. *Journal of Experimental Psychology: Applied, 24*, 196–206.

Xie, G. X., & Boush, D. M. (2011). How susceptible are consumers to deceptive advertising claims? A retrospective look at the experimental research literature. *The Marketing Review, 11*(3), 293–314.

Vulnerability to Financial Exploitation in Older Age: A Neuropsychology Perspective 7

S. Duke Han

Introduction

Older adults hold a significantly large portion of the United States' net worth (Agarwal et al., 2009), and because of this, they are at significantly higher risk for being targets of financial scam and fraud (AARP, 2020). The effects of scams and fraud are particularly deleterious in old age since life savings accrued over a long period of time might be impacted, resulting in a threat to living independently (Templeton and Kirkman, 2007). Additionally, older age presents with fewer job prospects and declining health and functional abilities to offset financial damages (Dessin, 2000; Jackson and Hafemeister, 2011). Scam and fraud in old age have also been associated with poorer health outcomes, perhaps most notably higher incident Alzheimer's Disease (Boyle et al., 2019) and poorer psychological functioning (James et al., 2014; Weissberger et al., 2020b). These health associations drive home the need to better understand what makes certain older adults more susceptible to financial exploitation.

This chapter is dedicated to providing a model for understanding susceptibility to financial exploitation in old age from the perspective of a clinical

DOI: 10.4324/9781003017189-7

neuropsychologist who has had the privilege of working with a team of investigators from a diverse set of disciplines, including but not limited to behavioral economics, geriatrics, neurology, biostatistics, experimental psychology, gerontology, and neuroimaging. For the purposes of this chapter, "financial exploitation" is defined as the misuse of a person's funds in order to primarily benefit someone other than the owner of the funds. First, the role of cognition in financial exploitation vulnerability in old age will be reviewed and discussed. Second, the rationale for brain considerations will be argued and neuroimaging studies will be reviewed. Third, a model will be proposed through which to understand financial exploitation vulnerability in old age. Finally, the chapter will end with concluding thoughts and suggested future directions.

Cognition and Financial Exploitation Vulnerability in Old Age

I was first introduced to the issue of financial exploitation in old age in the context of my clinical activities as a neuropsychologist. I routinely conduct clinical neuropsychological assessments for the purpose of ruling out possible early dementia. Over a decade ago, I started receiving referrals in clinic to rule out possible early dementia because it was discovered by a caregiver or family member that the older adult was giving away large sums of money to a perpetrator. This behavior was identified as a shift from previous patterns of behavior, and consequently the caregivers or family members believed this was a sign of cognitive decline consistent with encroaching Alzheimer's dementia. Interestingly and unexpectedly, I would find no signs of overt cognitive impairment in these patients, even after an exhaustive battery of cognitive measures that would sometimes take as long as 6 to 8 hours to administer. This feedback of seemingly intact cognition to caregivers and family members would often be received with confusion and frustration, and as a neuropsychologist, it left me often wondering what was being missed in the evaluation.

When the financial exploitation or scamming of an older adult occurs, a common assumption is that it is largely due to age-related cognitive decline or cognitive decline secondary to impending dementia. Research has supported cognitive impairment as a risk factor in scam, fraud, and financial exploitation, with much of this work spearheaded by Dr. Patricia Boyle (e.g., Boyle et al., 2019). In a group of over 700 community-dwelling older adults in the Chicago area who were deemed to be without dementia, we observed those with mild cognitive impairment (MCI) have poorer financial decision-making

(Han et al., 2015) and higher susceptibility to scams (Han et al., 2016b) in regression models controlling for the demographic factors of age, education, and sex. Susceptibility to scams has also been associated with overall poorer cognition in older adults, apart from impairment considerations (James et al., 2014). In considering cognitive domains of functioning, episodic memory and perceptual speed appear to be particularly salient for susceptibility to scams.

Although cognitive functioning can clearly be a factor in financial exploitation vulnerability, it must also be stated that poor or impaired cognitive functioning may not always be a reason for financial exploitation vulnerability. My specific clinical experiences described above illustrate this observation. In order to more fully investigate whether there are, in fact, discrepancies between overall cognitive ability and decision-making ability, we investigated statistical discrepancies between cognition and decision-making ability in a group of over 600 older adults without dementia from the same cohort (Han et al., 2016a). This work showed that about 25% of the group exhibited a significant discrepancy, phenomenologically confirming my clinical experiences. These findings are not isolated. Other clinicians have also reported typical cognitive measures do not appear to be sensitive to changes in financial exploitation vulnerability in some older adults. We previously discussed multiple factors that could be involved in making an older adult more vulnerable to financial exploitation in addition to considerations of cognition, including psychological factors, social factors, and environment factors (Lachs and Han, 2015). The result of these discussions led to the coining of the term "Age Associated Financial Vulnerability" as a way to catalyze research on the diverse interaction of factors that make an older adult more vulnerable to financial exploitation.

In considering older adults who test in the normal range on cognitive measures yet still exhibit changes in behavior that lead to financial exploitation vulnerability, a number of reasons might be entertained. One possibility is that cognition may not be a factor, and another factor, such as loneliness or isolation, might be the mechanism for vulnerability. Certainly, this is always a possibility and should be a consideration. Another possibility is that the cognitive measures typically utilized in a clinical assessment for cognitive impairment do not adequately capture the behavior in question. This notion deserves more attention, as most standard neuropsychological measures are designed to be sensitive to particular functions such as basic memory, attention, visuospatial, and language abilities generally ascribed to lateral parietal, medial and lateral temporal, and lateral frontal lobes of the brain. In many models of decision-making, the medial frontal, insular, and anterior basal ganglia regions are considered of high importance; however, these regions are often missed by traditional cognitive assessment batteries (as noted in Damasio et al., 1996). Neuropsychological measures sensitive to these brain regions and networks are crucial for moving the clinical assessment field forward in regards to ascertaining financial exploitation vulnerability.

Neuroimaging of Financial Exploitation Vulnerability in Old Age

As stated above, many clinical cognitive measures do not robustly assess the integrity of brain regions specifically implicated in financial decision-making. In the context of aging, it is well-established that neuropathologies (such as beta-amyloid plaques and neurofibrillary tangles) can accumulate in the brain progressively during the latter half of the life course. These age-related neuropathologies have been robustly associated with prospective cognitive decline in the context of Alzheimer's Disease (Sperling et al., 2019), and interestingly have demonstrable effects on brain function and structure years ahead of any perceivable cognitive impairment (e.g., Palmqvist et al., 2017; Hahn et al., 2019). Since many traditional cognitive measures are not sensitive to brain regions key to financial decision-making, and changes in the brain may precede noticeable changes in cognitive function, neuroimaging can be a useful tool to try and identify early markers of scam susceptibility and vulnerability to financial exploitation in older age that can be missed by traditional clinical neuropsychological measures.

Although decision-making has been for many years a popular topic of neuroimaging research in younger college-age samples, there has been a growing number of neuroimaging studies in older adults relevant to the topic of financial exploitation vulnerability. The review of all relevant neuroimaging studies is beyond the scope of this chapter, though particular studies are notable. Castle et al. (2012) conducted a study of younger and older participants as they reviewed faces and rated how trustworthy they appeared. Activity in the insula was associated with trust ratings, and older adults had less insula activity than young adults. The authors described this difference in trust perception as a possible neural mechanism for why certain aging adults might become more susceptible to financial scams. In a series of experiments, Samanez-Larkin and Knutson (2015) elegantly implicated the functioning of the nucleus accumbens, anterior insula, and medial prefrontal cortex as a circuit that may change in the context of aging. In particular, they implicated a reduction in sensitivity to monetary losses corresponding with less activity of the insula cortex in older adults. In perhaps the first neuroimaging study directly focused on financially exploited older adults, Spreng et al. (2017) showed cortical thinning of the anterior insula and posterior superior temporal cortices, and reduced functional connectivity in the salience and default networks using an independent components analysis (ICA) approach, in older persons who were victims of financial exploitation versus those who were demographically matched.

Our group has also been actively involved in identifying neuroimaging macrostructure (grey matter integrity), microstructure (white matter integrity), and functional connectivity (brain network integrity) correlates of financial exploitation vulnerability in old age. In a group of 123 older adults without dementia, we demonstrated that functional connectivity of the ventromedial prefrontal cortex, right paraphippocampal gyrus, and cerebellum were associated with temporal discounting in models adjusted for age, education, sex, and cognitive function (Han et al., 2013). The ventromedial prefrontal cortex and right medial temporal regions were again implicated by a follow-up study that assessed brain microstructure using diffusion tensor imaging (DTI) in 302 older adults without dementia that showed correlations between temporal discounting responses and multiple white matter integrity indicators, again adjusting for demographics and cognitive function (Han et al., 2018). In a study of brain macrostructure, we observed in 327 older adults without dementia lower grey matter density in the right medial temporal region (hippocampus) associated with greater susceptibility to scams, after accounting for the effects of demographics and cognitive function (Han et al., 2016c). This work was again followed up with a DTI study, which similarly implicated white matter integrity in the right temporal region as associated with susceptibility to scams in similarly adjusted models (Lamar et al., 2019). In a currently ongoing research initiative called the Finance, Cognition, and Health in Elders Study (FINCHES) focused on identifying the factors associated with financial exploitation in old age, we observed differential connectivity of the medial prefrontal cortex, insula, and hippocampus in older adults who reported having financial exploitation experiences versus those who do not (Weissberger et al., 2020a). Interestingly, the medial prefrontal cortex, insula, and hippocampus have also been implicated in studies of psychological and emotional distress (Sinha et al., 2004; Reis et al., 2020), an associated factor of financial vulnerability in older age.

An interesting consistency that has resulted from our neuroimaging work is the implication of right hemisphere brain regions. It is difficult to assess the significance of this laterality in our findings. Our findings may suggest that age-related pathological changes in right hemisphere regions or networks beginning in middle age and progressing into older age might be sensitive to financial exploitation vulnerability. Some researchers believe that since right hemisphere regions develop earlier than left hemisphere regions, then they might be more sensitive to pathological aspects of aging (Dolcos et al., 2002). It remains to be seen whether this laterality is indeed significant to the discussion of financial vulnerability in aging.

Model of Financial Exploitation Vulnerability in Old Age

Although the nascent state of the field precludes a comprehensive model of financial exploitation vulnerability in older age, a working hypothetical model informed by the fields of neuropsychology and behavioral neuroscience may be developed based on the work of our group and others. As stated before, scam susceptibility in old age has been established as one of the earliest predictors of incident Alzheimer's Disease even ahead of cognitive impairment (Boyle et al., 2019). Alzheimer's Disease is defined by the presence of amyloid plaque and neurofibrillary tangle neuropathology and its clinical syndrome is marked by early episodic memory impairment ahead of broader cognitive decline (Jack et al., 2016, 2018). In models of Alzheimer's Disease progression, amyloid plaque accumulation precedes neurofibrillary tangle accumulation (Jack et al., 2010, 2013), and amyloid accumulates early in a brain region-specific pattern that has frequently been identified as the Default Network (also known as the Default Mode Network, Buckner et al., 2008; Hedden et al., 2009; Palmqvist et al., 2017; Gordon et al., 2018). The Default Network includes the posterior cingulate cortex, precuneus, lateral parietal region, medial temporal region, and medial frontal region, and has been described as a functional network that structurally maps onto the pattern of cortical deterioration early in the course of Alzheimer's Disease (Buckner et al., 2008). However, it is infrequently acknowledged in the scientific literature that the pattern of cortical deterioration in early Alzheimer's Disease only maps onto the posterior portion of the Default Network (posterior cingulate, precuneus, lateral parietal region, and medial temporal) and does not include the anterior portion of the Default Network, particularly the medial frontal cortex. The posterior portion of the Default Network includes brain regions that support episodic memory function, and episodic memory decline is one of the first clinically observed signs of Alzheimer's Disease. The anterior portion of the Default Network (medial frontal cortex) does not structurally deteriorate early in the course of Alzheimer's Disease; however, it is a region of early significant amyloid accumulation and is functionally connected to other regions in the Default Network and other networks like the Frontoparietal

Network (Marek and Dosenbach, 2018) which serve certain higher-order cognitive functions (e.g., those that support specific executive functions).

One important function strongly ascribed to the medial frontal cortex and its broad functional connections is financial decision-making (Knutson et al., 2000; Knutson et al., 2001; Ernst and Paulus, 2005; Knutson et al., 2005; Clark et al., 2008; Hare et al., 2009; Kable and Glimcher, 2009; Luhmann, 2009; Wittmann et al., 2010; Gupta et al., 2011; Castle et al., 2012; Peters and Buchel, 2012; Han et al., 2013; Sakaki et al., 2013; Benningfield et al., 2014; Denny et al., 2014; Dolcos et al., 2014; Samenez-Larkin et al., 2014). Since amyloid accumulation is known to impact brain functional connectivity and corresponding functions ahead of structural changes (Palmqvist et al., 2017; Hahn et al., 2019), we posit that (1) early neuropathological accumulation in the medial frontal regions of the Default Network results in functional impact on financial decision-making, (2) declines in financial decision-making may lead to greater financial exploitation vulnerability and even precede noticeable cognitive (specifically episodic memory) changes, and (3) declines in both of these functions correspond with changes in the functional connectivity (and possibly other neuroimaging metrics) of their corresponding brain components. More specifically, financial decision-making declines will correspond with anterior Default Network (medial frontal) functional connectivity declines, and episodic memory declines will correspond with posterior Default Network (medial temporal and parietal) functional connectivity declines. A recent review of high-resolution neuroimaging studies of individuals and direct neuronal recording studies in both humans and monkeys supports a two-component conceptualization of the Default Network very similar to our conceptual model (Buckner and DiNocola, 2019). In this review, theory of mind was cited as an example function ascribed to the anterior Default Network, and autobiographical memory was a function ascribed to the posterior Default Network. We argue financial decision-making is another function that can be ascribed to the anterior Default Network given the medial prefrontal cortex's prominent role in financial decision-making, and the integrity of the posterior Default Network is also important for optimal financial decision-making (see Figure 7.1).

Our neuroimaging work on susceptibility to scams, temporal discounting, and differences between financial exploited and non-exploited older adults supports this model (Han et al., 2013; Han et al., 2016c; Han et al., 2018; Lamar et al., 2019; Weissberger et al., 2020a). We observed the macrostructure, microstructure, and functional connectivity of the medial temporal lobes (particularly in the right hemisphere) as importantly associated or differentiating regions, and these regions are well-known to be susceptible to the impact of

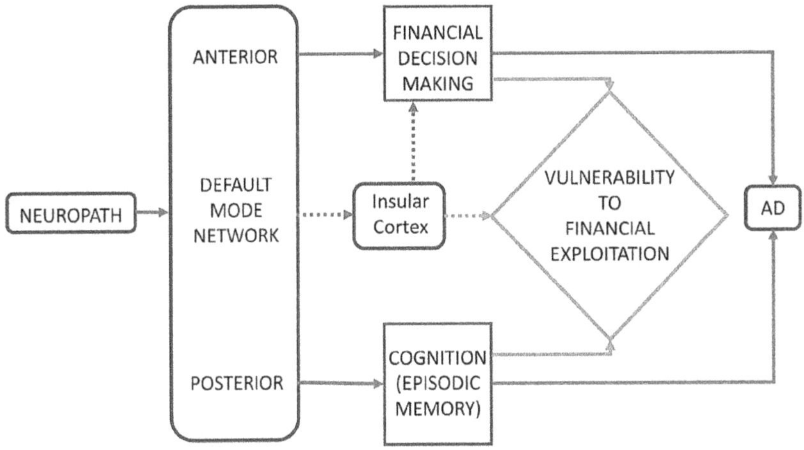

Figure 7.1 Model of financial exploitation vulnerability in old age and association with Alzheimer's disease (AD) risk.

age-related neuropathology, episodic memory decline, and in the context of the Default Network, represent the mechanism by which autobiographical memory is accessed (Buckner and DiNocola, 2019). It is understandable that if an older adult has difficulty accessing autobiographical memory for what a scam may look like, then that older adult will be more vulnerable to financial exploitation. Our work and others have also implicated medial frontal or associated frontal regions in decision-making work relevant to older adult susceptibility to financial exploitation (Han et al., 2013; Samenez-Larkin et al., 2014; Han et al., 2016c; Spreng et al., 2017), and this region is well-known for its role in self-management and self-control in decision-making (Hare et al., 2009), as well as sensitivity to calculations of expected value via frontostriatal feedback loops (e.g., Knutson et al., 2005; Samenez-Larkin et al., 2014). Certainly, any deficit in self-control or a miscalculation of expected value will result in a more vulnerable older adult.

In addition to the integrity of medial temporal lobe and medial frontal lobe structures, there is a growing consensus of the insula's involvement in financial decision-making in old age (Clark et al., 2008; Han et al., 2013; Samenez-Larkin et al., 2014; Spreng et al., 2017). The insula is a key brain region for emotional regulation and has been implicated in a number of higher-order cognitive, emotional, and perceptual functions (Jones et al., 2010). The insula represents an anatomical overlap of multiple functional brain systems devoted to multisensory perception, socioemotional processing, and cognitive processing, and therefore it can be argued this region is key for maintaining the integrated subjective experience of an individual's world (Kurth et al., 2010). It is believed that the insula assists with the development of a "gut" reaction to a perceived situation or stimuli (Jones et al., 2010). This region, and its associated functions, represents a neuroanatomical departure from the Default Network considerations described above (which include the medial frontal and temporal cortices sensitive to age-related neuropathological accumulation). However, it should be noted that the insula and medial temporal cortex share strong reciprocal connections (e.g., Gallo et al., 1992). Also, when asked in qualitative interviews about the point in time when an older adult discovers he or she might be falling prey to a scam, the responses are often that he or she starting having a "gut" feeling about the circumstances not being right. Given this, a possible set of brain regions that might mechanistically explain financial exploitation vulnerability in old age might be the Default Network plus the Insula Cortex. For the purposes of this chapter and for future discussions, this will heretofore be known as the DNIC network (Default Network + Insular Cortex).

Our theoretical model of financial exploitation vulnerability in older age is as follows. Neuropathologies accumulate with age and vary in the amount of accumulation according to factors known to have an impact (physical activity, cognitive activity, diet, social engagement, genetics, etc.). Age-related neuropathological changes impact first the connectivity, and then the volumetrics, of the DNIC network, particularly the medial frontal lobe, the medial temporal lobe, and the insula. The temporal sequence to which these particular brain regions become affected determines the course of presentation. If the medial frontal and insula regions are affected first, then the older adult may show declines in financial decision-making ahead of any noticeable memory or cognitive impairment. If the medial temporal regions are affected first, then the older adult may show memory declines ahead of any noticeable financial decision-making changes. If all of these brain regions decline together, then the older adult will show concurrent declines in both memory and financial decision-making. In all three scenarios, vulnerability to financial exploitation is increased in the older adult.

Conclusion and Future Directions

In conclusion, changes in financial exploitation vulnerability in older age apart from any noticeable cognitive decline may indicate accumulating age-related neuropathology in key brain regions involved decision-making and cognitive function. These regions include the medial frontal and medial temporal cortices of the Default Network and the Insular Cortex, collectively referred to as the DNIC network. Financial exploitation vulnerability in older age may therefore be one of the earliest signs of progressing Alzheimer's Disease and impending dementia (Boyle et al., 2019), and because of this, older adults who exhibit significant changes in financial behavior should be monitored closely.

A number of future directions are recommended:

1. Neuropathology – This model of financial vulnerability in old age is predicated on the notion that age-related neuropathology is the mechanism by which brain changes occur. This needs to be directly examined. Ideally a longitudinal cohort with regular neuropathological imaging or cerebrospinal fluid metrics might be leveraged to measure susceptibility to scam or fraud to determine if an increase in one results in an increase in another prior to any cognitive decline or impairment.
2. Neuroimaging – This model implicates the integrity of specific brain regions (medial frontal, medial temporal, insula) as involved in financial exploitation vulnerability in old age. Differential impact on particular structures, or the connections between structures, may result in different profiles of vulnerability. This needs to be explored and clarified.
3. Diversity – The vast majority of neuroimaging knowledge regarding decision-making has been acquired on primarily White, well-educated, young college participants. It is imperative that study samples represent the diversity of the population. Study samples need to be broadened in terms of age, education, race, and socioeconomic status. Our laboratory and others are actively pursuing this.
4. Neuropsychology – As stated above, the vast majority of clinical cognitive measures address brain regions and networks that are not typically those implicated in financial decision-making. The field of neuropsychology should actively pursue the development of clinical neuropsychology measures that are sensitive to the integrity of the medial frontal and insular cortices. If a test or measure could be developed as described, this would be a significant contribution.
5. Neurochemical and neurocellular elements – This model currently does not incorporate age-related neurochemical and neurocellular changes. These need to be addressed and incorporated.
6. Intervention – Officials and leaders in government, public policy, and the private sector are keenly interested in what interventions might be effective for older adults who may be or may become vulnerable to financial exploitation. Greater clarity on the mechanisms that contribute to vulnerability will inform the development of better interventions.

Acknowledgements

Funding support for this work includes the National Institute on Aging at the National Institutes of Health grants R01AG055430 and RF1AG068166, as well as the Elder Justice Foundation, and the Department of Family Medicine at the Keck School of Medicine of the University of Southern California. A special thank you to all of the collaborators I have worked with over the years, and in particular, Dr. David Bennet, Dr. Patricia Boyle, Dr. Lisa Barnes, Dr. Mark Lachs, and Dr. Laura Mosequeda for support and mentorship on these and related topics.

References

AARP. (2020). *The impostors: Stealing money, damaging lives*. Washington, DC: AARP Research.

Agarwal, S., Driscoll, J.C., Gabaix, X., Laibson, D. (2009). The age of reason: financial decisions over the lifecycle with implications for regulation. *Brookings Papers on Economic Activity, 2*, 51–117.

Benningfield, M.M., Blackford, J.U., Ellsworth, M.E., Samanez-Larkin, G.R., Martin, P.R., Cowan, R.L., & Zald, D.H. (2014). Caudate responses to reward anticipation associated with delay discounting behavior in healthy youth. *Developmental Cognitive Neuroscience, 7*, 43–52.

Boyle, P.A., Yu, L., Schneider, J.A., Wilson, R.S., & Bennett, D.A. (2019). Scam awareness related to incident Alzheimer dementia and mild cognitive impairment: a prospective cohort study. *Annals of Internal Medicine, 170(10)*, 702–709.

Buckner, R.L., & DiNocola, L.M. (2019). The brain's default network: updated anatomy, physiology and evolving insights. *Nature Reviews Neuroscience, 20*, 593–608.

Buckner, R.L., Andrews-Hanna, J.R., & Schacter, D.L. (2008). The brain's default network anatomy, function, and relevance to disease. *Annals of the New York Academy of Sciences, 1124*, 1–38.

Castle, E., Eisenberger, N.I., Seeman, T.E., Moons, W.G., Boggero, I.A., Grinblatt, M.S., & Taylor, S.E. (2012). Neural and behavioral bases of age differences in perceptions of trust. *Proceedings of the National Academy of Sciences, 109(51)*, 20848–20852.

Clark, L., Bechara, A., Damasio, H., Aitken, M.R., Sahakian, B.J., & Robbins, T.W. (2008). Differential effects of insular and ventromedial prefrontal cortex lesions on risky decision-making. *Brain, 131*, 1311–1322.

Damasio, A.R., Everitt, B.J., & Bishop, D. (1996). The Somatic Marker Hypothesis and the possible functions of the prefrontal cortex [and Discussion]. *Philosophical Transactions: Biological Sciences, 351(1346)*, 1413–1420, *Executive and Cognitive Functions of the Prefrontal Cortex*.

Denny, B.T., Fan, J., Liu, X., Guerreri, S., Mayson, S.J., Rimsky, L., New, A.S., Siever, L.J., & Koenigsberg, H.W. (2014). Insula-amygdala functional connectivity is correlated with habituation to repeated negative images. *Social Cognitive and Affective Neuroscience, 9*, 1160–1667.

Dessin, C.L. (2000). Financial abuse of the elderly. *Idaho Law Review, 36(2)*, 203–226.

Dolcos, S., Katsumi, Y., & Dixon, R.A. (2014). The role of arousal in the spontaneous regulation of emotions in healthy aging: a fMRI investigation. *Frontiers in Psychology, 5*, 681.

Dolcos, F., Rice, H.J., & Cabeza, R. (2002). Hemispheric asymmetry and aging: right hemisphere decline or asymmetry reduction. *Neuroscience and Biobehavioral Reviews, 26*, 819–825.

Ernst, M., & Paulus, M.P. (2005). Neurobiology of decision making: a selective review from a neurocognitive and clinical perspective. *Biological Psychiatry, 58(8)*, 597–604.

Gallo, M., Roldan, G., & Bures, J. (1992). Differential involvement of gustatory insular cortex and amygdala in the acquisition and retrieval of conditioned taste aversion in rats. *Behavioral Brain Research, 52*, 91–97.

Gordon, B.A., Blazey, T.M., Su, Y., et al. (2018). Spatial patterns of neuroimaging biomarker change in individuals from families with autosomal dominant Alzheimer's disease: a longitudinal study. *The Lancet Neurology, 17*, 241–250.

Gupta, R., Koscik, T.R., Bechara, A., & Tranel, D. (2011). The amygdala and decision-making. *Neuropsychologia, 49(4)*, 760–766.

Hahn, A., Strandberg, T.O., Stomrud, E., et al. (2019). Association between earliest amyloid uptake and functional connectivity in cognitively unimpaired elderly. *Cerebral Cortex, 29*, 2173–2182.

Han, S.D., Arfanakis, K., Fleischman, D.A., Yu, L., Bennett, D.A., & Boyle, P.A. (2018). White matter correlates of temporal discounting in older adults. *Brain Structure and Function, 223*, 3653–3663.

Han, S.D., Boyle, P.A., James, B.D., Yu, L., Barnes, L.L., & Bennett, D.A. (2016b). Discrepancies between cognition and decision making in older adults. *Aging Clinical and Experimental Research, 28*, 99–108.

Han, S.D., Boyle, P.A., James, B.D., Yu, L., & Bennett, D.A. (2015). Mild cognitive impairment is associated with poorer decision making in community-based older persons. *Journal of the American Geriatrics Society, 63*, 676–683.

Han, S.D., Boyle, P.A., James, B.D., Yu, L., & Bennett, D.A. (2016a). Mild cognitive impairment and susceptibility to scams in old age. *Journal of Alzheimer's Disease, 49*, 845–851.

Han, S.D., Boyle, P.A., Yu, L., Arfanakis, K., James, B.D., Fleischman, D.A., & Bennett, D.A. (2016c). Grey matter correlates of susceptibility to scam in community-dwelling older adults. *Brain Imaging and Behavior, 10(2)*, 524–532.

Han, S.D., Boyle, P.A., Yu, L., Fleischman, D.A., Arfanakis, K., & Bennett, D.A. (2013). Ventromedial PFC, parahippocampal, and cerebellar connectivity are associated with temporal discounting in old age. *Experimental Gerontology, 48*, 1489–1498.

Hare, T.A., Camerer, C.F., & Rangel, A. (2009). Self-control in decision-making involves modulation of the vmPFC valuation system. *Science, 324*, 646–648.

Hedden, T., Van Dijk, K.R., Becker, J.A., et al. (2009). Disruption of functional connectivity in clinically normal older adults harboring amyloid burden. *Journal of Neuroscience, 29(40)*, 12686–12694.

Jack, C.R., Jr., Bennett, D.A., Blennow, K., et al. (2016). A/T/N: an unbiased descriptive classification scheme for Alzheimer disease biomarkers. *Neurology, 87(5)*, 539–547.

Jack, C.R., Jr., Bennett, D.A., Blennow, K., et al. (2018). NIA-AA research framework: toward a biological definition of Alzheimer's disease. *Alzheimer's and Dementia, 14(4)*, 535–562.

Jack, C.R., Jr., Knopman, D.S., Jagust, W.J., et al. (2010). Hypothetical model of dynamic biomarkers of the Alzheimer's pathological cascade. *The Lancet Neurology, 9*, 119–128.

Jack, C.R., Jr., Knopman, D.S., Jagust, W.J., et al. (2013). Update on hypothetical model of Alzheimer's disease biomarkers. *The Lancet Neurology, 12(2)*, 207–216.

Jackson, S.L., & Hafemeister, T.L. (2011). *Financial abuse of elderly people vs. other forms of elder abuse: assessing their dynamics, risk factors, and society's response*. Final Report Presented to the National Institute of Justice.

James, B.D., Boyle, P.A., & Bennett, D.A. (2014). Correlates of susceptibility to scams in older adults without dementia. *Journal of Elder Abuse and Neglect, 26*, 107–122.

Jones, C.L., Ward, J., & Critchley, H.D. (2010). The neuropsychological impact of insular cortex lesions. *Journal of Neurol Neurosurg Psychiatry, 81*, 611–618.

Kable, J.W., & Glimcher, P.W. (2009). The neurobiology of decision: consensus and controversy. *Neuron, 63*, 733–745.

Knutson, B., & Bossaerts, P. (2007). Neural antecedents of financial decisions. *Journal of Neuroscience, 27*, 8174–8177.

Knutson, B., Adams, C.M., Fong, G.W., & Hommer, D. (2001). Anticipation of increasing monetary reward selectively recruits nucleus accumbens. *Journal of Neuroscience, 21*, 1–5.

Knutson, B., Taylor, J., Kaufman, M., Peterson, R., & Glover, G. (2005). Distributed neural representation of expected value. *Journal of Neuroscience, 25(19)*, 4806–4812.

Knutson, B., Westdrop, A., Kaiser, E., & Hommer, D. (2000). FMRI visualization of brain activity during a monetary incentive delay task. *NeuroImage, 12*, 20–27.

Krawitz, A., Fukunaga, R., & Brown, J.W. (2010). Anterior insula activity predicts the influence of positively framed messages on decision making. *Cognitive Affective Behavioral Neuroscience, 10(3)*, 392–405.

Kurth, F., Zilles, K., Fox, P.T., Laird, A.R., & Eickhoff, S.B. (2010). A link between the systems: functional differentiation and integration within the human insula revealed by meta-analysis. *Brain Structure and Function, 214*, 519–534.

Lachs, M.S., & Han, S.D. (2015). Age associated financial vulnerability: an emerging public health issue. *Annals of Internal Medicine, 163(11)*, 877–878.

Lamar, M., Arfanakis, K., Yu, L., et al. (2019). White matter correlates of scam susceptibility in community-dwelling older adults. *Brain Imaging Behav, 14*, 1521–1530.

Luhmann, C.C. (2009). Temporal decision-making: insights from cognitive neuroscience. *Frontiers in Behavioral Neuroscience, 39*, 1–9.

Marek, S., & Dosenbach, N.U.F. (2018). The frontoparietal network: function, electrophysiology, and importance of individual precision mapping. *Dialogues in Clinical Neuroscience, 20*, 133–140.

Palmqvist, S., Scholl, M., Strandberg, O., et al. (2017). Earliest accumulation of beta amyloid occurs within the default-mode network and concurrently affects brain connectivity. *Nature Communications, 8*, 1214.

Peters, J., & Buchel, C. (2012). The neural mechanisms of inter-temporal decision-making: understanding variability. *Trends in Cognitive Sciences, 15*, 207–239.

Reis, J.C., Antoni, M.H., & Travado, L. (2020). Emotional distress, brain functioning, and biobehavioral processes in cancer patients: a neuroimaging review and future directions. *CNS Spectrums, 25*, 79–100.

Sakaki, M., Nga, L., & Mather, M. (2013). Amygdala functional connectivity with medial prefrontal cortex at rest predicts the positivity effect in older adults' memory. *Journal of Cognitive Neuroscience, 25*, 1206–1224.

Samanez-Larkin, G.R., & Knutson, B. (2015). Decision making in the ageing brain: changes in affective and motivational circuits. *Nature Reviews Neuroscience, 16(5)*, 278–289.

Samenez-Larkin, G.R., Worthy, D.A., Mata, R., McClure, S.M., & Knutson, B. (2014). Adult age differences in frontostriatal representation of prediction error but not reward outcome. *Cognitive, Affective, & Behavioral Neuroscience, 14*, 672–682.

Sinha, R., Lacadie, C., Skudlarski, P., & Wexler, B.E. (2004). Neural circuits underlying emotional distress in humans. *Annals of the New York Academy of Sciences, 1032*, 254–257.

Sperling, R.A., Mormino, E.C., Schultz, A.P., et al. (2019). The impact of amyloid-beta and tau on prospective cognitive decline in older individuals. *Annals of Neurology, 85(2)*, 181–193.

Spreng, R.N., Cassidy, B.N., Darboh, B.S., DuPre, E., Lockrow, A.W., Setton, R., & Turner, G.R. (2017). Financial exploitation is associated with structural and functional brain differences in healthy older adults. *The Journals of Gerontology Series A Biological Sciences and Medical Sciences, 72(10)*, 1365–1368.

Templeton, V.H., & Kirkman, D.N. (2007). Fraud, vulnerability, and aging. *Alzheimer's Care Today, 8(3)*, 265–277.

Weissberger, G.H., Mosqueda, L., Nguyen, A.L., Axelrod, J., Nguyen, C.P., Boyle, P.A., Spreng, N., & Han, S.D. (2020a). Functional connectivity correlates of perceived financial exploitation in older adults. *Frontiers in Aging Neuroscience, 12*, 583433.

Weissberger, G.H., Mosqueda, L., Nguyen, A.L., Samek, A., Boyle, P.A., Nguyen, C.P., & Han, S.D. (2020b). Physical and mental health correlates of perceived financial exploitation in older adults: preliminary findings from the Finance, Cognition, and Health in Elders Study (FINCHES). *Aging and Mental Health, 24(5)*, 740–746.

Wittmann, M., Lovero, K.L., Lane, S.D., & Paulus, M.P. (2010). Now or later? Striatum and insula activation to immediate versus delayed rewards. *Journal of Neuroscience, Psychology, and Economics, 1*, 15–26.

8 Do Not Distract Me While I Am Winning This Auction: The Psychology of Auction Fraud

David Modic

Introduction

Internet fraud in general

The term fraud derives from mid-14th century French *fraude*, as well as the Latin term *fraudāre* meaning to cause deceit or injury (Fraud, 2011). Another commonly used synonym—*scam* is more recent. The term was probably first used by the actor Steve McQueen in an interview for *Time* magazine in 1963, when he talked about his former carnival boss as someone who scammed the public (Luce, 1963; Merriam-Webster, 2005). Auction fraud, a subset of the type of fraud that uses the Internet as a conduit (e.g., Nigerian scams, lottery and investment scams, lonely hearts swindles and others), is a low-probability event (Modic & Lea, 2011; Shadel & Pak, 2007; Titus, Heinzelmann, & Boyle, 1995). By low probability we mean that it is often written about in the mainstream media, while at the same time it does not happen very often. Research shows that the incidence rates of losing something that has value to us (money, sleep, hope, inner peace, feeling of safety) to scams ranges from

DOI: 10.4324/9781003017189-8

1.6% (Modic & Lea, 2011) to over 7.7% (Shadel & Pak, 2007, p. 33) to 15% (Titus & Dover, 2001, p. 141). The relatively large discrepancies in frequency are dependent on the definition of loss, time frame, sampled populations, and willingness to disclose being a victim.

It is a common misconception that money is the primary component of loss. Even the scientific community usually defines the loss estimates of fraud in monetary values (e.g. Deevy, Lucich, & Beals, 2012; Fischer, Lea, & Evans, 2009; Shadel, 2012). However, recent research by Modic and Anderson (2015), for example, shows that emotional impact of being victimised is consistently perceived to be higher by the victims, compared to perceived financial losses. Therefore, when we talk about loss in this chapter, we will use the economic term *utility* (Bernoulli, 1954, initially published in 1738). Loosely defined, utility is any kind of good that has value to us (free time, money, trust, relaxant, etc.). As such, this broadly defined concept is ideally suited to be used when we talk about losses from fraud.

Similar to other crimes, reporting that one has been a victim of fraud is relatively rare. For example, in childhood sexual abuse 27% of females and 16% of males self-report (Finkelhor, Hotaling, Lewis, & Smith, 1990) for fear of being victimized, because of the sole fact that they are already victimized (i.e. secondary victimization). Reporting sexual abuse also stigmatizes victims (they become 'damaged goods'). Sexual assault is seldomly reported in prisons and in the general population, as the victims (amongst other factors) fear being stigmatized (Miller, 2010). In fraud, for similar reasons, the reporting rate on average is 25% (Copes, Kerley, Mason, & Van Wyk, 2001), even though substantial losses are incurred, according to various reports (Anderson et al., 2012; Fischer, Lea, & Evans, 2013).

The category of loss of some sort of personal good, like money, sleep, or hope (i.e. loss of utility), can be used as one of the taxonomical determinants of stages of complying with scammers (i.e. scam compliance). There are several definitions of the stages of scam compliance from simplistic, where an individual is either a victim, or not (e.g. Rusch, 1999; Titus, 1999) to more complex ones. The consensus among fraud researchers is that simple on/off models do not offer enough granularity. Rather, fraudsters proceed in stages. Shadel (2012, p. 29) uses these terms to describe scam compliance: (a) *the front*, (b) *the drive*, (c) *the close*, and (d) *the load*. *The front* describes the initial contact where the scammers use various techniques to gain trust. *The drive* is the stage where the scammer forces victims into complying with their demands and they offer incentives. In *the close* the fraudster gains utility from the victim; and in *the load* the scammers scam the victim again.

Cukier, Nesselroth, and Cody (2007) define the stages of falling for an advance fee fraud scheme as (a) the initial contact and building up of the relationship, (b) the convincing of the mark of participating in a legitimate transaction, and (b) the final stage of closing the transaction to the detriment of the victim.

Correspondingly, becoming a victim of any fraud, while not a perfect parallel, can also be seen as a staged process (Dyrud, 2005; Shadel & Pak, 2007, p. 52; Titus & Dover, 2001), where (a) the potential victims first find a fraudulent offer to be *plausible*, then (b) *respond* to it with private information (e.g. full name, address, telephone number, credit card information…), and (c) *lose utility*. We have confirmed this staged process in different contexts, for example in general Internet fraud scam compliance (Modic & Anderson, 2015; Modic & Lea, 2011), and in theoretical models (Modic, Anderson, & Palomäki, 2018). Our model of scam compliance does not significantly differ from that of Shadel (2012), with the exception that we did not take repeat victimization into account, due to the space, time and resource constraints.

To summarize, roping someone into stock fraud, or swindling a lonely person, or selling someone an imaginary van on eBay is a low-probability event, victims are reluctant to report victimization to scams, and scam compliance proceeds in stages.

Auction scams

Online auctions are quite a lucrative business for auction platform providers. For example eBay had a yearly net revenue of $10.7 billion in 2018 (eBay Financial, 2019, p. 33). These annual revenues are greater than GDP of more than 50% of world's nations (Hergert, 2009). The business is not that lucrative for the sellers since there is a large amount of competition and a certain amount of price undercutting (Anwar, McMillan, & Zheng, 2006; Hasker & Sickles, 2010), but the buyers have some distinct advantages. First, they have copious amounts of choice (and thus lower seller margins; Anwar et al., 2006) that leads to buying more reasonably priced goods (Browne, Durrett, & Wetherbe, 2004; Kauffman & Wood, 2000; Moe & Fader, 2001; Senecal, Kalczynski, & Nantel, 2005). The buyers are also able to comparison shop, which is one of the important factors in online/offline shopping choice (Browne et al., 2004; Senecal et al., 2005).

The sheer volume of daily transactions on large online auction sites is telling. If we look at eBay, for example, they completed, on average, five hundred million auction sales per month (eBay Metrics, 2012). In recent years, eBay has made accessing their transactions figures less accessible. However, since their NET revenue is roughly the same as in years when data were freely available, we posit that more recent figures are of the same order of magnitude. More transactions mean a greater chance of an individual encountering a fraudulent one and since substantial sums of currency change hands daily on auction platforms, they hold an interest not only for consumers but also for scammers.

There is very little data on auction fraud readily available, neither on its rate of being committed nor on its rate of being prevented by online auction sites (Smith, Grabosky, & Urbas, 2004, p. 13; Wall, 2005). Internet auction scams (goods misrepresented or not delivered) represented approximately 2% of Internet scams in 2009, according to the American National Consumer League's Fraud Center (2009), with an average loss of approximately £800 per "successful" scam. These figures are both old and not contextualized enough. A more pertinent information would be how many individuals who encounter auction fraud lose utility to it (i.e. the effectiveness of a fraudulent category, *cf.* previous section).

Although auction scams do not constitute a large percentage of Internet scams, the issue is with the definition, not with the incidence rates. Many auction scams include subverting payment methods in one way, for example by using fake cheques. These types of fraud represented 44% of the online scam landscape in recent years (National Consumer League's Fraud Center, 2009). Research has also shown that at the beginning of the century, 41% of online auction buyers had experienced difficulties in receiving goods bought on auction sites (Kauffman & Wood, 2000). Exact incidence data is not available, as online auction houses do not see it to be in their interest to disclose this. However, in other crime contexts the availability of marks, ease of access, low chance of being caught and others (Wall, 2005, 2007) led to increase in crime frequencies.

Exogenous factors influencing decision-making in eBay auctions

Feedback score as a trust cue

Feedback score (i.e. the percentage of individuals giving a positive mark to an eBay transaction.100% feedback score means every single transaction by a member was rated as positive) and the frequency and amount of rated transactions play an important role in establishing credibility and trust in an online shopping process (Diekmann & Wyder, 2002; Green, 2007; Hergert, 2009). Feedback score is important both in establishing trust (Resnick, Kuwabara, Zeckhauser, & Friedman, 2000; Resnick & Zeckhauser, 2002; Utz, Matzat, & Snijders, 2009) and in setting the price of an item (i.e. sellers with lower feedback scores have to lower their prices; Bapna, Jank, & Shmueli, 2008; Hergert, 2009; Lee, Im, & Lee, 2000). As a corollary, individuals are willing to pay a premium on an item, if the seller's feedback score is high enough (Ba & Pavlou, 2002). We can infer from this that a non-perfect feedback score is both a risk factor in itself and a possible influence on other risk factors (such as price or location).

In the context of online auction scams, where at the onset the buyer does not know whether they are facing a legitimate transaction or not, a high feedback score should play a significant role in the determination of whether the buyer is facing a scam and the decision on whether it makes sense to continue with the transaction.

Cross-cultural factors

Geographical proximity plays an important role in establishing trust in online commerce, with individuals being more likely to engage in a transaction if the seller is near them or at least in the same country (Hergert, 2009). At the same time, the border effect (i.e. the perceived possible impact of different taxes and import duties on an auction item price; Maier, 2010) is one of the factors strengthening price disparity.

Country-of-origin effects play a role in a global market—consumers from more developed countries (like the U.S. or the U.K.) are less likely to buy products originating from countries that are perceived to be less developed (e.g. China; Verlegh & Steenkamp, 1999). There is research showing that in an online marketplace, the country of origin concept is equivalent to the seller's location (Hu & Wang, 2010)—this also makes sense, because in a global economy, a majority of brand products is manufactured in Asia, regardless of the origin of the brand (e.g. Apple has almost no manufacturing plants in the US—most of the parts for their product catalogue are manufactured in China and Taiwan; Skapinker, 2011), making the seller's location more salient than where the item was produced in the first place.

Price

Stakes influence risk perception in any transaction (Kahneman, 2003). The amount itself plays a role in risk perception only in relative terms, depending on the impact of the item price on personal utility (i.e. an individual who is wealthier would not be as likely to perceive high price as risky by itself; Neumann & Morgenstern, 1944, p. 162).

Several factors should be considered when talking about the price of an item. Uncommonly low price could be perceived as risky by some individuals (i.e. they might believe that an offer is *too good to be true*; Dodds & Monroe,

1985). At the same time, a reasonably priced item should lower the perceived risk. This is, because in general, the perceived benefit is inversely correlated with the perceived risk (i.e. the more an individual believes to be gaining, the likelier they are to ignore the risk of something going wrong; Alhakami & Slovic, 1994; Finucane, Alhakami, Slovic, & Johnson, 2000)

In the context of a scam, an experienced scammer would construct an offer that would present itself as a very good value. It could be a known brand name object, which is commonly sold for a higher price than listed in a fraudulent auction. The price would be reduced enough to be enticing, but not too much, as that would make the object less desirable. Research by Dodds and Monroe (1985), for example, shows that significantly lower prices decrease chances of a sale. Furthermore, the item in question would be presented as flawed in a way that has absolutely no impact on its desirability (e.g., *unwanted gift* or *brand new without tags*), thus making it a good value for money.

Endogenous factors influencing decision-making in auctions

There is growing evidence that psychological mechanisms influence overall scam compliance, as has been shown by, for example, Fischer et al. (2013), Duffield and Grabosky (2001), Shadel and Pak (2007), and Whitty & Buchanan, (2012). There is no reason to believe that auction fraud would be any different, but psychological research on this topic is rare. In the present chapter, we fill this gap by using two scales: (1) Susceptibility to Persuasion—II (i.e. StP-II; Modic et al., 2018); and (2) HEXACO personality scale (Ashton & Lee, 2009). The StP-II (Modic et al., 2018) has been used across various contexts from measuring persuadability of nuclear deterrent contractors, to marketing agencies. It has ten sub-scales, each based on mechanisms of persuasion that have been repeatedly shown to impact behaviour modification. It was primarily developed to measure scam compliance. StP-II (Modic et al., 2018) has been primarily developed to measure scam compliance across different stages and categories of fraud. The constructs that it contains have all been shown to significantly influence behaviour, like for example replying to fraudulent offer.

HEXACO (Ashton & Lee, 2009) is a personality scale, based on the NEO-PI-R (McCrae & Costa, 1987) five-factor model of personality, with an added sixth domain, titled Honesty—Humility, that in simplified terms measures the propensity of an individual to be truthful. As such, it is particularly well suited to measure personality traits in the contexts where deception is likely to occur, such as fraud.

The effectiveness of auction fraud

While online auctions are lucrative, it is unclear how effective auction scams are. By effectiveness, we mean the ratio between the incidence rates and the likelihood of losing utility. In this respect, it does not matter whether individuals all over the world get hundreds of thousands of Nigerian emails, if less than 1% respond to them (Modic & Lea, 2011, 2013), much less lose utility. Therefore, one of the aims of this chapter will be to establish the effectiveness of auction fraud. We estimate that more than one individual in three who encounter auction fraud will lose utility to it, for two reasons: (a) we tend to confuse the reputation of the overall entity with the reputation of the particular individual, when we are unfamiliar with them (Selin, 2006). Transporting this into the context of eBay auctions, if we do not know the seller, we trust them as much as we trust eBay, which means that scammers may be more effective than usual. (b) The auctions are *solicited* in a way. When we get an unsolicited offer over email or the phone, we need to first decide how plausible it is. On a reputable auction site, we will be more likely to assume that we are participating in a legitimate transaction.

Proposed research

While we know that large amounts of money are involved in online auctions and that alone tends to attract individuals, there is a relative scarcity of psychological research into what makes fraudulent auctions attractive. Therefore, our aim in this chapter is to answer the following: (1) What are the salient psychological mechanisms of persuasion influencing compliance with fraudulent auctioneers? (2) What are the particulars of fraudulent auctions? Are there any products or services particularly suited to auction fraud? (3) How much money is lost? (4) Which personality traits are salient, and specifically (5) Are there any differences in psychological traits across the individuals who respond only and those who lose utility?

Method 1

Participants

Our participants self-selected to fill out an online questionnaire that was advertised on a well-known news site. They could opt in for a follow-up study,

Table 8.1 Scam Compliance in Auction Fraud for Those Who Encountered It (n = 2701)

Stage	*n*	%
Plausible	359	13
Responded	407	15
Lost	325	12

Note. 82 participants (3%) responded but did not lose utility in auction fraud.

which is described as Study 2 in the present chapter. Initially, we collected 10,493 responses. Out of those, we discarded 3,884 responses as they were incomplete. We ended up with 6,609 responses, out of which 2,701 encountered Auction fraud. Scam compliance levels for auction fraud are listed in Table 8.1.

In demographics, age was skewed negatively, with the biggest group (23%) aged 41–50, followed by 22% of those aged 51–60. Gender ratio was also somewhat skewed—71% of participants were male. More than three-quarters of participants (76%) reported having a University degree or higher. Majority of participants were in a long-term relationship (57%).

Design

To establish the relationship between Auction Fraud scam compliance and psychological mechanisms affecting separate stages, we ran a nominal logistic regression on the data.

The DV Scam Compliance with Auction Fraud was a nominal variable with four levels (1—not compliant, 2—found plausible, 3—interacted, 4—lost utility). In the subsequent analysis, reference group was non-compliant (i.e. those who did not find scams plausible, have not responded to them and have not lost utility to them).

The Independent Variables were derived from the Susceptibility to Persuasion scale—StP-II (Modic et al., 2018), with 54 items and 10 subdomains (with a further 6 sub-sub domains). The independent variables were: Ability to Premeditate, (Need for) Consistency, Self-Control, Need for Similarity, Attitude towards Advertising, (Need for) Cognition, (Need for) Uniqueness, Sensation seeking (Novelty, Intensity), Social Influence (Normative, Informative), Attitudes towards Risk (Ethical domain, Financial domain). The reliability of scales for each domain was adequate (.671 to .817), with overall reliability of StP-II at .820.

Results 1

Out of 2,701 respondents who encountered auction fraud, 327 (12%) lost utility to it. This is below our estimates and it is addressed in the discussion.

Because the principal dependent variable was measured on four ranked with indeterminable intervals among the levels (no compliance, plausibility, responded and lost) nominal logistic regression was employed to help determine which persuasive mechanisms measured by the StP-II (Modic et al., 2018) could be used to inform Auction Fraud scam compliance.

Initially, Pearson correlations across the independent variables were examined. Most were significant, ranging from moderate to small – Similarity × Uniqueness, $r_{6587} = .456$, $p < .001$ to Consistency ×x Risk –– Ethical, $r_{6537} = .029$, $p = .017$.

The correlations between the dependent variable and the independent ones were small (none were above absolute .06), therefore nominal logistic regression was appropriate (cf. Norusis, 2010). Results of the analysis are presented in Table 8.2.

Our model yields eight significant predictors of plausibility (Need for Consistency, Need for Cognition, Need for Uniqueness, Sensation Seeking—Intensity,

Table 8.2 Regressors of Fake Auction Scam Compliance in the Nominal Logistic Regression (n = 6609)

		B	*Exp(B)*	*Std. Error*	*Wald*
Plausible	Consistency	−0.07	0.93	0.03	7.755**
	Cognition	−0.07	0.93	0.03	5.201**
	Uniqueness	0.15	1.16	0.03	32.06***
	Sensa. Seek. (intensity)	0.09	1.10	0.02	17.917***
	Soc. Inf. (normative)	0.10	1.11	0.03	13.288***
	Soc. Inf. (informative)	0.06	1.06	0.02	8.597**
	Risk (financial)	0.07	1.07	0.03	5.196**
	Risk (ethical)	0.09	1.09	0.04	6.262**
Responded	Uniqueness	0.25	1.28	0.11	5.491**
	Sensa. Seek. (intensity)	0.20	1.22	0.09	4.801**
	Risk (ethical)	0.37	1.45	0.13	8.622**
Lost	Attitude towards Adv.	−0.12	0.89	0.05	5.97**
	Uniqueness	0.21	1.23	0.06	14.588***

Note. Reference category is non-compliant.
*p < .1, **p < .05, ***p < .001.

Social Influence—Normative, Social Influence—Informative, Attitudes towards Risk—Financial, Attitudes towards Risk—Ethical), three significant predictors to Responding (Uniqueness, Sensation Seeking—Intensity, Attitudes towards Risk—Ethical) and two significant predictors to Losing Utility to Auction Fraud (Attitude towards Advertising, Need for Uniqueness). The model had a low predictive strength (Nagelkerke pseudo $R^2 = .030$).

Discussion 1

The effectiveness of auction fraud in this sample is below our estimates, which were based on the results of unrelated research at the University of Cambridge (in preparation), where we have conducted an internal survey, measuring the effectiveness of different types of Internet fraud. In that sample of 1,012 students and staff, 68% have not encountered auction fraud, but out of those who did, more than one in two (>55%) lost utility.

As has been previously shown, for example by Modic and Lea (2011), there is a linear progression between the stages of Auction Fraud scam compliance, with different persuasive mechanisms affecting the level of compliance. The results show that for a buyer to find a fraudulent auction believable it must evoke the Need for Consistency; therefore, it should look as run-of-the-mill as possible. Furthermore, the Auction should be clear and not overly cognitively challenging to understand, while it should avoid being simplistic. The scammer should claim that this is a unique opportunity, and the object being sold should be presented as one of a kind, in some way. Purchasing this object should present an opportunity to have an intensive experience, while purchase should be presented as something that the buyers in-group thinks is both an objectively smart purchase and something that every self-respecting member of said group should possess. Finally, those potential buyers who have a somewhat lax financial and ethical attitude towards risk, should find fraudulent auctions more believable. The strongest predictor of Plausibility was Uniqueness, confirming findings that unique or scarce items are more desirable by consumers and thus inhibit rational decision-making (e.g. Eisend, 2008; Fischer, Greitemeyer, & Frey, 2008; Kramer & Carroll, 2009; Shirai & Bettman, 2005).

Once a potential victim has found a fraudulent offer plausible, they are likely to respond, although, as research and the present analysis shows, sometimes they will respond even if they believe that an offer is fraudulent from the start. This might stem from over-confidence (DellaVigna, 2009; Fischer et al., 2013) or from under-estimation of risks involved, which is a signal scammers are happy to project (Herley, 2012). Once a fraudulent offer has been accepted as plausible, a subset of persuasive mechanisms applies. For the mark to engage with the scam, the offer should be presented as scarce or unique, it should appeal to intense experiences and it helps if the mark prefers to be less than perfectly ethical. In addition, those individuals who lose utility in the end are likely to dislike advertisements but still prefer unique or scarce offers.

The goal of Study 1 was to uncover salient StP-II mechanisms when it comes to auction fraud scam compliance. The self-reported auction fraud victims from Study 1, who indicated the willingness to be contacted for a follow-up study, were subsequently contacted again to explore their cases in more detail.

Method 2

Participants

The participants in Study 2 were chosen from the pool of participants in Study 1, who agreed to take part in a follow-up study. Out of those who agreed to participate again (n = 2,131), 280 indicated they lost utility from fraudulent auctions or from counterfeit goods. Those who indicated they lost utility purchasing fake goods, were initially asked whether this occurred on an auction site. If it did, they were included in the auction fraud pool. Out of 280 contacted victims, 114 responded. We removed those who were scammed as sellers, those who were not victimized through auction sites and those who did not complete the survey. We ended up with a sample of 81 confirmed victims of Auction fraud. While the sample in this instance was small, it shared some similar characteristics with victims of financial fraud described by Deliema, Shadel, and Pak (2020)—the ratio of males to females was similar, as was the educational levels ratio.

Procedure

The online survey can be roughly divided into three logical parts.

1. Demographic and incident data (in addition to demographics, we were interested in what was purchased, how much it was worth in percentage of respondents' income, were there any clues that would in retrospect

show that this was potentially fraudulent, how did the scam progress and what did the respondents do after the fraud took place, i.e. did they report the fraud, whom to, did they recover their funds, how much did they recover).

2. Psychological instruments: HEXACO (Ashton & Lee, 2009) personality scale and the UPPS-IBS (Whiteside et al., 2005) Impulsivity scale that was shortened, revalidated and re-tested for reliability by Modic and Lea (2011).
3. Final part (demand characteristics questions, debrief, etc).

Design

There was one dependent variable. Lost was a two-level variable (1—responded only, 2—responded and lost utility). Since this was a pool of victims, there was not enough variance to include those who found the scam implausible.

The independent variables were derived from means of HEXACO (Ashton & Lee, 2009) domains and subdomains; the six main domains are: Honesty—humility (H), Emotionality (E), Extraversion (X), Agreeableness (A), Conscientiousness (C), and Openness to Experience (O). Their subdomains are: H (Sincerity, Fairness, Greed—avoidance, Modesty), E (Fearfulness, Anxiety, Dependence, Sentimentality), X (Social Self-esteem, Boldness, Sociability, Liveliness), A (Forgiveness, Gentleness, Flexibility, Patience), C (Organization, Diligence, Perfectionism, Prudence), O (Aesthetic Appreciation, Inquisitiveness, Creativity, Unconventionality).

Furthermore, the independent variables were derived from the means of modified UPPS-IBS (Whiteside et al., 2005) subscales: Urgency, Premeditation (lack of), Perseverance (lack of), Sensation Seeking.

A series of Logistic Regression models were run to establish the differences in psychological traits between those who interacted with Auction Fraudsters and those who lost utility to them. Initially, all the IV's were entered into the Model and pruned out in order of insignificance. The final Model was reached in three steps.

Results 2

Fraud progression

We were first interested in the potential victims' familiarity with online auction sites (eBay in our case). Data show that 30% of victims were new, having conducted less than 10 transactions. An additional 30% conducted less than 50 transactions. Only 9% of respondents conducted more than 500 transactions on Auction sites.

We initially looked at which objects individuals were buying in online auctions. The relatively small sample did not yield enough variance, to find out whether there were specific items that were more likely to feature in a fraudulent auction. Victims attempted to purchase everything from toilet paper rolls to a time-share apartment in an online auction.

While we did not manage to find the objects, we investigated the financial impact of fraudulent auctions. Since financial impact is best measured in the context of prior utility (i.e. how financially secure an individual is in the first place), we needed to relativize the cost. In Table 8.3 we present the losses as a fraction of an individual's monthly income.

We were interested in which parameters of a fraudulent online auction are enticing, and to what extent, to a buyer. To this effect we asked the participants the following question: "We would like you to still focus on the fraudulent auction we were discussing before. Which of the below influenced your decision to participate in that particular auction?" We then listed items that could potentially indicate a fraudulent auction (cf. *Introduction*). In Table 8.4, we list the results.

A well-described object, even if it is all lies, is the best incentive, closely followed by price and visual presentation. It seems that no one cares much about the duration of the membership or whether the seller sells in bulk.

In the aftermath, after the fraudulent Auction took place and money changed hands, we were interested in finding out whether the victims filed a claim, and if not, why not. Less than half (n = 22, 45%) respondents who lost

Table 8.3 Size of Financial Impact of Auction Fraud (n = 79)

	Frequency	%
Less than 1% of my monthly earnings	47	59.5
Around 10%	20	25.3
Around 20%	6	7.6
Around 30%	1	1.3
Around 80%	1	1.3
More than a 100% (had to save or borrow to pay for the item)	1	1.3
Several times my monthly earnings	3	3.8

Note. Item text: "Regardless of whether you lost some money or not in the end (in the auction we are discussing), please think about the price of the item and try to recall what proportion of your monthly earnings..."

Table 8.4 Which Items Did the Victim of an Auction Fraud Pay Attention to in Fraudulent Auction (n = 81)

	[%][a]
The description of the item (how plausible it is)	62
The price of the item	58
The pictures of the item	58
Condition of the item (new, new without tags, used...)	57
The seller's feedback score	47
Auction / listing type (was it an auction or buy it now type of listing)	38
Spelling mistakes in the listing	36
The number of transactions the seller made in the past	35
The reported location of the item	33
Status of the seller (shop or individual)	24
Number of Sellers offering this item (general availability of the item)	22
Time remaining in the listing	21
Number of items available (in that listing)	15
The length of membership (that is: Member since ...)	14

a How many participants decided to participate in based on the item.

utility filed a claim. They overwhelmingly (n = 15, 68%) did not think it worth it. Three individuals (14%) were refunded before opening a dispute. Some were unaware of being able to file a claim, and some were too late.

Out of those who filed a claim, 50% (n = 11), got nothing, 9% (n = 2) got back some funds and 36% (n = 8) recovered all the funds. Out of those who got refund in full or in part, practically all (n = 8, 80%) got refunded by the auction company or their subsidiaries, and 1 (20%) got refunded by the seller.

Personality differences across those who responded and those who lost

In order to run the logistic regression model, we first screened the datafile for outliers, but none were removed as they were all inside the 2 SD margin. To establish whether the logistic regression model is warranted, we ran a series of Spearman rho bivariate correlations across the DV, HEXACO domain and sub-domain means, and UPPS-IBS subscale means. There was only one significant moderate correlation between the DV, and a subscale sub-domain mean – Lost × Modesty – $\rho_{81} = .318$, $p = .004$. There were significant and strong correlations between members of sub-domains, which is not unexpected, as they do describe the sane HEXACO domains.

Table 8.5 Logistic Regression Model for Personality Traits Influencing the Transition from Responding to Buying (n = 78)

	B	*S.E.*	*Exp(B)*	*Wald*
HEXACO				
Modesty (HON)	1.812	0.588	6.12	9.500**
Social self-esteem (EXTR)	1.028	0.585	2.795	3.083*
Sociability (EXTR)	−1.193	0.507	0.303	5.540**
Gentleness (AGRE)	1.717	0.634	5.57	7.327**
Flexibility (AGRE)	−2.034	0.801	0.131	6.440**
Organization (CONSCI)	1.592	0.579	4.916	7.553**
Diligence (CONSCI)	−1.497	0.599	0.224	6.240**
Aesthetic Apprecia. (OPE)	−1.064	0.494	0.345	4.640**
Creativity (OPE)	1.762	0.605	5.826	8.482**
UPPS-IBS				
Premeditation	−2.197	0.797	0.111	7.601**
Sensation seeking	0.737	0.434	2.089	2.881*

Note. *p < .1, **p < .05, ***p < .001.
NONE of the HEXACO domains was statistically significant as a full construct.

Initially, we ran a logistic regression model with Lost DV × HEXACO and UPPS-IBS domains. None of the full domains were significant predictors of transition from responding to losing. We subsequently ran several more models, including HEXACO sub-domains and in steps removed the non-significant predictors. The final model is listed in Table 8.5.

The model was significant with $\chi_{11}^2 = 42.314$, $p < .001$; Nagelkerke's $R^2 = .59$. The Hosmer and Lemeshow Test was not significant, indicating a good fit at $\chi_8^2 = 9.432$, $p = .307$. The likelihood of transitioning from responding to a full victim were significantly predicted by 9 HEXACO subdomains and 2 UPPS-IBS domains. Overall strongest regressor was Modesty (subdomain of Honesty—humility domain), indicating that modest individuals are more likely to progress from responding to losing utility.

Most Respondents (98% of the sample) were willing to disclose the item they thought they were buying. However, the items ranged wildly in price and category and there were no duplicate items. The funds invested were skewed as 3 out of every 5 (60%) items purchased represented were worth less than 1% of the respondent's monthly income. However, 4% of respondents did invest several times their monthly income. Half of those who lost utility to Auction Fraud filed a claim and out of those, half got some, or all, of the funds back, signifying that chances of recovering funds are 25% with the proviso that you do need to file a claim first. A majority of respondents did not file a claim, as they did not feel it was worth the hassle; this has implications on the policy level, since one of the underlying causes of the effectiveness of criminal activities that defraud a large amount of individuals for very small amounts (i.e. *micro-crime*; Wall, 2011) is that most victims will not bother reporting them, as the amounts they lost were negligible to them.

Discussion 2

Several personality traits significantly influence the likelihood of progressing from responding to a fraudulent offer to losing utility to it. Some significant HEXACO sub-domains were negative predictors, indicating that individuals more likely to lose utility are those who are less sociable, inflexible, somewhat less likely to carefully check a listing, and those who do not care as much about the aesthetic merits of an item. This is in line with other research on Internet fraud, by, for example, Fischer et al. (2013) or Whitty and Buchanan (2012), who show similar findings.

The strongest predictor of the likelihood of progressing from responding to losing utility in the context of impulsivity is the lack of the ability to premeditate. Those who have a hard time thinking things through and considering the future consequences of their actions will be more likely to engage in risky behaviours that will result in a loss. That too, has some previous support in research, for example, by Modic et al. (2018), who, in the process of validating a scale of susceptibility to persuasion show, that lack of premeditation explains the most unexplained variance when it comes to the StP-II construct.

Conclusion

Our aim in this chapter was to increase our understanding of Auction fraud and which of the psychological mechanisms increase scam compliance in this context. We have uncovered several psychological mechanisms of persuasion that significantly impact the three stages of scam compliance and we have uncovered several personality traits that impact the likelihood of becoming a victim of Auction Fraud.

We were hoping to uncover specific objects that would be used more often fraudulent auctions. The relatively low response rates and sample size in Study 2 prevented us from drawing any firm conclusions. However, the present research indicates that items featuring in fraudulent auctions will overwhelmingly be lower-cost items. An argument can be made that this is not due to some deep insight of fraudsters, but simply because there are more of low-cost items featuring on eBay. While it may be true that lower-cost items are more frequently offered on eBay, the argument cannot be made that there is a scarcity of higher-cost items. We chose to interpret this more as a support for theories of micro-crime (e.g. Wall, 2011), where pursuit is less likely if the amounts gained by scammers are low on a per-person basis, but high in accumulation.

While we cannot directly infer anything from the present data about the effectiveness of crime-fighting authorities in the context of Auction fraud, the analysis shows that victims usually do not initially contact these authorities. They tend to first contact the businesses where they were defrauded, and these entities often reimburse the victims. This leads to a situation where being an auction fraudster is a lucrative proposition—the potential victims will be largely reimbursed if they apply themselves to it, making it likely that there will be no official pursuit of the fraudster, while the cost will be borne by the online businesses, who figure this to be the operational costs and are unlikely to vigorously pursue it.

We have found that several psychological mechanisms of persuasion influence the likelihood a potential victim losing utility in a fraudulent auction. Need for Uniqueness is the strongest overall predictor of Auction fraud scam compliance. It is well documented that in other contexts scarcity and uniqueness influence economic behaviour in the sense that they increase its desirability and perceived value (Lynn, 1989; Rusch, 1999; Suri, Kohli, & Monroe, 2007; Tan & Chua, 2004). Curiously, one can argue that if scarcity was an important predictor of scam compliance, then general availability would be important in the context of auctions. Our analysis did not seem to confirm this as an important factor. However, we would argue that desirability of an object is determined by the buyer before they visit an online auction site, not after. Therefore, economics of scale would dictate that in a huge marketplace most run-of-the-mill items are not scarce, which plays into the hands of a consumer, who can comparison shop. Uniqueness, however, is determined by the presentation of the sold item ("everyone has an iPhone, but only this one has a star shaped smudge just below the apple logo in the back!").

An argument could be made that scam compliance with fraudulent auctions is not a function of psychology, but rather of frequency of use, that is the victims are more vulnerable, because they use auction sites more than others. However, approximately one-third of the victims in our sample had conducted less than ten transactions on eBay, and another third (approximately) less than fifty. Only one in ten of our victims was a heavy auction site user. Therefore, the exposure is not the main driver of scam compliance.

A curious finding was that none of the HEXACO (Ashton & Lee, 2009) domains as a whole was salient in auction fraud scam compliance. This may be related to the finding that several sub-domains are inversely correlated (e.g., Extraversion: +Social Self Esteem vs. −Sociability; Agreeableness: +Gentleness vs. −Flexibility and so on). This finding would explain why the whole domains do not predict scam compliance, but it would not explain why there is an inverse correlation in the first place. This would require further study with a larger sample of actual victims. However, even this analysis shows that the HEXACO (Ashton & Lee, 2009) domains are perhaps too coarse to be able to determine scam compliance. For example, while both Gentleness and Flexibility are well placed inside the Agreeableness sub-domain, according to Ashton and Lee (2009), the analysis shows that gentler individuals are more likely to fall for Auction fraud, as well as those who are less flexible. In this vein, most HEXACO (Ashton & Lee, 2009) domains contain positive and negative regressors.

What can be done additionally to increase our understanding of psychology auction fraud? Larger, more representative samples should give us more data about items that present greater likelihood of featuring in fraudulent auctions. Developing and testing specific deterrence mechanisms based on our understanding of psychology of auction fraud would decrease the likelihood of auction fraud. However, online auction houses are traditionally reluctant to collaborate with academic researchers for fear of public misperception. However, eBay is not the only large auction house available. Chinese auction houses like AliExpress are also growing steadily. Comparing fraud mechanics across these enterprises would be interesting.

We have previously shown that mechanisms of persuasion, personality traits, and emotional consequences of victimization impact overall scam compliance stages (Modic & Anderson, 2015; Modic & Lea, 2011; Modic et al., 2018). In this chapter we show that auction fraud is similar to other types of fraud in the sense that scam compliance stages are impacted by mechanisms of persuasion and personality traits. It is also dissimilar in the sense that different persuasive mechanisms impact different types of fraud and different personality traits influence compliance across categories of fraud (cf. Whitty & Buchanan, 2012 for a study of personality traits salient in victims of romance scams). As is often the case in fraud research, the results support decisions that are intuitive enough, but while perfect hindsight is valuable, it is perhaps not as useful as actual empirical evidence. So, should we distract those who participate in online auctions? There seems to be no need; the scammers are doing that successfully already.

References

Alhakami, A. S., & Slovic, P. (1994). A Psychological Study of the Inverse Relationship between Perceived Risk and Perceived Benefit. *Risk Analysis, 14*(6), 1085–1096. doi:10.1111/j.1539-6924.1994.tb00080.x.

Anderson, R., Barton, C., Böhme, R., Clayton, R., van Eeten, M., Levi, M., … Savage, S. (2012). *Measuring the Cost of Cybercrime. Paper presented at the 11th Annual Workshop on the Economics of Information Security WEIS 2012*, Berlin, Germany. http://weis2012.econinfosec.org/papers/Anderson_WEIS2012.pdf

Anwar, S., McMillan, R., & Zheng, M. (2006). Bidding Behavior in Competing Auctions: Evidence from eBay. *European Economic Review, 50*(2), 307–322. Retrieved from http://ejournals.ebsco.com/direct.asp?ArticleID=4DCAA744A667B5B1DCA5

Ashton, M. C., & Lee, K. (2009). The HEXACO–60: A Short Measure of the Major Dimensions of Personality. *Journal of Personality Assessment, 91*(4), 340–345. doi:10.1080/00223890902935878.

Ba, S., & Pavlou, P. A. (2002). Evidence of the Effect of Trust Building Technology in Electronic Markets: Price Premiums and Buyer Behavior. *Mis Quarterly, 26*(3), 243–268. Retrieved from http://www.jstor.org/stable/4132332

Bapna, R., Jank, W., & Shmueli, G. (2008). Price Formation and Its Dynamics in Online Auctions. *Decision Support Systems, 44*(3), 641–656. Retrieved from http://ejournals.ebsco.com/direct.asp?ArticleID=416E9F8E6615AD97BF91

Bernoulli, D. (1954). Exposition of a New Theory on the Measurement of Risk. *Econometrica, 22*(1), 23–36. Retrieved from http://www.jstor.org/stable/1909829

Browne, G. J., Durrett, J. R., & Wetherbe, J. C. (2004). Consumer Reactions toward Clicks and Bricks: Investigating Buying Behaviour On-line and at Stores. *Behaviour & Information Technology, 23*(4), 237–245. Retrieved from <Go to ISI>://000222083900002.

Copes, H., Kerley, K. R., Mason, K. A., & Van Wyk, J. (2001). Reporting Behavior of Fraud Victims and Black's Theory of Law: An Empirical Assessment. *Justice Quarterly, 18*(2), 343–363. doi:10.1080/07418820100094931.

Cukier, W. L., Nesselroth, E. J., & Cody, S. (2007). *Genre, Narrative and the "Nigerian Letter" in Electronic Mail. Paper presented at the 40th Annual Hawaii International Conference on System Sciences (HICSS'07)*, Hilton Waikoloa Village, Big Island. http://www2.computer.org/portal/web/csdl/proceedings/h#5

Deevy, M., Lucich, S., & Beals, M. (2012). *Scams, Schemes & Swindles: A Review of Consumer Financial Fraud Research*. Retrieved from Financial Fraud Research Center: http://fraudresearchcenter.org/wp-content/uploads/2012/11/Scams-Schemes-Swindles-FINAL-On-Website.pdf

Deliema, M., Shadel, D., & Pak, K. (2020). Profiling Victims of Investment Fraud: Mindsets and Risky Behaviors. *Journal of Consumer Research, 46*(5), 904–914. doi:10.1093/jcr/ucz020.

DellaVigna, S. (2009). Psychology and Economics: Evidence from the Field. *Journal of Economic Literature, 47*(2), 315–372. doi:10.1257/jel.47.2.315.

Diekmann, A., & Wyder, D. (2002). Vertrauen und Reputationseffekte bei Internet-Auktionen. *KZfSS Kölner Zeitschrift für Soziologie und Sozialpsychologie, 54*(4), 674–693. doi:10.1007/s11577-002-0104-z.

Dodds, W. B., & Monroe, K. B. (1985). The Effect of Brand and Price Information on Subjective Product Evaluations. *Advances in Consumer Research, 12*(1), 85–90. Retrieved from http://search.ebscohost.com/login.aspx?direct=true&db=bth&AN=6430942&site=ehost-live

Duffield, G. M., & Grabosky, P. N. (March, 2001). The Psychology of Fraud. *Trends and Issues in Crime and Criminal Justice, 199*(199), 1–6. Retrieved from http://www.aic.gov.au/publications/tandi/ti199.pdf

Dyrud, M. A. (2005). *I Brought You a Good News: An Analysis of Nigerian 419 Letters. Paper presented at the 70th Annual Convention of The Association for Business Communication*, Irvine, CA. Analysis retrieved from http://www.businesscommunication.org/conventions/Proceedings/2005/PDFs/07ABC05.pdf

eBay Financial. (2019). *eBay Annual Report 2018*. Retrieved from https://ebay.q4cdn.com/610426115/files/doc_financials/financials/2018/annual/2018_eBay_Annual_Report.pdf

eBay Metrics. (2012). *eBay Unaudited Supplemental Operating Data (Metrics)*. Retrieved from http://investor.ebay.com/financial_history.cfm

Eisend, M. (2008). Explaining the Impact of Scarcity Appeals in Advertising. *Journal of Advertising, 37*(3), 33–40. Retrieved from http://search.ebscohost.com/login.aspx?direct=true&db=bth&AN=34462736&site=ehost-live

Finkelhor, D., Hotaling, G., Lewis, I. A., & Smith, C. (1990). Sexual Abuse in a National Survey of Adult Men and Women - Prevalence, Characteristics, and Risk-Factors. *Child Abuse & Neglect, 14*(1), 19–28. doi:10.1016/0145-2134(90)90077-7.

Finucane, M. L., Alhakami, A., Slovic, P., & Johnson, S. M. (2000). The Affect Heuristic in Judgments of Risks and Benefits. *Journal of Behavioral Decision Making, 13*(1), 1–17. doi:10.1002/(sici)1099-0771(200001/03)13:1<1::aid-bdm333>3.0.co;2-s.

Fischer, P., Greitemeyer, T., & Frey, D. (2008). Self-Regulation and Selective Exposure: The Impact of Depleted Self-Regulation Resources on Confirmatory Information Processing. *Journal of Personality and Social Psychology, 94*(3), 382–395. doi:10.1037/0022-3514.94.3.382.

Fischer, P., Lea, S., & Evans, K. (2009). *The Psychology of Scams: Provoking and Committing Errors of Judgement. Research for the Office of Fair Trading* (OFT1070). Retrieved from Exeter, UK: http://www.oft.gov.uk/shared_oft/reports/consumer_protection/oft1070.pdf

Fischer, P., Lea, S. E. G., & Evans, K. M. (2013). Why do Individuals Respond to Fraudulent Scam Communication and Lose Money? The Psychological Determinants of Scam Compliance. *Journal of Applied Social Psychology, 43*(10), 2060–2072. doi:10.1111/jasp.12158.

Fraud. (2011). *Oxford English Dictionary Online*. Oxford University Press. Retrieved July 30, 2012, from http://www.oed.com/view/Entry/74299?rskey=AHrCD1&result=2#eid

Green, M. C. (2007). Trust and Social Interaction on the Internet. In A. N. Joinson, K. Y. A. McKenna, T. Postmes, & U.-D. Reips (Eds.), *The Oxford Handbook of Internet Psychology* (pp. 43–53). Oxford and New York: Oxford University Press.

Hasker, K., & Sickles, R. (2010). eBay in the Economic Literature: Analysis of an Auction Marketplace. *Review of Industrial Organization, 37*(1), 3–42. doi:10.1007/s11151-010-9257-5.

Hergert, M. (2009). International Vendors and Trust in Electronic Auctions. *Journal of Global Business Management, 5*(1). Retrieved from http://www.jgbm.org/page/28%20Michael%20Hergert%20.pdf

Herley, C. (2012). *Why do Nigerian Scammers Say They Are from Nigeria?* Paper presented at the WEIS 2012, Berlin, Germanz. Conference article retrieved from http://research.microsoft.com/pubs/167719/WhyFromNigeria.pdf

Hu, Y., & Wang, X. (2010). Country-of-Origin Premiums for Retailers in International Trades: Evidence from eBay's International Markets. *Journal of Retailing, 86*(2), 200–207. Retrieved from http://ejournals.ebsco.com/direct.asp?ArticleID=47CDB694ABBF2BA7517F

Kahneman, D. (2003). Maps of Bounded Rationality: Psychology for Behavioral Economics. *The American Economic Review, 93*(5), 1449–1475. Retrieved from http://www.jstor.org/stable/3132137

Kauffman, R. J., & Wood, C. A. (2000). *Running up the Bid: Modeling Seller Opportunism in Internet Auctions. Paper presented at the Sixth Americas Conference in Information Systems,* Long Beach, CA. http://aisel.aisnet.org/amcis2000/376

Kramer, T., & Carroll, R. (2009). The Effect of Incidental Out-of-Stock Options on Preferences. *Marketing Letters, 20*(2), 197–208. doi:10.1007/s11002-008-9059-9.

Lee, Z., Im, I., & Lee, S. J. (2000). *The Effect of Negative Buyer Feedback on Prices in Internet Auction MarkeEts. Paper presented at the Proceedings of the twenty first international conference on information systems*, Brisbane, Queensland, Australia.

Luce, H. R. (June 28, 1963). Actors: The Mild One. *Time Magazine, LXXXI/26*(26). Retrieved from http://www.time.com/time/magazine/article/0,9171,874969,00.html

Lynn, M. (1989). Scarcity Effects on Desirability: Mediated by Assumed Expensiveness? *Journal of Economic Psychology, 10*(2), 257–274. doi:10.1016/0167-4870(89)90023-8.

Maier, P. (2010). An Analysis of International Price Differentials on eBay. *Contemporary Economic Policy, 28*(3), 307–321. doi:10.1111/j.1465-7287.2009.00179.x.

McCrae, R. R., & Costa, P. T. (1987). Validation of the Five-Factor Model of Personality across Instruments and Observers. *Journal of Personality and Social Psychology, 52*(1), 81–90. doi:10.1037/0022-3514.52.1.81.

Merriam-Webster (Ed.) (2005) *The Merriam-Webster Dictionary*. Springfield, MA: Merriam-Webster.

Miller, K. L. (2010). The Darkest Figure of Crime: Perceptions of Reasons for Male Inmates to Not Report Sexual Assault. *Justice Quarterly, 27*(5), 692–712. doi:10.1080/07418820903292284.

Modic, D., & Anderson, R. (2015). It's All Over but the Crying: The Emotional and Financial Impact of Internet Fraud. *Ieee Security & Privacy, 13*(5), 99–103. doi:10.1109/MSP.2015.107.

Modic, D., Anderson, R., & Palomäki, J. (2018). We Will Make You Like Our Research: The Development of a Susceptibility-to-Persuasion Scale. *PLoS One, 13*(3), e0194119. doi:10.1371/journal.pone.0194119.

Modic, D., & Lea, S. E. G. (2011). *How Neurotic Are Scam Victims, Really? The Big Five and Internet Scams. Paper presented at the 2011 Conference of the International Confederation for the Advancement of Behavioral Economics and Economic Psychology, Exeter*, United Kingdom. https://papers.ssrn.com/sol3/Delivery.cfm/SSRN_ID2448130_code1448306.pdf?abstractid=2448130&mirid=1

Modic, D., & Lea, S. E. G. (2013). Scam Compliance and the Psychology of Persuasion [pre-print]. *Social Sciences Research Network*. Available at SSRN: http://ssrn.com/abstract=2364464. Retrieved from http://ssrn.com/abstract=2364464

Moe, W. W., & Fader, P. S. (2001). Uncovering Patterns in Cybershopping. *California Management Review, 43*(4), 106.

National Consumer League's Fraud Center. (2009). *Fraud Trends January - June 2009*. Washington, DC. Retrieved from www.nclnet.org/news/2009/2008%20fraud%20stats.pdf.

Neumann, J. V., & Morgenstern, O. (1944). *Theory of Games and Economic Behaviour*. Princeton, NJ: Princeton University Press.

Norusis, M. J. (2010). Chapter 4: Ordinal Regression. In *PASW Statistics 18 Guide to Data Analysis* (pp. 69–89). Upper Saddle River, NJ: Prentice Hall.

Resnick, P., Kuwabara, K., Zeckhauser, R., & Friedman, E. (2000). Reputation Systems. *Commun. ACM, 43*(12), 45–48. doi:10.1145/355112.355122.

Resnick, P., & Zeckhauser, R. (2002). Trust among Strangers in Internet Transactions: Empirical Analysis of eBay's Reputation System. In *The Economics of the Internet and E-commerce* (Vol. 11, pp. 127–157). Emerald Group Publishing Limited.

Rusch, J. J. (1999). *The "Social Engineering" of Internet Fraud*. Paper presented at the Internet Global Summit - INET 99, San Jose, CA. Policy paper retrieved from http://www.isoc.org/isoc/conferences/inet/99/proceedings/3g/3g_2.htm

Selin, C. (2006). Trust and the Illusive Force of Scenarios. *Futures, 38*(1), 1–14. doi:10.1016/j.futures.2005.04.001.

Senecal, S., Kalczynski, P. J., & Nantel, J. (2005). Consumers' Decision-Making Process and Their Online Shopping Behavior: A Clickstream Analysis. *Journal of Business Research, 58*(11), 1599–1608. Retrieved from http://ejournals.ebsco.com/direct.asp?ArticleID=4D8EAF944E67F882AD25

Shadel, D. P. (2012). *Outsmarting the Scam Artists: How to Protect Yourself from the Most Clever Cons*. Hoboken, NJ: John Wiley & Sons.

Shadel, D. P., & Pak, K. B. S. (2007). *The Psychology of Consumer Fraud*. (PhD). Tillbrook University, Stanford Center on Longevity.

Shirai, M., & Bettman, J. R. (2005). Consumer Expectations Concerning Timing and Depth of the Next Deal. *Psychology and Marketing, 22*(6), 457–472. Retrieved from http://ejournals.ebsco.com/direct.asp?ArticleID=415CB2010D11DC220121

Skapinker, M. (2011). Time for Apple to Open Its Factories [Analysis]. *Financial Times*. Retrieved from http://www.ft.com/cms/s/0/14a97ace-d870-11e0-8f0a-00144feabdc0.html#axzz1naPIO81Z

Smith, R. G., Grabosky, P., & Urbas, G. (2004). *Cyber Criminals on Trial*. Cambridge: Cambridge University Press.

Suri, R., Kohli, C., & Monroe, K. (2007). The Effects of Perceived Scarcity on Consumers' Processing of Price Information. *Journal of the Academy of Marketing Science, 35*(1), 89–100. Retrieved from http://dx.doi.org/10.1007/s11747-006-0008-y

Tan, S.-J., & Chua, S. H. (2004). "While Stocks Last!" Impact of Framing on Consumers' Perception of Sales Promotions. *Journal of Consumer Marketing, 21*(5), 343–355. doi:10.1108/07363760410549168.

Titus, R. M. (1999). *The Victimology of Fraud. Paper presented at the restoration for victims of crime: contemporary challenges*, Melbourne, Australia. Report retrieved from http://www.aic.gov.au/conferences/rvc/titus.pdf

Titus, R. M., & Dover, A. R. (2001). Personal Fraud: The Victims and the Scams. *Crime Prevention Studies, 12*, 133–151.

Titus, R. M., Heinzelmann, F., & Boyle, J. M. (1995). Victimization of Persons by Fraud. *Crime & Delinquency, 41*(1), 54–72. Retrieved from http://cad.sagepub.com/content/41/1/54.abstract

Utz, S., Matzat, U., & Snijders, C. (2009). On-line Reputation Systems: The Effects of Feedback Comments and Reactions on Building and Rebuilding Trust in On-line Auctions. *International Journal of Electronic Commerce, 13*(3), 95–118. doi:10.2753/jec1086-4415130304.

Verlegh, P. W. J., & Steenkamp, J.-B. E. M. (1999). A Review and Meta-Analysis of Country-of-Origin Research. *Journal of Economic Psychology, 20*(5), 521–546. doi:10.1016/s0167-4870(99)00023-9.

Wall, D. S. (2005). The Internet as a Conduit for Criminal Activity. In A. Pattavina (Ed.), *Information Technology and the Criminal Justice System* (pp. 77–98). Thousand Oaks, CA: Sage Publications, Inc.

Wall, D. S. (2007). Policing Cybercrimes: Situating the Public Police in Networks of Security within Cyberspace (Revised February 2011). *Police Practice and Research: An International Journal, 8*(2), 183–205. Retrieved from http://ssrn.com/paper=853225

Wall, D. S. (2011). Micro-Frauds: Virtual Robberies, Stings and Scams in the Information Age. In T. Holt & B. Schell (Eds.), *Corporate Hacking and Technology-Driven Crime: Social Dynamics and Implications* (pp. 68–85). Hershey, PA: IGI Global.

Whiteside, S. P., Lynam, D. R., Miller, J. D., & Reynolds, S. K. (2005). Validation of the UPPS Impulsive Behaviour Scale: A Four-Factor Model of Impulsivity. *European Journal of Personality, 19*(7), 559–574. doi:10.1002/per.556.

Whitty, M. T., & Buchanan, T. (2012). *The Psychology of the Online Dating Romance Scam. A Report for the ESRC*. Retrieved from Leicester, UK.

9 Trends in online consumer fraud: A data science perspective

Felix Soldner, Bennett Kleinberg, and Shane Johnson

Following the advent of the Internet, the interaction between sellers and consumers is increasingly shifting from a face-to-face towards an online environment. With that shift, new forms of consumer fraud have emerged (Rusch, 1991). Such fraud, as well as cybercrime as a whole, seems to be increasing, generating costs to society, including direct monetary losses, criminal revenues, and opportunity costs (Ablon et al., 2014; Anderson et al., 2013; van Wegberg et al., 2018). For example, a report by the FBI (2018), which examined complaints and messages from Internet crime victims in the US, found a steady increase for all types of cybercrime, with an estimated total monetary loss of $2.71 billion in 2018. Additionally, estimates suggest that consumer products and services account for 42.6% of all financial fraud incidents, with the Internet being the dominant solicitation method (30%) in the US (DeLiema et al., 2017). Although accurate estimates of online consumer fraud are difficult to compute due to the lack of, and granularity of, data, estimates such as that above give a sense of the scale of the problem. In terms of prevention, difficulties come from the nature of the online environment, which enables fraudsters to reach individuals at scale, making traditional ways of manually detecting and preventing such fraud inefficient (Herley, 2010).

DOI: 10.4324/9781003017189-9

The chapter is organized as follows. We will first examine what online consumer fraud is, revisiting the definition and common fraud schemes described in the chapter by Anderson (2022). This is followed by a review of some of the current approaches (non-)governmental and commercial institutions take to detect and prevent online consumer fraud. We will then discuss darknet markets – internet platforms that, amongst other things, sell both legal and illicit goods while providing anonymity (Christin, 2013) – and how they facilitating online consumer fraud. The chapter closes with a discussion of how methods from data science can be applied to support the detection and prevention of online consumer fraud.

Common online consumer fraud types on the surface web

For this chapter, we focus on online consumer fraud committed on the surface web (e.g. on eBay, Amazon, etc.) and define fraud in this context as transactions in which the consumer is deceived in some way and during which they are unaware that fraudulent activity is taking place. We limit our attention to fraud such as unauthorized billing, the non-delivery of goods ordered or services from legitimate or fraudulent websites, or fraud that requires the theft of their credentials (e.g. via phishing websites) (Anderson, 2019). Such types of fraud can often be deployed at scale (as discussed in the chapter by Anderson, 2022) and require little sustained attention from the fraudster. These types of offenses differ from other types of fraud such as romance or advanced fees scams, which require sustained effort on the part of the fraudster and typically include activity that cannot be automated easily. We focus our attention on the former because we believe that these types of offenses – which generally involve only one or no interaction with a victim – will be easier to address using approaches from data science. Data science approaches often rely on automated detection systems, which are difficult to deploy if a personal conversation between individuals is taking place (with the exceptions of e-mail spam filters). Furthermore, to successfully implement automated detection methods, the required data need to be accessible and usable, as in open or public domains, such as online marketplaces. Thus, we will discuss common online consumer fraud types, which are more suitable to be addressed by data science methods.

Fraudulent billings

One of the most common fraud schemes involves billings for products or services that the customer did not agree to (Anderson, 2019). They can occur on websites where a customer believes they are making a one-time order and payment but are in fact signing up for a subscription of some kind. Similarly, free trials for which a subscription is about to terminate can be extended without the approval of – but at a cost to – the customer. It has been estimated that unapproved billings through fraudulent websites accounted for a monetary loss of $48 million in the USA alone in 2018 FBI (2018). However, such estimates are based solely on complaints made to the FBI and – given that most (online) crime goes unreported (up to 85%) (Office for National Statistics, 2020) – provide only a partial picture. Different forms of such web pages exist but include those that masquerade as pages created by legitimate companies or governments, with consumers being directed to them in various ways including false advertisements on social media platforms, e-mails, text messages,[1] and so on. These pages generally mimic the appearance of the official websites in a convincing manner which contributes to consumers being lured in.[2]

Non-deliveries

Another common form of online consumer fraud is non-delivery fraud. In the simplest form of this type of offending online, the buyer and seller transact in an online marketplace, but while the seller receives payment, the product is never sent to the buyer (Anderson, 2019). For some online platforms (e.g. eBay), the buyer has the option of writing a negative seller review and flagging the fraud quickly, which can make it difficult for offenders to sustain their activity using the same seller account over a prolonged period (Bauerly, 2009). However, this does not prevent fraud from taking place in the first place. According to the FBI, this type of offending accounts for monetary losses of more than $180 million per annum in the USA (FBI, 2017, 2018).

In other variations of this offense, the seller convinces the customer to pay for the goods or service outside of the marketplace on which it was advertised (e.g., using a cheque, cash, or fake escrow). This type of fraud involves more effort on the part of the seller because it requires them to convince the customer to transact outside of the original platform. However, where successful, the online platform cannot confirm purchases, which makes the flagging of the fraud more difficult, allowing fraudsters to maintain their account for longer.

In other instances of this type of offense, the product may be misrepresented, with the customer receiving an item of lower value, they may receive the packaging but not the actual item, or the product may be wrongly delivered on purpose. In the latter case, the seller has proof that an item was delivered and can shift the blame toward the delivery service, which makes it more difficult to resolve the problem.

Commonalities in online fraud schemes

The above-mentioned fraud schemes differ in how they are executed, but they all typically involve or require the presence of open or publicly available websites. Since these websites can be observed and data scraped from them, this presents the opportunity to do something about them using techniques from data science. Moreover, since such methods can be automated, with appropriate planning, they might be addressed in a scalable way. Such techniques can also be applied to other types of fraud not mentioned above, such as fraudulent computer repairs (Miramirkhani et al., 2017) or fraud-related phishing websites, which can be prompted through pop-ups or false advertisements on any webpage (Anderson, 2019, 2022; Christin et al., 2010).

Current strategies to prevent and resolve online consumer fraud

Online consumer fraud takes place in an environment in which many different industries and sectors converge. Commercial enterprises, non-governmental and governmental organizations adopt different strategies to deal with such fraud, and these are outlined in Table 9.1.

The commercial sector aims to maximize profit by deploying brand protection methods and removing fraudsters from "seller" webpages. This is mostly achieved by actively searching for violations manually or using semi-automated approaches (Ganguly, 2015; Pointer Brand Protection, 2019; Yellow Brand Protection, 2019). In turn, non-governmental organizations mostly focus on trying to support (vulnerable) customers by informing them about different types of fraud to heighten their awareness of them. The goal with such strategies is to increase the likelihood that customers will spot fraudulent activities or listings while they are online and act accordingly (Beals et al., 2015; Deevy & Beals, 2013; DeLiema et al., 2019; Peaston, 2019; Stanford Center on Longevity, 2019). The success of such strategies requires guidance to be up to date, for consumers to be exposed to it, and for them to act upon it. While this approach is undoubtedly useful, a lot has to go right for it to work and it should be noted that awareness does not equate with effectiveness (in

Table 9.1 Summary of How Different Sectors Address Online Consumer Fraud

Sector	*Motivation*	*Strategy*	*Actions/Controls*	*How to Resolve Fraud*
Commercial industry (Ganguly, 2015; Pointer Brand Protection, 2019; Vistalworks, 2019; Yellow Brand Protection, 2019)	• Maximizing profit	• Hiring brand protection companies	• Searching for brand violations (manually, semi-automatically – "AI") in product/service domain • Reacting to complaints	• Contacting fraudsters • Notifying fraud to company/platform • pursuing legal actions
		• Creating internal divisions to detect fraud (e.g. eBay, Amazon)	• In-person visits • Test purchases • Customer flagging systems • Automated monitoring of item sales, transactions, and product view ratios	• Removing sellers from the webpage
Non-governmental (e.g. Cifas) (Beals et al., 2015; Deevy & Beals, 2013; DeLiema et al., 2019; Peaston, 2019; Stanford Center on Longevity, 2019)	• Protect (vulnerable) customers	• Using surveys to estimate fraud prevalence and to identify vulnerable customers • Creating fraud avoidance guidelines	Recommending individuals to scrutinize: • seller feedback and comments • price and seller history	• Increase the likelihood of consumers spotting suspicious listings

Sector	Motivation	Strategy	Actions/Controls	How to Resolve Fraud
Law enforcement (e.g. FBI, Trading Standards) (FBI, 2018; Great Britain & National Audit Office, 2016; Intellectual Property Office, personal communication, 2019; Raine et al., 2015; Trading Standards UK, personal communication, February 26, 2019a, personal communication, May 17, 2019b)	• Deter/detect criminals, reduce the negative financial impact on society	• Respond to fraud complaints, intelligence about fraud • Prioritizing fraud types and cases depending on financial damage	• Manual investigation of received intelligence • Cross-referencing of product and seller information	• Find, identify, and deter fraudsters • Inform affected platform

prevention). Law enforcement takes a more reactive approach by responding to complaints and intelligence about fraud, which are investigated to find, prosecute and subsequently deter fraudsters (FBI, 2018; Intellectual Property Office, personal communication, 2019; Trading Standards UK, personal communication, February 26, 2019a, personal communication, May 17, 2019b) (see Table 9.1).

Current strategies used to combat online consumer fraud by the commercial sector and law enforcement are heavily reliant on identifiable information about online users and vendors. In a non-anonymous space, such as the surface web, identifying individuals is generally feasible, as long as users register for accounts using names, e-mails, or other information that can be used to identify them. In addition, the activity of their computers can be tracked through their IP address, making geolocation possible, unless they use techniques to obscure this. Thus, authorities have some tools at hand to move against fraudsters. However, these approaches become extremely difficult on the dark web, in which users and vendors have anonymity and no trackable IP address. With this anonymity, the dark web provides a supportive space for online consumer fraud, in which individuals not only openly sell counterfeits but also sell fraud enabling services (e.g. high-rated eBay accounts, defrauding strategies, etc.). Therefore, it is important to examine the dark web to explore the prevalence of consumer fraud-enabling products and services in this space and to find methods of combating it. To do so, we will first describe what the dark web is, how it can be accessed, and how users sell goods as well as interact with each other on it. As will be seen, exploring each of these aspects provides potential insight as to how to tackle consumer fraud on the surface web.

The dark web

The Internet can be segmented into three sections which are characterized by how it can be accessed and how users communicate with each other: the surface web, the deep web, and the dark web (Figure 9.1) (Biddle et al., 2003; Mansfield-Devine, 2009).

The surface web is the Internet we usually encounter and includes platforms such as eBay, YouTube, and news sites. Put differently, it contains the online content that is indexed by openly accessible search engines (Bergman, 2001; He et al., 2007) such as Google's.

The deep web represents the part of the internet that is not indexed by search engines and cannot easily be accessed. Content is often password-protected or restricted in other ways (e.g., requiring authentication). Online banking, webmail, or paywall content would fall within this category. Historic estimates (Bergman, 2001; He et al., 2007) suggest that the deep web is

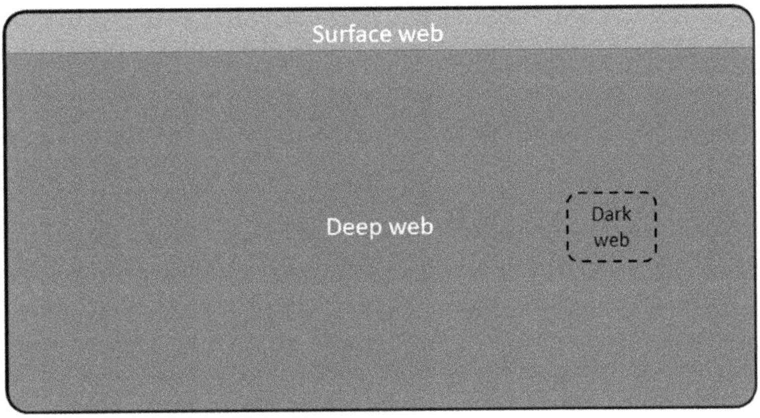

Figure 9.1 The World Wide Web subdivided into the surface, deep, and dark web. The domain proportions are approximations, as the deep web would dwarf the other domains to be unrecognizable.

400–550 times larger than the surface web in terms of the amount of information (data) and web pages stored. The deep web is believed to be the fastest-growing category of the internet, but it is difficult to estimate its current size precisely, as it is not openly indexed. For both the surface and deep web individual users and servers are not automatically anonymous.

The dark web represents a small portion of the deep web, on which users and hosts are anonymized. Anonymization can be facilitated through different technologies, such as The Onion Router (Tor) (The Tor Project, Inc., 2020) or the Invisible Internet Project (I2P) (The Invisible Internet Project, 2020). Such methods hide the identities of users by sending their data through a network of computers and servers that use protocols to conceal their IP addresses and serve as relays (Gehl, 2018). Hosts using this system can provide web pages called "onion sites". Navigating to an onion site requires an exact address, as they are not indexed by search engines and the administrative markers, such as ".com", ".net", or country codes, such as ".de" (Germany), ".us" (United States) are replaced by ".onion" (Ghosh et al., 2017b). While the darknet was not developed with malicious intent in mind, the safety of anonymous communications makes illegal activities less dangerous as some of the usual information that is used to track fraudsters is removed (see Figure 9.1).

The Tor network, which is perhaps the most widely known, can be accessed through the Tor client which functions like a regular browser. The ease of entering the dark web makes it accessible to many individuals, some of whom will want to engage in fraudulent activities. Estimates of the number of ".onion" web pages range from 3700 to 32,000, with a maximum of around 13,000 exhibiting prolonged activity (Ghosh et al., 2017b; Hyperion Gray, 2019; Lewis, 2016).

Markets on the dark web

The dark web harbors selling platforms, which are called "black markets," "cryptomarkets," or "dark(net) markets," which offer various products and services (Christin, 2013; Gehl, 2018). These platforms are not online shops but — like markets such as eBay — provide spaces for users to transact (Soska & Christin, 2015). Similarly, like eBay, platform providers receive a small margin of each monetary transaction. Darknet market transactions are anonymized through the use of cryptocurrencies, which can be obtained from online exchanges (e.g., Coinbase). Most of these currencies are based on a peer-to-peer system that does not rely on a bank or other centralized third party (Soska & Christin, 2015) (for more information on cryptocurrencies, see Chapter 10 of this book by Kamps et al., 2021). The use of cryptocurrencies as well as anonymized communications further facilitates illegal activity and makes tracking fraudsters very difficult. The Silk Road, which was the first commonly known darknet market, started operating in February 2011 and used Bitcoin (BTC) as a medium of transaction. Buyers did not pay the seller directly but used an escrow system — a form of holding area — embedded within the platform. Escrow systems allow platform operators to compute commissions as well as to supervise transactions between buyers and sellers to ensure that products are shipped (or services are provided) only after payments have been received (Christin, 2013). Thus, transactions can be completed in a highly anonymized space, in which accountability is otherwise almost absent.

Estimates suggest that for larger markets (e.g., Silk Road 1 & 2, Agora, AlphaBay), about 50–80% of all category listings (Demant et al., 2018; Europol, 2017; Soska & Christin, 2015) are for various forms of drugs (e.g. marijuana, amphetamines). However, a large range of other products are also typically offered including weapons, counterfeit goods, guides for malicious activities, stolen credit or debit card information, other personal data (e.g. log-in credentials), or services such as hacking attacks, or secure hosting (Adamsson, 2017; Du et al., 2018; van Wegberg et al., 2018). By way of an example, Figure 9.2 shows a screenshot from one darknet market – AlphaBay.

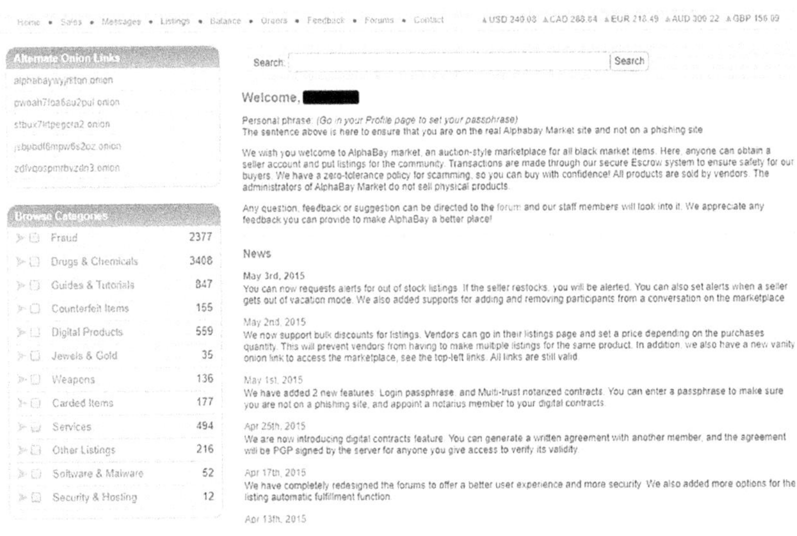

Figure 9.2 Screenshot of the homepage from AlphaBay (Branwen et al., 2015).

Examining darknet markets more closely is important as doing so offers a lens through which to understand online consumer fraud from a different perspective than the surface web. However, since all communication is anonymized, it is very difficult to retrieve market or user information (see Figure 9.2).

Obtaining darknet market data

Collecting darknet market data can be complicated as such data are rarely shared by the platforms. One way of collecting darknet market data is by visiting the websites as a user and retrieve it manually. However, the most commonly used method is to employ a web scraper that revisits markets at set intervals (e.g., once a day) over weeks, months, or longer (Ghosh et al., 2017a). Such web scrapers retrieve information from a web page and download it to a local machine. Employing web scrapers is relatively straightforward on the open web, it is time-consuming on the dark web due to the rerouting of page requests – necessary to create anonymity – through the Tor network, which takes significantly longer than on the surface web. Moreover, since darknet market sites often have different layouts, almost all scrapers need to be coded individually for each website (Du et al., 2018; Hayes et al., 2018). Also, researchers are often faced with unexpected problems during the scraping process, which requires a constant review of the collected data. This can entail changes in accessibility credentials, changes in the layout of the page, or downtime of the host (Ball et al., 2019; Ghosh et al., 2017b). Given that scraping is the predominant method of obtaining darknet market data, discussions of these challenges are well-rehearsed elsewhere and the interested reader is referred to in many studies (Ball et al., 2019; Du et al., 2018; Ghosh et al., 2017b; Van Buskirk et al., 2014, 2015, 2016).

Darknet markets economies

The Silk Road 1 operated from 2011 to 2013 and was the first darknet market studied by researchers, who examined what and how much was being sold (Christin, 2013). This darknet market had between 30,000 and 150,000 active customers, 220 distinct product categories, and vendors who made an overall monthly revenue of $1.2 million in 2012 (Christin, 2013). Drugs were predominately offered, and half of all products sold were shipped worldwide, mostly originating from the US (43%), followed by the UK (10%), and the Netherlands (6%). In their study, Soska and Christin (2015) estimated transactional and sales volumes through the analysis of product feedback for 32 different marketplaces for the period 2014–2015. They concluded that sales volumes typically varied between $300,000–$500,000 per day. With an estimation of 9,386 unique vendors across markets, 70% made less than $1,000 during their active time on the platform, while 1% accounted for more than half of all sales (Soska & Christin, 2015).

Baravalle and Lee (2018) examined AlphaBay between 2015 and 2017 and estimated sales to reach $79.8 million over the two years, with $69.2 million of this attributed to drugs & chemicals alone. They also estimated that $1.7 million of sales were generated from fraud (e.g., the sale of fake IDs, or accounts), $1.6 million from counterfeit items, $1.4 million from hacking attacks or server hosting, $748,544 from software & malware, $210,000 from guides & tutorials about committing fraud, $198,000 from digital products, $35,990 from security & hosting, and $125,472 from other listings. This suggested that counterfeit goods and goods and services related to fraud were well represented on the market.

A study by van Wegberg et al. (2018) investigating cybercrime commodities on eight darknet markets between 2011 and 2017, and estimated a revenue of at least $15 million. The study showed that business-to-consumer rather than business-to-business transactions were taken place and that cybercrime commodity trade exhibits some overall growth.

Multinational governmental institutions, such as Europol, are increasingly interested in darknet markets, particularly those associated with the drug economy, but also those that facilitate intellectual property (IP) crimes (EMCDDA-Europol, 2017; Europol, 2017). Based on data from five darknet markets (AlphaBay, Dream Market, Hansa, TradeRoute, and Valhalla), Europol estimate that fraud and counterfeits accounted for around 17% of all listings. Examining AlphaBay specifically, EMCDDA-Europol (2017) estimated that 10,000 products were counterfeit goods. Fake banknotes and IDs were the most frequent, but clothes, electronics, jewelry, software, e-books, subscriptions, and watches were also common. Fraud seemed to be well represented too, accounting for around 22% of all listings on Alphabay (Adamsson, 2017). Europol (2017) reports that vendors often sold small amounts, mostly specialized in one type of product, but were present in several different markets at the same time. EMCDDA-Europol (2017) concluded that IP crimes were increasing in darknet markets, but that products are not always clearly categorized, which makes it difficult to accurately estimate volumes of offers and sales.

Vendor and user behavior

The sale of products or services on the Internet requires a level of trust between the customer and vendor. This is true on both the surface and dark web, with trust often established through feedback systems such as reviews or ratings. For most dark web markets, reviews can only be submitted after a verified purchase (verified by the escrow system) and some markets make reviews mandatory (Calis, 2018). Since everyone is anonymous and no public or physical stores exist, the review system is a particularly important feature of dark web markets, along with escrow. Although there are no findings of fraud on darknet markets, the presence of such review, escrow, and registration procedures seem to suggest that fraud occurs frequently. Such security procedures are not new but are still often missing on regular surface web platforms; it would be interesting to investigate their effects on the prevalence of fraud on the surface web.

Methods of vendor identification

Identifying individuals on the dark web is inherently difficult due to their anonymity (Gehl, 2018; The Invisible Internet Project, 2020; The Tor Project, Inc., 2020). Nonetheless, some studies have analyzed text data or product photos to attempt to identify individuals or vendors with different user names that operate across platforms (Ho & Ng, 2016; Wang, 2018; Wang et al., 2018). Photos are important in markets since they serve as a form of proof that the vendor owns the product advertised. At the same time, pictures are only one aspect of building trust and they should be identifiably different from one vendor to the next, to highlight ownership. Therefore, Wang et al. (2018) suggested that photo styles could serve as an identification of vendors across markets. To examine whether this was plausible, they used transfer learning, for which a machine learning classifier was pre-trained on a large data set (ImageNet) and further fine-tuned by retraining it on a smaller data set (vendor-specific photos). The task for the classifier was to identify whether two or more vendors were the same based on nothing but the images used. The model performed well for a single market for which a subset of vendor and photo associations were known. However, the performance was more difficult to assess for matches across markets as their true association was unknown. Nevertheless, the approach offers a possible identification methodology for an otherwise anonymized environment, which, although not suggested by the authors, could also prove useful on the surface web. For example, once a fraudulent vendor is identified, other vendor accounts across platforms (e.g. eBay, Amazon) operated by the same fraudster(s) might also be identified in that manner.

In a different study, a series of automated methods, combined with manual investigations, were used to identify vendors on darknet markets (Hayes et al., 2018). The researchers collected data from vendors and their associated listings from an undisclosed collection of darknet markets. Using Maltego, which conducts automated surface web cross-referencing (Paterva, 2019), they searched for obtained (darknet) e-mail addresses, usernames, and other personally identifiable information, and were able to identify some darknet market vendors on the surface web. As noted by the authors, this approach has some limitations associated with identifiers, which are similar to high-frequency words. For example, a username, which resembles a popular brand or product name (e.g., Coca-Cola), would lead to meaningless cross-referencing. Nevertheless, their results suggest that the automated identification of some individuals is possible, but can be easily disrupted when users employ countermeasures, such as adapting their identifiable information (e.g. username, e-mail address) accordingly.

Importantly, the methods outlined show possible ways of identifying vendors across darknet markets, which might also be applicable, in some circumstances, for the identification of fraudsters across markets on the surface web as well as fraudulent products between the dark and the surface web.

The role of data science

Data science has been previously defined as "a set of fundamental principles that support and guide the principled extraction of information and knowledge from data" (Provost & Fawcett, 2013, p. 2). This definition captures a high-level perspective, but data science also involves "statistics, or the systematic study of the organization, properties, and analysis of data and its role in inference, including our confidence in the inference" (Dhar, 2013, p. 1). Thus, data science draws from many disciplines, including computer science, mathematics, statistics, and, importantly, the knowledge domain of the data in question (Dhar, 2013; Provost & Fawcett, 2013). In the realm of online consumer fraud, data science can be utilized to speed up or scale up manual processes, such as collecting, cross-referencing, and analyzing information from advertisements, product listings, sellers, or webpages to identify if they are likely to be fraudulent. Such methods will be reviewed in this section by looking at current and possible future applications and their associated advantages and disadvantages.

Current data science approaches in the academic literature

Current data science methods applied to online consumer fraud on the surface web mainly focus on the automated detection of specific types of fraud. For example, Pandit et al. (2007) collected eBay data and modeled the topological connections (i.e. the network) between sellers and buyers using transaction data. They hypothesized that fraudsters, who commit the crime, should be heavily connected to accomplices, whose role is to boost the fraudsters' feedback ratings. Accomplices are needed as they can continue to operate once the fraudster is banned from the site, retaining any positive ratings they accumulate. As such, fraudsters would be expected to have fewer connections to honest users than they would have to accomplices. Thus, the authors describe that fraudsters have many connections to accomplices, but the accomplices nor the fraudsters are interconnected, forming near bipartite cores, instead of cliques, which exhibit strong interconnectedness. The automated detection of such bipartite cores was evaluated on a synthetic network, containing over 66,000 nodes and 795,000 edges. The network was filled with artificial fraudster-accomplice structures of random sizes, which were detect with around 90% accuracy. An additional network was created from scraped eBay data, which contained ten known fraudsters who were identified through manual inspections and investigative media reports. All ten fraudsters were automatically detected by the authors' devised model. As the researchers discuss, the evaluation based on the analysis of the eBay data set has limitations since no fraud detections (other than those already detected through a manual investigation) could be verified. As such, additional verification of the models' performance through a well-labeled data set would be needed to determine its applicability (Pandit et al., 2007).

Hernandez-Castro and Roberts (2015) used an automated detection method that can process data without human interventions, to try to identify illegal sales of elephant ivory on eBay. Two former law enforcement officers annotated 1,159 product listings as selling ivory or not. Utilizing the CN2 induction algorithm (Clark & Niblett, 1989), which made decisions based on metadata parameters of the listings (e.g., item price, number of reviews), the framework was able to categorize almost all listings correctly. The advantage of the CN2 algorithm (a supervised machine learning method) is that it induces decision rules, which can be inspected to gain an understanding of the sale strategies of the potential fraudsters. Other supervised machine learning methods, such as random forest or logistic regressions, are also interpretable, but many others, such as neural networks, can be black boxes, since the decision rules are generated automatically, making it difficult to understand the inner workings of the classification system and hence the possible fraud strategies. While the system developed by Hernandez-Castro and Roberts (2015) could find suspicious online listings quickly, without manual searchers, it is difficult to assess the reliability of their current classifier, as the true labels of the listings (selling ivory or not) were not known and no interrater reliability score between the annotators was reported (Hernandez-Castro & Roberts, 2015). However, a similar approach of using domain experts to label instances of online consumer fraud (e.g. counterfeits on eBay) could be helpful. For example, classifiers trained using these data could then act as a pre-selection (or triaging) tool by labeling suspicious listings. Although such an approach does not eliminate the problem of falsely labeled fraudsters, it could reduce the number of listings experts subsequently have to investigate, reducing the overall workload. The model could then be updated after each investigation to increase its performances and reduce false positives.

Other researchers have utilized supervised classification methods. These are trained and tested on different subsets of labeled data (Chang & Chang, 2012; Sahingoz et al., 2019; Xu et al., 2016). In the training phase, supervised machine learning classifiers learn to infer from the features (e.g., metadata or writing style of the advertisements) what the corresponding label (e.g. fraudulent versus legitimate, or same versus different account holder of a vendor profile) of a data point is likely to be. The goal is typically to find a combination of features that enable the best discrimination of the outcome labels. The labels are obtained through manual annotations, which can be time-consuming, particularly where a large volume of labels is required. However, the advantage of such approaches is that they can uncover previously unknown patterns within the data and utilize these to classify unlabeled data. Such methods find a wide range of applications that can be utilized on the dark as well as the surface web, depending on the discriminatory problem.

Chang and Chang (2012) used decision trees, another type of supervised classification method, to detect fraud on the Yahoo Taiwan online auction site. The method was trained on the history of sellers' activities and the sellers were labeled as legitimate or fraudulent, depending upon whether they had been blacklisted from the auction site or not. While the performance of the model was promising, the labeling process makes the evaluation problematic. That is, it remains unclear why users were blacklisted and whether and how many genuine sellers were falsely blacklisted. Supervised machine learning methods have also been employed to detect phishing websites by examining their URL (Sahingoz et al., 2019) or HTML-structure (Xu et al., 2016). The approach is the same as that described above – using an annotated data set the algorithm learns to associate the URLs or the webpage's HTML structure with the correct label to infer a decision rule. This is then used to classify new incoming data (webpages) that do not have labels. A similar approach can also be applied to classify webpages on the dark web, to automatically identify what type of webpage it is (e.g. a marketplace versus a discussion forum), and what is being discussed or sold (Ghosh et al., 2017b).

An important aspect of machine learning is that many (but not all) supervised methods rely on the selection and crafting of informative features, which are the parameters the algorithms learn from. Thus, the goal is often to create features that are readable by the algorithm and convey a high amount of information. Machine learning methods need numerical features to work, which means that in the case of non-numerical data, such as text, the creation of features becomes more complicated as it requires the data to be converted to numerical representations. This can be achieved using Natural Language Processing (NLP) methods, which essentially work at the intersection of computer and human language, to bridge the understanding of the two domains (Jurafsky & Martin, 2019; Nadkarni et al., 2011). By utilizing NLP methods, text (e.g., characters, words, sentences) can be converted to numerical data, which can be processed and analyzed by a computer. This can be as simple as creating frequencies of words that occur in the text, but also includes numerical representations of grammatical structures or semantic meanings (Goldberg & Levy, 2014). For a more detailed overview of NLP methods and how they function, readers are referred to Goldberg (2016), Jurafsky and Martin (2019), and Nadkarni et al. (2011).

Supervised machine learning methods are powerful tools, which can uncover previously unknown patterns in large amounts of data. However, they need well-created data sets, with suitable features and labels, which are not always easy to obtain. In particular, the labeling process is often problematic as the "ground-truth" of the labels is often unknown (see above).

Ground-truth

In the context of this chapter, ground-truth refers to the true labels of a data set. The knowledge about ground-truth or certainty of the label could be about an item on a selling platform, a confession, or anything else. In an experimental setting, in which researchers have full control, true labels can be obtained. For example, participants might be asked to test a pair of purchased headphones, followed by instructions to write an honest and fake review (with opposing sentiments) about them. However, outside of an experimental setting, and in most other cases, the ground-truth is not as unambiguous and only a level of certainty can be attributed to a particular data point. For example, how would we know if a shoe advertised on an online platform was counterfeit or legitimate? A common strategy employed by consumers is to choose a reputable seller by inspecting their ratings and reviews (Dellarocas, 2006; Houser & Wooders, 2006; Melnik & Alm, 2003; Resnick et al., 2000). To provide a better label, an expert could assess the listing, or, better still, order a pair of shoes and compare them to a sample purchased directly from the manufacturer. Each method will provide an assessment of the listing with different levels of certainty about the labels (counterfeit vs. genuine) associated with an item or event.

In many cases, obtaining labels with a high degree of certainty will either be impossible or costly in terms of time, money, or both (Raine et al., 2015). In some instances officials from online marketplaces or law enforcement (e.g. Trading Standards) order products from sellers or visit the sellers' physical locations to conduct manual inspections (Ganguly, 2015; Raine et al., 2015) but this is costly. Furthermore, transparency during the labeling process is important as is the clear conveyance of the label's limitations, to ensure that a judgment about the associated certainty of the labels is possible, without needing further expert knowledge. This is especially important to law enforcement, for whom resources are limited and misallocations can be costly. The strategy to minimize mislabeling is to reduce false positives labels (e.g., mislabeling a genuine product to be fraudulent) and false-negative labels (e.g., mislabeling a fraudulent product to be genuine). Training a model to work well on a poorly labeled data set is of little value and, consequently, the determination of the data labels on which a supervised model is trained is paramount. Therefore, the value of a model should not be judged on performance metrics alone, but also on how the data were acquired and labeled for each context.

Possible future data science applications

As described above, current data science approaches often focus on supervised machine learning methods which would support a proactive approach to the detection of possible frauds on the surface web before people are affected. However, given how the labels used for these approaches are obtained, it is unclear if such detections should always warrant a lawful intervention (Chang & Chang, 2012; Hernandez-Castro & Roberts, 2015; Pandit et al., 2007; Xu et al., 2016). That said, these approaches could be used to presort and prioritize cases (e.g. suspicious advertisements, sellers, webpages) which authorities could then focus on manually, making better use of limited resources.

Other areas in which data science methods could alleviate the current workload of law enforcement are in gathering, pooling, and analyzing information about reported items, services, sellers, or webpages (Great Britain & National Audit Office, 2016; Raine et al., 2015; Trading Standards UK, personal communication, February 26, 2019a).

Automation of manual tasks

An initial step in alleviating the workload would be to automate the standard processes of gathering and pooling information relevant to a reported online fraud, (e.g. reported from a consumer or a company). Information gathering and pooling could be addressed by using rule-based systems that could automatically collect information (e.g. telephone numbers, e-mail addresses, prices, product or seller names) from webpages. Additional automated web searches could supplement and cross-reference the existing information, including whether they exist and in what capacity they are registered (e.g., does the physical address of the seller exist, and is the business legally registered with the relevant authority?).

Uncovering unknown patterns in existing data

Existing data could be analyzed using unsupervised machine learning methods that do not rely on labeled training data. Here, the idea is to cluster the data based on inherent traits to find common features or properties that may not be directly apparent (Arthur & Vassilvitskii, 2006; Ester et al., 1996; Liu et al., 2012). For example, a consumer-reported incident of fraud or counterfeit items on shopping platforms might be clustered into several groups. These groups could be based on similarities in their descriptions, prices, item locations, and so on. Such similarities could point toward meaningful associations, which may open up new leads in an investigation. For example, where items are identified as sharing features, such as similar descriptions, seller locations, and images, but that are advertised by sellers with different usernames, might point to a common seller that wishes to conceal their identity and fraudulent activity.

Understanding online markets at scale

It is important to understand the online markets in which consumer fraud occurs as it places the reported fraud cases into context and may inform new fraud detection strategies. Data science can help in accumulating, structuring, and analyzing data for online markets, such as eBay, Amazon, Alibaba, or any darknet market. By devising scraping methods for these markets, large amounts of data for products and sellers can be collected. Through NLP methods it is also possible to operationalize and measure text characteristics and styles from titles, descriptions, reviews, and so on. Understanding markets with such data will (we hope) enable us to update our beliefs about common product and seller characteristics, and determine what constitutes "normal", and understand how fraudsters might behave.

Utilizing darknet markets to identify consumer fraud on the surface web

Identifying illegal activity on the surface web is a challenge since most products and services are advertised as being genuine or legal. In contrast, on the dark web, most of the services are, by definition, illegal, and generally advertised with no effort made to conceal this. This raises an interesting possibility — could information found on the dark web serve as a source of intelligence to determine what illegal activity is or might happen on the surface web. Although categories on dark markets surrounding consumer fraud only represent a small portion (17%) of what is sold or traded (EMCDDA-Europol, 2017; Europol, 2017), they are often labeled as such. Thus, such information could serve as a source of ground-truth data for illegal products and services on the surface web, where most fraudulent sales occur. Moreover, to increase profits, it appears that vendors sell on multiple darknet markets *and* the surface web (Europol, 2017), suggesting that cross-domain referencing could be of value.

As far as we are aware, to date, research has not examined this possibility of using such data to inform fraudulent product identification on the surface web. The focus of such cross-referencing would be the identification of counterfeit goods, which is the main category of items on the dark web that also appears on the surface web. However, fraud-related categories, such as personal credentials, guides, and tutorials, may also be of interest. For example, if hacked seller accounts (e.g., eBay) or specific fraud strategies are frequently advertised, their occurrence could represent an indicator of security breaches, which might be worth investigating. To examine the feasibility of such a cross-referencing approach, historical darknet data could be compared to law enforcement data sets of online consumer fraud for the same periods. In the case that such connections can be made, further work could focus on monitoring current darknet markets and cross-referencing them with current listings on the surface web. Since counterfeits on darknet markets are mostly clearly labeled and contain many product details (e.g. name, price, pictures, and description), a similar automated cross-referencing approach could be taken as has previously been described in studies (see above) that have sought to identify individual vendors (Hayes et al., 2018). Identifying fraud (enabling) services, such as hosting phishing sites or well established eBay accounts from the dark web on the surface web, might not be as easy to identify, as they often do not have similar listed details as fraudulent products before the sale (Thomas et al., 2015). However, depending on the level of details provided by vendors offering such services, these listings could also serve as an informative tool for researchers seeking to identify illegal activity on the surface web.

Conclusion

The costs associated with online consumer fraud are significant and the detection and their prevention using data science approaches have seen some progress. However, they are not yet well integrated or used outside of the academic literature. Using and implementing data science methods is complicated by a range of factors, such as the interplay of different sectors and jurisdictions that are affected, seller anonymity, and data labeling. A pressing issue is the volume of fraud complaints, most of which cannot be dealt with appropriately due to the lack of personnel and the highly time-consuming manual processing of such cases. Data science approaches would offer some help in automating and speeding up this (currently) manual work. Furthermore, darknet markets are increasingly utilized to sell fraudulent products online, such as counterfeits, or fraud enabling services. However, it is still unclear to what extent and how fraudulent transactions on these markets are related to those on the surface web. Nevertheless, such dark web listings could serve as an informative tool for detecting and identifying fraudulent behavior on the surface web.

Notes

1 For example, https://www.actionfraud.police.uk/alert/fake-dpd-messages-lead-to-over-200000-in-losses-since-june.
2 For an example, https://www.gov.uk/government/publications/phishing-and-bogus-emails-hm-revenue-and-customs-examples/phishing-emails-and-bogus-contact-hm-revenue-and-customs-examples.

References

Ablon, L., Libicki, M., & Abler, A. (2014). *Markets for Cybercrime Tools and Stolen Data: Hackers' Bazaar*. RAND Corporation. https://doi.org/10.7249/RR610

Adamsson, H. (2017). *Classification of Illegal Advertisement*. Uppsala University.

Anderson, K. (2019). *Mass-Market Consumer Fraud in the United States: A 2017 Update*. Bureau of Economics, Federal Trade Commission.

Anderson, K. (2022). Mass-Market Consumer Frauds: What the Data Show. In S. Wood & Y. Hanoch (ed.) *A Fresh Look at Fraud: Theoretical and Applied Approaches*. Routledge.

Anderson, R., Barton, C., Böhme, R., Clayton, R., van Eeten, M. J. G., Levi, M., Moore, T., & Savage, S. (2013). Measuring the Cost of Cybercrime. In R. Böhme (Ed.), *The Economics of Information Security and Privacy* (pp. 265–300). Springer: Berlin Heidelberg. https://doi.org/10.1007/978-3-642-39498-0_12

Arthur, D., & Vassilvitskii, S. (2006). *k-means++: The Advantages of Careful Seeding*. Stanford.

Ball, M., Broadhurst, R., Niven, A., & Trivedi, H. (2019). *Data Capture and Analysis of Darknet Markets*.

Baravalle, A., & Lee, S. W. (2018). Dark Web Markets: Turning the Lights on AlphaBay. In H. Hacid, W. Cellary, H. Wang, H.-Y. Paik, & R. Zhou (Eds.), *Web Information Systems Engineering – WISE 2018* (Vol. 11234, pp. 502–514). Springer International Publishing. http://link.springer.com/10.1007/978-3-030-02925-8_35

Bauerly, R. J. (2009). Online Auction Fraud and Ebay. *Marketing Management Journal*, 19(1).

Beals, M., DeLiema, M., & Deevy, M. (2015). *Framework for a Taxonomy of Fraud* (p. 40). Financial Fraud Research Center; Stanford Center on Longevity; FINRA Investor Education Foundation. http://162.144.124.243/~longevl0/wp-content/uploads/2016/03/Full-Taxonomy-report.pdf

Bergman, M. K. (2001). White Paper: The Deep Web: Surfacing Hidden Value. *Journal of Electronic Publishing*, *7*(1). http://dx.doi.org/10.3998/3336451.0007.104

Biddle, P., England, P., Peinado, M., & Willman, B. (2003). The Darknet and the Future of Content Protection. In J. Feigenbaum (Ed.), *Digital Rights Management* (Vol. 2696, pp. 155–176). Springer: Berlin, Heidelberg. https://doi.org/10.1007/978-3-540-44993-5_10

Branwen, G., Christin, N., Décary-Hétu, D., Andersen, R. M., StExo, El Presidente, Anonymous, Lau, D., Sohhlz, Kratunov, D., Cakic, V., Whom, McKenna, M., & Goode, S. (2015). *Dark Net Market archives, 2011–2015* (2015-07-12). https://www.gwern.net/DNM-archives

Calis, T. (2018). *Multi-Homing Sellers and Loyal Buyers on Darknet Markets*.

Chang, W.-H., & Chang, J.-S. (2012). An Effective Early Fraud Detection Method for Online Auctions. *Electronic Commerce Research and Applications*, *11*(4), 346–360. https://doi.org/10.1016/j.elerap.2012.02.005

Christin, N. (2013). Traveling the Silk Road: A Measurement Analysis of a Large Anonymous Online Marketplace. *Proceedings of the 22nd International Conference on World Wide Web – WWW '13*, 213–224. https://doi.org/10.1145/2488388.2488408

Christin, N., Yanagihara, S. S., & Kamataki, K. (2010). Dissecting One Click Frauds. *Proceedings of the 17th ACM Conference on Computer and Communications Security – CCS'10*, 15. https://doi.org/10.1145/1866307.1866310

Clark, P., & Niblett, T. (1989). The CN2 Induction Algorithm. *Machine Learning*, *3*(4), 261–283. https://doi.org/10.1007/BF00116835

Deevy, M., & Beals, M. (2013). *The Scope of the Problem*. Financial Fraud Research Center; Stanford Center on Longevity; FINRA Investor Education Foundation.

DeLiema, M., Fletcher, E., Kieffer, C. N., Mottola, G. R., & Pessanha, R. (2019). *Exposed to Scams. What Separates Victims from Non-victims?* (p. 24). Stanford Center on Longevity, Federal Trade Commission, FINRA Foundation, International Association of Better Business Bureaus, BBB Institute for Marketplace Trust.

DeLiema, M. I., Mottola, G. R., & Deevy, M. (2017). *Findings from a Pilot Study to Measure Financial Fraud in the United States*. Stanford Center on Longevity; FINRA Investor Education Foundation. https://www.ssrn.com/abstract=2914560

Dellarocas, C. (2006). Reputation Mechanisms. In T. Hendershott (Ed.), *Handbook on Economics and Information Systems* (pp. 629–660). Elsevier.

Demant, J., Munksgaard, R., & Houborg, E. (2018). Personal Use, Social Supply or Redistribution? Cryptomarket Demand on Silk Road 2 and Agora. *Trends in Organized Crime, 21*(1), 42–61. https://doi.org/10.1007/s12117-016-9281-4

Dhar, V. (2013). Data Science and Prediction. *Communications of the ACM, 56*(12), 64–73. https://doi.org/10.1145/2500499

Du, P.-Y., Zhang, N., Ebrahimi, M., Samtani, S., Lazarine, B., Arnold, N., Dunn, R., Suntwal, S., Angeles, G., Schweitzer, R., & Chen, H. (2018). Identifying, Collecting, and Presenting Hacker Community Data: Forums, IRC, Carding Shops, and DNMs. *2018 IEEE International Conference on Intelligence and Security Informatics (ISI)*, 70–75. https://doi.org/10.1109/ISI.2018.8587327

EMCDDA-Europol. (2017). *Drugs and the Darknet: Perspectives for Enforcement, Research and Policy*. Publications Office of the European Union.

Ester, M., Kriegel, H.-P., & Xu, X. (1996). A Density-Based Algorithm for Discovering Clusters in Large Spatial Databases with Noise. *Proceedings of the 2nd International Conference on Knowledge Discovery and Data Mining*, Ortland, OR, AAAI Press, 226–231.

Europol. (2017). *Intellectual Property Crime on the Darknet*. Enforcement Cooperation. https://www.europol.europa.eu/publications-documents/intellectual-property-crime-darknet.

FBI. (2017). *2017 Internet Crime Report* (p. 29). Federal Bureau of Investigation.

FBI. (2018). *Internet Crime Report*. Federal Bureau of Investigation. https://pdf.ic3.gov/2018_IC3Report.pdf

Ganguly, P. (January 8, 2015). How E-retailers Such as Flipkart, Amazon Are Keeping the Fake Products at Bay. *The Economic Times*; New Delhi, 2.

Gehl, R. W. (2018). Archives for the Dark Web: A Field Guide for Study. In Lewis Levenberg, T. Neilson, & D. Rheams (Eds.), *Research Methods for the Digital Humanities* (pp. 31–51). Springer International Publishing. https://doi.org/10.1007/978-3-319-96713-4_3

Ghosh, S., Das, A., Porras, P., Yegneswaran, V., & Gehani, A. (2017a). Automated Categorization of Onion Sites for Analyzing the Darkweb Ecosystem. *Proceedings of the 23rd ACM SIGKDD International Conference on Knowledge Discovery and Data Mining – KDD '17*, 1793–1802. https://doi.org/10.1145/3097983.3098193

Ghosh, S., Porras, P., Yegneswaran, V., Nitz, K., & Das, A. (2017b). *ATOL: A Framework for Automated Analysis and Categorization of the Darkweb Ecosystem*. In *Workshops at the Thirty-First AAAI Conference on Artificial Intelligence*.

Goldberg, Y. (2016). A Primer on Neural Network Models for Natural Language Processing. *Journal of Artificial Intelligence Research (JAIR), 57*, 345–420.

Goldberg, Y., & Levy, O. (2014). word2vec Explained: Deriving Mikolov et al.'s Negative-Sampling Word-Embedding Method. *ArXiv:1402.3722 [Cs, Stat]*. http://arxiv.org/abs/1402.3722

Great Britain & National Audit Office. (2016). *Protecting Consumers from Scams, Unfair Trading and Unsafe Goods* (HC 851). National Audit Office; Department for Business, Energy & Industrial Strategy.

Hayes, D., Cappa, F., & Cardon, J. (2018). A Framework for More Effective Dark Web Marketplace Investigations. *Information, 9*(8), 186. https://doi.org/10.3390/info9080186

He, B., Patel, M., Zhang, Z., & Chang, K. C.-C. (2007). Accessing the Deep Web. *Communications of the ACM, 50*(5), 94–101. https://doi.org/10.1145/1230819.1241670

Herley, C. (2010). The Plight of the Targeted Attacker in a World of Scale. *The Ninth Workshop on the Economics of Information Security (WEIS) 2010*, Harvard University, USA, 12.

Hernandez-Castro, J., & Roberts, D. L. (2015). Automatic Detection of Potentially Illegal Online Sales of Elephant Ivory via Data Mining. *PeerJ Computer Science, 1*, e10. https://doi.org/10.7717/peerj-cs.10

Ho, T. N., & Ng, W. K. (2016). Application of Stylometry to DarkWeb Forum User Identification. In K.-Y. Lam, C.-H. Chi, & S. Qing (Eds.), *Information and Communications Security* (Vol. 9977, pp. 173–183). Springer International Publishing. https://doi.org/10.1007/978-3-319-50011-9_14

Houser, D., & Wooders, J. (2006). Reputation in Auctions: Theory, and Evidence from eBay. *Journal of Economics Management Strategy, 15*(2), 353–369. https://doi.org/10.1111/j.1530-9134.2006.00103.x

Hyperion Gray. (2019). *Dark Web Map*. https://www.hyperiongray.com/dark-web-map/#zoom=0.8521016982969332&x=0.5064520330563047&y=0.572866049039204

Intellectual Property Office. (2019). *Annotation Task* [Letter to Felix Soldner].

Jurafsky, D., & Martin, J. H. (2019). *Speech and Language Processing an Introduction to Natural Language Processing, Computational Linguistics, and Speech Recognition—Third Edition Draft*. https://web.stanford.edu/~jurafsky/slp3/

Lewis, S. J. (July 3, 2016). *OnionScan Report June 2016—Snapshots of the Dark Web*. Mascherari Press. https://mascherari.press/onionscan-report-june-2016/

Liu, F. T., Ting, K. M., & Zhou, Z.-H. (2012). Isolation-Based Anomaly Detection. *ACM Transactions on Knowledge Discovery from Data, 6*(1), 1–39. https://doi.org/10.1145/2133360.2133363.

Mansfield-Devine, S. (2009). Darknets. *Computer Fraud & Security, 2009*(12), 4–6. https://doi.org/10.1016/S1361-3723(09)70150-2

Melnik, M. I., & Alm, J. (2003). Does a Seller's eCommerce Reputation Matter? Evidence from eBay Auctions. *The Journal of Industrial Economics, 50*(3), 337–349. https://doi.org/10.1111/1467-6451.00180

Miramirkhani, N., Starov, O., & Nikiforakis, N. (2017). Dial One for Scam: A Large-Scale Analysis of Technical Support Scams. *Proceedings 2017 Network and Distributed System Security Symposium*. Network and Distributed System Security Symposium, San Diego, CA. https://doi.org/10.14722/ndss.2017.23163

Nadkarni, P. M., Ohno-Machado, L., & Chapman, W. W. (2011). Natural Language Processing: An Introduction. *Journal of the American Medical Informatics Association, 18*(5), 544–551. https://doi.org/10.1136/amiajnl-2011-000464

Office for National Statistics. (2020). *Nature of Fraud and Computer Misuse in England and Wales: Year Ending March 2019* (p. 29). Office for National Statistics.

Pandit, S., Chau, D. H., Wang, S., & Faloutsos, C. (2007). Netprobe: A Fast and Scalable System for Fraud Detection in Online Auction Networks. *Proceedings of the 16th International Conference on World Wide Web – WWW '07*, 201. https://doi.org/10.1145/1242572.1242600.

Paterva. (2019). *Paterva Home*. Paterva a New Train of Thought. https://www.paterva.com/index.php

Peaston, S. (2019). *The Fraudscape* (p. 19). Cifas. https://www.cifas.org.uk/secure/contentPORT/uploads/documents/Cifas%20Fraudscape%202019%20Full%20Digital%20Report%20.pdf

Pointer Brand Protection. (2019). *Online Brand Protection with an Impact*. Pointer Brand Protection. https://pointerbrandprotection.com/

Provost, F., & Fawcett, T. (2013). Data Science and Its Relationship to Big Data and Data-Driven Decision Making. *Big Data*, *1*(1), 51–59. https://doi.org/10.1089/big.2013.1508

Raine, J., Mangan, C., & Watt, P. (2015). *The Impact of Local Authority Trading Standards in Challenging Times* (p. 148). The Department for Business, Innovation and Skills and The Trading Standards Institute.

Resnick, P., Kuwabara, K., Zeckhauser, R., & Friedman, E. (2000). Reputation Systems. *Communications of the ACM*, *43*(12), 45–48. https://doi.org/10.1145/355112.355122

Rusch, J. J. (1991). *The "Social Engineering" of Internet Fraud*. 12. http://www.isoc.org/isoc/conferences/inet/99/proceedings/3g/3g_2.htm

Sahingoz, O. K., Buber, E., Demir, O., & Diri, B. (2019). Machine Learning Based Phishing Detection from URLs. *Expert Systems with Applications*, *117*, 345–357. https://doi.org/10.1016/j.eswa.2018.09.029

Soska, K., & Christin, N. (2015). Measuring the Longitudinal Evolution of the Online Anonymous Marketplace Ecosystem. *Proceedings of the 24th USENIX Security Symposium*, 33–48. USENIX Association, Baltimore, MD .

Stanford Center on Longevity. (2019). *Financial Fraud – Stanford Center on Longevity*. http://longevity.stanford.edu/2017/03/29/safeguarding-clients-from-financial-fraud-and-exploitation/.

The Invisible Internet Project. (2020). *I2P Anonymous Network*. https://geti2p.net/en/

The Tor Project, Inc. (2020). *The Tor Project | Privacy & Freedom Online*. https://torproject.org

Thomas, K., Huang, D. Y., Wang, D., Bursztein, E., Grier, C., Holt, T. J., Kruegel, C., McCoy, D., Savage, S., & Vigna, G. (2015). Framing Dependencies Introduced by Underground Commoditization. *14th Workshop on the Economics of Information Security*. WEIS 2015, Delft, Netherlands.

Trading Standards UK. (February 26, 2019a). *Interview about Possible Data Science Solutions* [Personal communication]. London, UK.

Trading Standards UK. (May 17, 2019b). *Interview about Trading Standards Areas of Operations, and Current Issues Concerning Online Crime* [Personal communication]. Northallerton, UK.

Van Buskirk, J., Naicker, S., Bruno, R. B., Breen, C., & Roxburgh. (2016). *Drugs and the Internet*. https://www.drugsandalcohol.ie/20369/1/NDARC_Drugs&TheInternet_Bulletin1.pdf

Van Buskirk, J., Roxburgh, A., Farrell, M., & Burns, L. (2014). The Closure of the Silk Road: What Has This Meant for Online Drug Trading? Editorial. *Addiction*, *109*(4), 517–518. https://doi.org/10.1111/add.12422

Van Buskirk, J., Roxburgh, A., Naicker, S., & Burns, L. (2015). A Response to Dolliver's "Evaluating Drug Trafficking on the Tor Network." *International Journal of Drug Policy*, *26*(11), 1126–1127. https://doi.org/10.1016/j.drugpo.2015.07.001

van Wegberg, R., Tajalizadehkhoob, S., Soska, K., Akyazi, U., Ganan, C., Klievink, B., Christin, N., & van Eeten, M. (2018). Plug and Prey? Measuring the Commoditization of Cybercrime via Online Anonymous Markets. *Proceedings of the 27th USENIX Security Symposium (USENIX Security'18)*, 1009–1026. USENIX Association, Baltimore, MD.

Vistalworks. (2019). *Vistalworks—Keeps Online Shoppers Safe from Harm*. Vistalworks. https://vistalworks.com

Wang, X. (2018). *Photo-Based Vendor Re-identification on Darknet Marketplaces Using Deep Neural Networks* [Master Thesis] Faculty of the Virginia Polytechnic Institute and State University.

Wang, X., Peng, P., Wang, C., & Wang, G. (2018). You Are Your Photographs: Detecting Multiple Identities of Vendors in the Darknet Marketplaces. *Proceedings of the 2018 on Asia Conference on Computer and Communications Security – ASIACCS '18*, 431–442. https://doi.org/10.1145/3196494.3196529

Xu, J.-C., Shin, K., & Liu, Y.-L. (2016). Detecting Fake Sites Based on HTML Structure Analysis. *Proceedings of the 6th International Conference on Communication and Network Security – ICCNS '16*, 86–90. https://doi.org/10.1145/3017971.3017980

Yellow Brand Protection. (2019). *Anti-Counterfeiting | Yellow Brand Protection*. https://www.yellowbrandprotection.com/services/anti-counterfeiting

Cryptocurrencies: Boons and curses for fraud prevention

10

Josh Kamps, Arianna Trozze, and Bennett Kleinberg

Introduction

Cryptocurrencies blend finance and technology. While the long-term success of this has yet to be ascertained, its influence is undeniable; as of February 2021, cryptocurrencies have a market cap of over a trillion dollars (CoinGecko, 2021).

> In a world of fiat currencies, Bitcoin is the victor.

Coined by Guy Adami on CNBC's "Fast Money" program in February 2020, this positive analysis of Bitcoin's achievements succinctly captures the sentiment many actors in the cryptocurrency sector share. This notion of cryptocurrencies' potential has spread from the small group of "cypherpunks" (individuals with a strong interest in privacy and cryptography) who have followed Bitcoin since its inception, to the wider public, all in the span of just 10 years.

While Bitcoin has become embedded in public discourse (which often centers on its notorious price volatility), at the time of writing over 6,000 other

DOI: 10.4324/9781003017189-10

cryptocurrencies and tokens have emerged (CoinGecko, 2021). During 2020, in particular, we witnessed the rise of not just cryptocurrencies, but an entire decentralized financial (DeFi) ecosystem (Schär, 2021; Werner et al., 2021). While intriguing, this marriage of technological complexity and finance may create new opportunities for financial fraud or exacerbate pre-existing ones. It is therefore imperative that as the cryptocurrency ecosystem matures, we investigate possibilities for fraud therein. This chapter is designed to provide an overview of cryptocurrencies and the wider decentralized financial ecosystem, from the perspective of fraud.

Cryptocurrency primer

In order to discuss cryptocurrency fraud, we first outline what cryptocurrencies are and some of their properties. The fundamentals are introduced using the example of Bitcoin, the first cryptocurrency. For more details, see the original Bitcoin whitepaper (Nakamoto, 2008) or for a full technical examination of Bitcoin see the book *Mastering Bitcoin* (Antonopoulos, 2015).

Bitcoin and the blockchain

In January 2009 an entity under the pseudonym Satoshi Nakamoto released the Bitcoin (₿) protocol, introducing cryptocurrencies to the world. Previous digital currency attempts suffered from the double spending problem. With money that can be sent like e-mail, there is nothing preventing an actor from sending the same money to multiple people. Bitcoin's solution to this obstacle was to combine cryptography, peer-to-peer networks, and proof-of-work algorithms. While these concepts previously existed, Satoshi united them with a data structure now known as a blockchain. Blockchain is a descriptive term: it is a series of blocks (i.e., information) which are linked together to form a chain. In the case of Bitcoin, the blocks contain information about financial transactions, and are linked together via a cryptographic hashing function. A hashing function takes some arbitrary input, and outputs a unique numeric identifier (i.e. a hash) for that input in a deterministic way such that the same input is always assigned the same hash. Blocks are thus linked by having each new block contains a hash of the previous block, as well as information about new transactions. Consequently, it is impossible to alter the contents of a block, without changing every block that comes after it. The principle is illustrated in Figure 10.1. If one modifies Block X, its hash (i.e., its

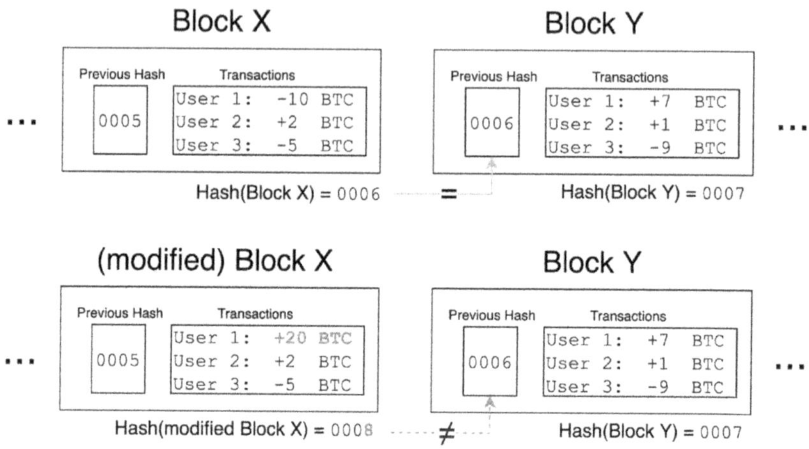

Figure 10.1 A *simplified* depiction of two blocks in the blockchain. Blocks are linked by having each block contain a hash of the previous one. If you modify a block, you modify its hash, thereby unlinking it from the next block.

numeric representation) will change, causing the link between Block X and Block Y to be broken. In order to rectify this, an actor would have to update Block Y with Block X's new hash, causing its hash to change. This means they would have to modify the next block with Block Y's new hash, which would cause its hash to change, and so on. This setup ensures a tamper-resistant record that is transparent and auditable, making it possible to verify that no double-spends have occurred (Nakamoto, 2008).

However, if the blockchain was under the control of a centralized entity, it would still be possible to tamper with it: one could just modify a block and then change every subsequent block as needed. In order to ensure the validity of the blockchain, copies of it need to be publicly distributed and accessible, so that everyone can monitor it and make sure it has not been tampered with. This is achieved by validating the information across a network of machines (i.e. a peer-to-peer network). The Bitcoin network is comprised of nodes (i.e., computers running communication software), and anyone can download the blockchain and become a node by obtaining and running the proper software.[1] The nodes in the Bitcoin network are the critical pieces of infrastructure that validate transactions and protect against double-spending. When you want to make a new transaction, it is sent to all the nodes in the network for verification. The nodes all adhere to the Bitcoin protocol, which is a set of rules that governs transactions. Amongst other things, this protocol defines the amount of Bitcoin that will ever exist (21 million) and states that a transaction cannot be double spent (Bitcoin Wiki, 2021). If the nodes receive a transaction that does not adhere to the Bitcoin protocol, it is rejected. This leaves another question: how do we uniformly add new transactions and update a blockchain spread across many computers around the globe?

Mining and consensus

When nodes receive a new transaction, they must know every other node got the same transaction in the same order. It is important that all blockchains reflect the same information, but whose copy of the blockchain does the network believe in case of disputes—in other words, how do we reach consensus? The answer is one of the great breakthroughs of Bitcoin: the network will always believe the blockchain with the most blocks, in other words, the longest one, with the most work put into it.

When new transactions are broadcast to the Bitcoin network, they are validated by all nodes in the network to make sure they adhere to the rules. After transactions are deemed legitimate, they are placed into a pool where they wait to be grouped together into a block and added to the blockchain. This action of grouping transaction into blocks, and then adding the blocks to the blockchain is the job of a special subset of nodes, known as miners. Miners will take validated transactions from the pool and organize them into blocks. These miners will then compete with other miners by performing a series of computationally intensive calculations until one miner has found the solution. This solution is known as a "proof-of-work," since holding the solution means they spent computational resources to find it. Once a miner holds this proof-of-work, they can add it to the block of transactions they compiled. They are then allowed to broadcast their block to the network and add it to the blockchain. This is how transactions are added to every copy of the blockchain in the correct order. The process is referred to as mining since whoever wins the right to add a new block to the blockchain is also allowed (by the protocol) to include a transaction to themselves, awarding them with Bitcoin for their contribution to the network (Nakamoto, 2008). This is how new Bitcoin are created.

It is impossible to add a block to the blockchain without first providing this proof-of-work. Not only does this process solve the issue of transaction ordering, it also disincentivizes a node from attempting to alter their copy of the blockchain and attempt to pass it off as the "real" blockchain [known as a 51% attack (Gervais et al., 2016)], due to the amount of computing power required to do so. Proof-of-work is known as a "consensus algorithm" since it defines how the network reaches consensus on the status of the blockchain (Bach et al., 2018).

Sending and receiving bitcoin

To send and receive bitcoin means to add transactions to the blockchain. It is therefore important that both the sender and receiver are identified in a secure manner, and that the transaction cannot be forged. Bitcoin uses public-key cryptography to achieve this. In order to send or receive bitcoin a key pair must be generated. The public key is not sensitive and is what you share with people if you wish to receive bitcoin. Any bitcoin sent to a public address can only be spent if one holds the corresponding private key, making private keys valuable and important to keep safe. The key generation and management process has been heavily simplified for users over the past few years, as keys are usually stored in a "bitcoin wallet," which takes care of the technicalities automatically, as well as allows for various forms of backup. Sending and receiving bitcoin today is a relatively straightforward task.

Summary and cryptocurrencies more broadly

Bitcoin uses a blockchain to store its transactions, and it distributes this blockchain across a peer-to-peer network of validator nodes to decentralize accounting. Mining and the consensus algorithm (proof-of-work) form the correct economic incentives to ensure the blockchain is not tampered with, while public-key cryptography insures transactions on the blockchain have integrity and cannot be forged. This fusion of blockchain, peer-to-peer networks, proof-of-work, and cryptography makes Bitcoin decentralized (and thus censorship-resistant), secure, permissionless (meaning anyone can send and receive on the network without permission from any third party), and borderless.

Since Bitcoin's inception, it has inspired a plethora of new cryptocurrencies, each with their own modifications, ranging from different coin limits to entirely new consensus algorithms and properties (Hileman & Rauchs, 2017). The number of alternative coins, often known as "altcoins", and tokens (cryptoassets powered by an existing blockchain), is constantly increasing as new projects are created. While it is hard to pin the exact number down, at the time of writing, there are over 11,000 different altcoins and tokens, with about 4,500 being described as "actively traded" by market data provider Nomics (Nomics, 2021). The term "cryptocurrency" is used broadly and colloquially throughout the remaining discussions to refer to a variety of cryptoassets, including Bitcoin, altcoins, and tokens. The following sections will examine cryptocurrencies from the perspective of fraud, outlining the types of fraud in which cryptocurrencies have been involved, as well as how cryptocurrencies' unique properties may offer both boons and curses for fraud detection and prevention.

Cryptocurrency fraud

Cryptocurrencies enable entirely new types of transactions and possibilities that simply do not exist in traditional finance: frictionless global payments and irreversible transactions are hallmarks of any cryptocurrency, with flash loans, decentralized exchanges, and more being enabled by decentralized finance (Schär, 2021). With this, cryptocurrencies present additional layers of complexity to financial fraud.

The unique properties of the cryptocurrency ecosystem offer both boons and curses when it comes to detecting and preventing fraud. As will be discussed later in this chapter, the utilization of the unique tools that the cryptocurrency ecosystem provides (such as transparency) is leading to an alternative financial sector where fraud can be monitored more effectively. This section introduces cryptocurrency fraud at a high level, distinguishing between schemes enabled by cryptocurrencies and those dependent on cryptocurrencies. Fraud is a broad term, especially in this context when the regulatory structure surrounding cryptocurrencies is still developing in most jurisdictions, and our liberal use of the term here is a reflection of that.

What does cryptocurrency fraud look like?

As a subset of financial fraud, much of cryptocurrency fraud is similar to the types of fraud often present in traditional financial markets for example: Ponzi schemes, phishing scams, and pump-and-dumps (Badawi & Jourdan, 2020). However, the uniquely digital nature of cryptocurrencies has caused the methods of some of these traditional frauds to evolve. Ponzi schemes can now operate automatically and immutably, as is the case with Ponzi schemes that run using smart contracts on Ethereum,[2] making it difficult for victims to seek recompense (Bartoletti et al., 2020; Chen et al., 2018). Phishing scams have modernized, taking advantage of irreversible transactions and preying on people's fear of missing out (Chainalysis, 2020). Pump-and-dump manipulations (buying a cheap asset and then getting others to buy it before you sell) also exhibit updated tactics, taking advantage of the large number of unregulated markets, low-value cryptocurrencies, and real-time chat communication (Kamps & Kleinberg, 2018).

While some of the fraud types are familiar, there are also new types of fraud dependent upon the characteristics of cryptocurrency ecosystem. Therefore, at the highest level, cryptocurrency fraud falls into two main categories: crypto-dependent and crypto-enabled. These groupings were inspired by the similar categorizations often used for cybercrime (McGuire & Dowling, 2013). Proposed definitions for crypto-dependent and crypto-enabled fraud are as follows:

> Crypto-dependent: Unique fraud types which rely on the properties of cryptocurrencies or the cryptocurrency ecosystem.
>
> Crypto-enabled: Fraud types which existed previously but have seen new applications or been further facilitated by cryptocurrencies.

Across crypto-dependent and crypto-enabled, we placed schemes into eight non-orthogonal and non-exhaustive sub-categories: market manipulation, extortion schemes, investment schemes, theft schemes, insider trading, fraudulent services, mining schemes, and tactics relating to decentralized finance. Figure 10.2 graphically presents these distinctions with examples of fraud types that belong to each category. The specific fraud types in Figure 10.2 were included where there is at least preliminary evidence that they have occurred, and they have been collected over time through observation of academic papers, news sources, and crypto-related chatrooms and message boards.

What impact has cryptocurrency fraud had?

In the context of traditional fraud, the exact impact can be hard to measure due to its uniquely broad nature, under-reporting, and lack of awareness around victimization (Blakeborough & Correia, 2017). Furthermore, a review of the data collection process used to measure the impact of fraud in the UK found that, amongst other things, inconsistent definitions of fraud, neglect of certain types of fraud, and the differing reasons and motivations for which the data were collected were all issues (Levi & Burrows, 2007). Considering these characteristics, as well as the lack of any cohesive public record of crypto fraud, any estimates are likely to be conservative and incomplete. Efforts at calculating the financial impact of cryptocurrency fraud have only begun in the last few years and are mainly being performed by a handful of blockchain analysis companies. CipherTrace and Chainalsysis both report the "total" loss due crypto fraud as increasing annually since 2017 and estimate

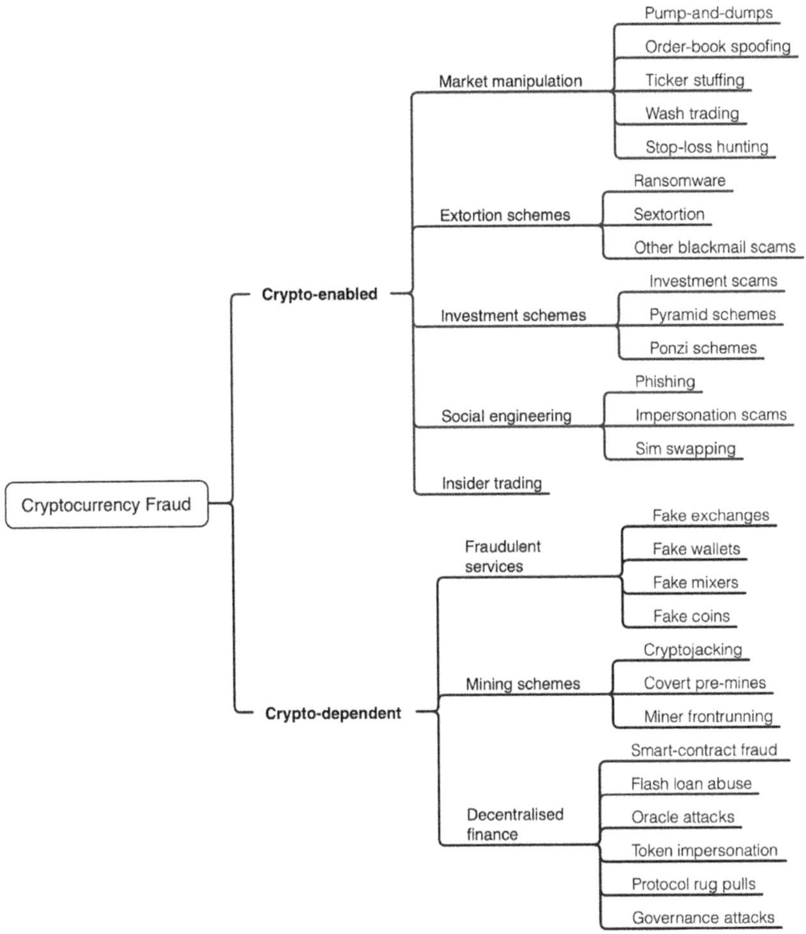

Figure 10.2 Fraud types split by whether they rely on the properties of cryptocurrencies (crypto-dependent) or are an existing scam which has seen new applications in crypto (crypto-enabled).

around $4.5 billion in losses for 2019 alone (Chainalysis, 2020; CipherTrace, 2020). However, the majority of that estimated figure can be attributed to billion-dollar Ponzi schemes (e.g., PlusToken[3]), and there may be other types of cryptocurrency fraud that are simply not tracked or reported. While these reports capture the largest-known scams, this section aims to highlight some of the other possible, though perhaps smaller and emerging fraud types. To get more accurate figures on the totality of crypto fraud, as discussed further in later sections, we propose better monitoring and reporting tools, as well as better recording standards for cryptocurrency-related fraud.

Descriptions of crypto-enabled fraud types

Market manipulation

Manipulation is a risk in any financial market. However, as an emerging ecosystem, the cryptocurrency sector has been lacking applicable regulations and operating standards such as those that are found in traditional markets, which attempt to alleviate the prevalence of such schemes. Classic market manipulation schemes have been observed to be occurring in crypto, sometimes in an evolved, but familiar format. **Pump-and-dumps** are a form of market manipulation where bad actors purchase a commodity, and then artificially inflate the price (often through misinformation) before selling off their holdings. In the cryptocurrency space, perpetrators will often organize in online chatrooms to purchase low market-cap cryptocurrencies and then attempt to inflate the price by spreading misinformation (Hamrick et al., 2018). The rate and speed of these manipulations has increased due to the inherently digital nature of cryptocurrencies (Kamps & Kleinberg, 2018). Methods for detecting these schemes have continued to develop, further utilizing techniques such as anomaly detection (Mansourifar et al., 2020) and machine learning (La Morgia et al., 2020; Mansourifar et al., 2020; Mirtaheri et al., 2019; Xu & Livshits, 2019).

The relevance of liquidity as a metric in crypto (due to exchange aggregator sites such as CoinMarketCap, which rank exchanges by liquidity), may have incentivized **wash trading**. This occurs when a single party (or a group acting together) buys and sells their own assets in order to give the appearance of authentic trading volume on a platform (CME, 2021). Aggregator sites rank cryptocurrency exchanges by liquidity, thus incentivizing exchanges to resort to wash trading in order to appear higher on the list, and thus attract more customers (Singer, 2020). Academic analysis is limited, but one study estimates that for unregulated exchanges, up to 70% of the volume may be from wash trading (Cong et al., 2020). For the same reason, and due to a lack of data integrity standards, **ticker-stuffing** (simply providing a ticker with fake volume numbers) has also been witnessed (Nomics, 2019).

Trading manipulation such as order-book spoofing and stop-loss hunting mainly target those who actively trade on exchanges. On many exchanges, users signal their intent to buy or sell at particular prices, and these buy and sell orders are recorded in what is called an order-book. **Order-book spoofing** occurs when an actor attempts to manipulate the market by advertising orders which they have no intent of actually filling (Lee et al., 2013; Twomey & Mann, 2020). These users advertise orders to buy or sell a commodity at a certain price, but then remove these orders before they can be filled. This is done to give the false impression of price movement. Cryptocurrency exchange BitMEX have introduced new trading restrictions that limit traders based on the proportion of orders they actually fill in an effort to combat this fraud type (BitMEX, 2020). **Stop-loss hunting** takes advantage of a market feature known as a "stop-loss", which is a tool that traders can use to automatically sell their assets if the price dips below a certain threshold. Academic research is thin, but it has been documented that those who hold large amounts of cryptocurrency will sometimes attempt to push the price of a coin below common stop-loss values, in order to trigger automatic sales and purchase large quantities of coins for a cheaper price (Banton, 2020; Coin Bureau, 2018).

Extortion schemes

Extortion-based schemes have seen an uptick since the advent of cryptocurrencies, due to their pseudonymous nature and since the ease of accepting global payment has widened the potential victim pool (Kshetri & Voas, 2017). **Ransom malware** (ransomware) is a form of extortion where a victim's computer is infected with malware which encrypts their files, making it impossible for them to access them (NCSC, 2020). In order to decrypt their files, the users must pay a ransom to the criminals, usually now with cryptocurrencies, though documented cases exist, where these rely on other relatively anonymous payment systems like PaysafeCards and Ukash (Dunn, 2014) and even SMS texts (McMillan, 2010). The transparency of the blockchain allows for data-driven research, which may prove useful for clustering ransomware families and tracking ransomware payments (Conti et al., 2018; Paquet-Clouston et al., 2018). **Blackmail scams** attempt to extract money out of a victim by threatening them. These can take many forms—including a recent COVID-19 variant where threats to infect the victim are made (Xia et al., 2020a)—but one of the more common types of blackmail scams that has been circulating is **sextortion**. The scammer claims to have some sort of sexual information about the victim, such as knowing they have visited adult websites or that they have hacked their webcam and obtained nude photos, and they then threaten to release these details unless the victim pays a ransom. While there may be multiple motives for sextortion (O'Malley & Holt, 2020), an increasing number of sextortion schemes have a profit-driven focus, requesting payment in cryptocurrency (Paquet-Clouston et al., 2019). By analysing the blockchain, researchers estimate that these scams brought in $146,000 in 60 days (Schultz, 2018), and, in another instance, over $1 million in under a year (Paquet-Clouston et al., 2019). Research further suggests that many of these schemes are controlled by a small number of distinct entities (Oggier et al., 2020; Paquet-Clouston et al., 2019).

Investment schemes

Investment scams are not new, but cryptocurrencies offer a salient new angle for scammers to abuse. While traditionally these would be perpetrated through by calling individuals without prior arrangement (i.e., cold calling) they are increasingly taking place online and utilizing cryptocurrencies, resulting in damages of over £197 million in 2018 according to the United Kingdom's Financial Conduct Authority (FCA, 2019). Cryptocurrency forms of this scam include trying to convince potential victims to buy a new cryptocurrency (often called an Initial Coin Offering or ICO) (SEC, 2017), investments into a cryptocurrency mining company (Vasek & Moore, 2015), or some other crypto-related scheme.

Social engineering schemes

Social engineering broadly refers to attacks carried out through manipulating or tricking people (Peltier, 2006). Some prominent examples of this in the cryptocurrency context will be discussed below: crypto wallet/website phishing scams, SIM swapping, and high-profile impersonation scams. **Phishing scams** attempt to fool victims into handing over funds or sensitive information by appearing as a legitimate actor. In the cryptocurrency context, usual targets are private keys or login details. There have been exchanges created for phishing purposes (Osborne, 2021) as well as phishing versions of crypto wallet extensions (Zmudinski, 2020), among others. Each of these is designed to steal your cryptocurrency, by either getting you to deposit it directly (such as with a phishing exchange), or by stealing your private keys (e.g., through fake wallet extensions). **SIM swapping** abuses telecom providers' ability to copy the information from your SIM card (i.e., phone number) to a new SIM in case of loss or damage. Attackers obtain information about a victim, then use this to trick telecom providers into copying the victim's SIM information onto a SIM card they control. A recent empirical study found that providers often use weak authentication mechanisms, making these attacks easier to perform (Lee et al., 2020). SIM swapping is often used to bypass two-factor authentication, and because many cryptocurrency services allow for account recovery with phone-based two-factor authentication, attackers can potentially drain the accounts of vulnerable individuals. In a high-profile case, telecom provider AT&T was sued for "assisting" in the theft of $23 million worth of the plaintiff's cryptocurrency (Chavez-Dreyfuss, 2019). In January 2020 a man was arrested for the alleged theft of $50 million worth of cryptocurrency using SIM swap attacks, targeting mainly attendees of the 2018 Consensus crypto conference in New York City (Duhaime, 2020). **Impersonation**

scams are often found on Twitter or YouTube, and often involve impersonating high-profile accounts of famous people (e.g. Elon Musk, Donald Trump), while bolstering their accounts with fake subscribers, views, likes, etc. (Gemini, 2020; Narang, 2020). The exact wording of the scams varies, but a common claim is that if you send some amount of cryptocurrency, they will send double the amount back. This technique was also used with the *real* accounts of high-profile twitter users in the large twitter hack in mid-2020, raking in over $120,000 (Robinson, 2020b). While seemingly obvious scams, some reports note damages in the millions (Redman, 2019) and blockchain analysis suggests these scams could have brought in $5,000 in a single night (Cimpanu, 2018), though the veracity of this information cannot be ascertained.

Insider trading

The cryptocurrency sector has vulnerabilities with respect to insider trading, stemming from the fact that as was described in the section on market manipulation, well-defined (and enforced) regulations and operating standards for crypto companies are lacking. With only a handful of large companies, announcements from key actors in the sector can sometimes cause the price of an asset to change. The most common example of this is the price rise that can occur when exchanges list new cryptocurrencies or tokens, such as when the price of COMP doubled after being listed on Coinbase (Martinez, 2020). This listing effect has also been documented empirically (Ante, 2019; Benedetti & Nikbakht, 2021). While most companies will have some sort of restrictions in place to minimize insider trading, with hundreds of coins, tokens, and projects, the potential for inside information to be leaked may be greater in the cryptocurrency space. Especially given the proclivity for crypto projects to communicate directly with users using chat platforms like Telegram or Discord. If employees of cryptocurrency exchanges, service providers, or other financial protocols were to even unintentionally leak non-public information, this could lead to insider trading implications.

Descriptions of crypto-dependent fraud types

Fraudulent services

In contrast to traditional financial exchanges, the permissionless nature of transactions with crypto means that the development ecosystem is more open and accessible. This has led to the creation of many legitimate exchanges and services, but has also made it easier for fraudulent exchanges to appear. Similarly, there have been many cryptocurrency wallet providers, and with them many fake ones that aim to scam users. **Fake exchanges** and **fake wallets** may either be a completely new service like the exchanges often advertised through chat platform Discord (Osborne, 2021) that steal deposits from victims; or they may impersonate existing ones through techniques such as typo-squatting (making a similar domain name) or fake apps (Xia et al., 2020b). **Fake mixers** are fraudulent versions of mixing services, which seek to group and mix cryptocurrency transactions of many users together in order to make blockchain analysis techniques harder to apply. They are often used by those who desire more financial privacy, but have become associated with money launderers (Möser et al., 2013). Like fake exchanges and fake wallets, instead of performing the advertised service, they steal the deposited money (Vasek & Moore, 2015). Often taking the form of an ICO (initial coin offering), **fake coins** are fraudulent cryptocurrencies with little or no utility designed to take your funds without delivering a product. Ruja Ignatova, famously called the "Cryptoqueen," made billions off of a Ponzi scheme promoting a fake cryptocurrency known as OneCoin before disappearing in 2017 (BBC, 2019). Fraudulent initial coin offerings often use social media and celebrity endorsements to reach a wide audience, alongside vague information and promises of high returns on investments; an estimated 10% of ICO funds have been lost to fraud (Tiwari et al., 2020).

Mining schemes

The unique mining mechanism through which many cryptocurrencies are secured and generated has created a unique vector for bad actors to exploit. **Cryptojacking** is a form of malware that hijacks a victim's computing power and uses it to mine (i.e., generate) cryptocurrency (ENISA, 2020). One of the largest costs in mining is electricity, thus the main benefit of cryptojacking is that you gain the mined currency without having to pay for the electrical overhead. The Monero cryptocurrency has often been a target for cryptojacking due to its algorithm being resistant to specialized mining hardware, allowing for a larger profit margin despite using ordinary devices and browsers (Eskandari et al., 2018; Zimba et al., 2019). Detection methods for these schemes have been investigated, with several approaches often using machine learning, harnessing the unique signatures that these types of attacks have to successfully detect these schemes (Hong et al., 2018; Kharraz et al., 2019; Ning et al., 2019; Petrov et al., 2020; Tahir et al., 2017). A report by the European Union Agency for Cybersecurity noted cryptojacking is declining, with a 78% decrease in the second half of 2019 compared to the first, likely due to better combatting efforts, decreased Monero price, and the closure of popular coin-mining software Coinhive (ENISA, 2020).

A **covert-premine** is another type of fraudulent mining scheme which occurs when a cryptocurrency advertises the supply cap of the coin to be a certain value, but some party is in fact able to mine additional currency. A known example of this occurred with Bitcoin Private, a coin based on Bitcoin with additional privacy features. Bitcoin Private was supposed to launch with a total supply cap of 21 million, but an additional two million were covertly pre-mined before the coin launched (approximately valued at $3.9m at the time) (CoinMetrics, 2018). The team behind Bitcoin Private later claimed this was an exploit and that the "source, purpose, and recipient" were unknown to them (Alexandre, 2018).

Miner front-running is a phenomenon that occurs (mainly on Ethereum, currently) when a miner notices a transaction that may make a profit, copies this transaction, and executes it before the original, thereby "stealing" the profit. This is possible because pending Ethereum transactions must wait in what is known as the *mempool* before they are added to the blockchain. Since the miners can see all the transactions in the mempool, they are able to see potential transactions *before* they have actually been executed (since they *are* the ones that execute them). This has led to the creation of arbitrage bots that will analyse pending transactions for profitable trades and execute them first, with profit estimations around $17 million (Qin et al., 2021). The mempool has been described as a treacherous "dark forest", in an account that attempts to evade these bots in order to re-claim $12,000 from a smart contract (Robinson, 2020a). This concept has been generalized academically as Miner Extractable Value (MEV), where it has been noted the revenue from such front-running attacks may disrupt cryptoeconomic incentives, posing a threat to the consensus mechanisms of Ethereum (Daian et al., 2019).

Decentralized finance

Decentralized finance (DeFi) is an emerging area in the cryptocurrency ecosystem that aims to decentralize not only payment, but also many other financial primitives such as derivatives, options, loans, insurance, and more (Schär, 2021; Werner et al., 2021). Decentralized finance is made possible due to the concept of smart contracts. Smart contracts are programs that function much as a traditional contract would, by enforcing certain properties to which both parties agree. Except, instead of these properties being upheld legally, they are enforced by code. Smart contracts are usually deployed on blockchains, the most popular being Ethereum, whose DeFi smart contracts currently hold nearly $40 billion (DeFi Pulse, 2021). If the conditions of a smart contract are met, then the outcome can occur. This is very similar to how traditional programs work, but because smart contracts are deployed on the blockchain, they inherit the security features it provides, such as immutability and transparency. The key idea behind smart contracts is that the code is visible for everyone to see, and, in theory, no one can change it once deployed, not even the original creators. This allows for programs that involve monetary funds to be trusted, without the need for a centralized intermediary to ensure that funds are not stolen. The possibilities of smart contracts are promising, and when properly implemented could even help to reduce fraud in certain situations, due to the transparent and automatic nature. However, **smart contract fraud** opportunities are also present. Automatic Ponzi schemes can be created (Bartoletti et al., 2020; Chen et al., 2018), and funds could be lost due to bugs or malicious contracts (Thompson, 2020). The fraud types in the remainder of this section will describe some of what has been witnessed in the emerging area of decentralized finance, and all involve smart contracts at some level.

Oracle attacks occur because smart contracts, in order to be useful, need access to changing outside data (e.g., the price of an asset). While the code of a smart contract is immutable, data coming in from what is known as an *oracle* leave room for vulnerabilities. It is possible for an attacker to profit off of such a data manipulation, such as when the Harvest Finance protocol was manipulated, resulting in a $25 million loss (Foxley, 2020). Solving oracle attacks in a decentralized way is an active research area, with protocols such as Chainlink[4] and Band[5] as examples. For a more detailed examination of oracles, see Liu & Szalachowski (2020). **Flash loan abuse** centers around a new type of financial primitive known as a flash loan, an uncollateralized loan that is borrowed and repaid in a single Ethereum transaction. This is possible because transactions can be reverted before they are completed. If the transaction is successful, then the loan is paid back; if not, then the transaction (and thus the loan) is reversed. This makes it possible to do things that would generate a profit, but which have capital constraints. Arbitrage, for example, is a common use case for flash loans. This feature is empowering and intriguing, but can also be abused, as it was when attackers exploited vulnerabilities on the bZx platform using capital derived from flash loans, making $900,000 in seconds (Qureshi, 2021). Academic analysis of flash loans reveals several other possible nefarious use cases for flash loans, including oracle manipulations and wash trading (Qin et al., 2020).

A **protocol rug pull** occurs when the founders of a protocol exit from a project or token with some or all of the money that has been deposited, either by stealing funds, or draining the liquidity. This is usually possible while the protocol is in a transition period to a fully decentralized state, because the founders may still have some control over a portion of the funds (e.g., a development fund). Many projects in DeFi also have anonymous founders, while this is largely in line with the ethos of the sector, it can have potential downsides. SushiSwap[6] is a decentralized exchanged that garnered a lot of attention when it began to reward its users for providing liquidity (often known as yield farming). The protocol had around $1 billion locked in its smart contracts, when the anonymous founder known as Chef Nomi was able to walk away with 37,400 ETH from the development fund, worth $13 million at the time (Keoun et al., 2020). Interestingly, he later returned the funds (Palmer & De, 2020), the project was taken over by the community, and SushiSwap is now one of the largest decentralized exchanges. Victims of similar "rug pulls," however, have not been so fortunate, with CipherTrace estimating $129 million lost to this mode of fraud in 2020 (CipherTrace, 2021).

Token impersonation takes advantage of the decentralized (and thus un-curated) nature of decentralized exchanges. Because anyone can "list" a token (this means providing starting liquidity for it), scammers have taken to "listing" fake tokens for real projects that do not (currently) have a token; or are very similar to existing tokens (Haig, 2020). If an unsuspecting buyer does not double-check with the official project, they may end up purchasing a token that they are unable to sell. Token lists[7] are one attempt at combatting this deception, by providing community-curated lists of tokens. This intervention highlights the important role that centralized entities play in curating official content, and the reputational struggle that decentralized protocols face. Many decentralized finance protocols are (or aim to be) run by their communities, often utilizing voting mechanisms to decide on the next steps the protocols should take. The exact details of these mechanisms vary, but they often involve voting power being related to the holding of the protocol's token. If these mechanisms can be manipulated (e.g., if an entity has enough tokens), then a **governance attack** could occur, leading to unwanted changes or even loss of funds. It has been demonstrated that $20m used maliciously in the MakerDAO[8] protocol could have led to a profit of $340m (Zoltu, 2020). Flash loans could potentially be used to aid in these attacks, which often require a certain amount of collateral to hit a dangerous threshold.

Cryptocurrency fraud detection and prevention

If cryptocurrencies are to thrive then fraud must be kept to a manageable level, even as the technology scales to an increasing number of users. While it is possible some types of cryptocurrency fraud can be managed using known techniques, as the cryptocurrency sector evolves so too will the means and methods of fraud perpetrators, perhaps making them less suited to traditional countermeasures. However, cryptocurrencies offer a unique and data-rich ecosystem that could be harnessed for fraud prevention.

The importance of prevention

Recovering funds lost to crypto fraud is difficult due to the inherent nature of cryptocurrency transactions, since they cannot be frozen or reversed. If one considers traditional finance and crypto finance on axis of centralization and opacity (as depicted in Figure 10.3), crypto finance trends toward being decentralized and transparent, whereas traditional finance trends toward being centralized and opaque, by the nature of their architectures. Various protocols of each may be in different positions on such a plane, but the general implication for fraud, as summarized in Table 10.1, is that crypto fraud has potential to be easier to detect, but harder to reverse. This implies that solutions need to be weighted toward prevention, since recompense for cryptocurrency fraud may be more difficult absent central authority. Not only does prevention appear to be more of a necessity when considering how best to approach cryptocurrency fraud, but one could also make the argument that the principles of the

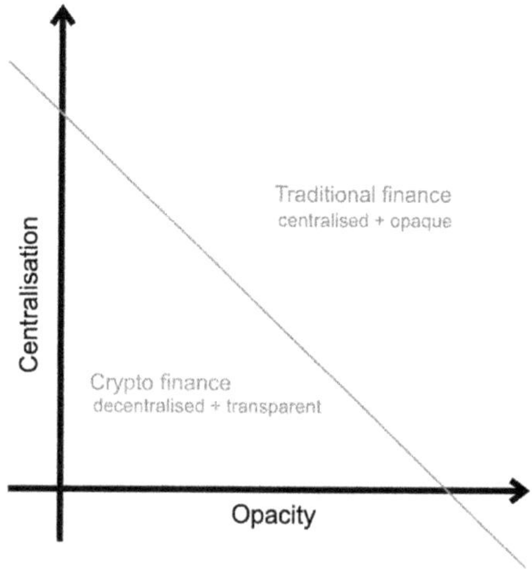

Figure 10.3 A depiction of crypto finance and traditional finance based on degree of decentralisation and opacity. We suggest a dimensionality here as decentralisation is not binary, but we purposefully refrain from adding specific examples due to the rapidly changing pace of the field.

Table 10.1 A Consideration of Traditional Fraud vs. Crypto Fraud Based on Degree of Centralisation and Opacity

Traditional Fraud	*Crypto Fraud*
In general, harder to detect (opaquer)	In general, easier to detect (more transparent)
Easier to reverse (more centralised)	Harder to reverse (more decentralised)

ecosystem support such an approach, since those properties (i.e., decentralisation and transparency) can be useful for detection.

Detection

The first step toward prevention is detection. The further development of monitoring systems may help to facilitate prevention efforts. Automatic mitigation or flagging systems are a necessity, with thousands of cryptocurrencies on hundreds of different markets and platforms, the plethora of data far exceeds what could reasonably be managed with manual effort.

The advantage for cryptocurrencies is that what might normally require data-sharing agreements between banks and other organizations can now be followed and tracked by anyone. Financial information can be independently verified, which makes it resistant to falsification, such as was seen in a recent SEC case dealing with a Ponzi scheme that was falsifying financial records (SEC, 2021). In a decentralized financial network, it is possible to create a record of financial statements completely transparently using on-chain data, making their authenticity verifiable.[9] However, just because it is possible to verify a variety of information that occurs on the blockchain, it does not mean that people do. Simplifying the path to verification by creating easy to use data tooling and integrating this in a user-friendly way will be a key challenge for researchers. While not the focus of this chapter, it should be noted that privacy concerns do arise if one imagines a future with a transparent financial system, with personal transactional privacy being a particular concern.

Linking transactions to identities

The transparency of the blockchain has naturally led to an area of research attempting to link identities to transactions. This is often used to try to trace certain transactions back to an identity in order to combat crimes such as terrorism financing, money laundering, and others. Address clustering heuristics are used to group different addresses together that may belong to one identity. The transactions can then be analysed to determine if the user interacted with anything that may identify them in the real world. These heuristics have been studied extensively in Bitcoin (Harrigan & Fretter, 2016; Meiklejohn et al., 2016; Spagnuolo, 2013), recently appeared in Ethereum (Victor, 2020), and have also been used to track payments across different cryptocurrency ledgers (Yousaf et al., 2019). The advancement of privacy-enhancing tools (e.g., ring signatures and stealth addresses) and cryptocurrencies could mitigate the effectiveness of these types of technologies; privacy coins such as Monero[10] and ZCash,[11] or tools such as CoinJoin[12] for Bitcoin and Tornado.cash[13] for Ethereum, all attempt to add some transactional privacy to the blockchain, but it remains to be seen whether these will become mainstream.

Focus areas for prevention

While not exhaustive, four main areas of focus emerge when considering cryptocurrency fraud prevention: data, protocol design, education, and regulation.

Data

Data integrity is a key issue when thinking about cryptocurrency fraud detection and prevention. While blockchains fundamentally help with the issue of data integrity, the data needs to be analysed and examined for veracity, and if off-chain data are used, this needs to be verifiable. Wash trading, for example, is an issue of data integrity. Off-chain wash trading, such as that performed by exchanges, has been shown as discussed previously. On-chain wash trading (which may be occurring with crypto-collectibles, see NonFungible [2020]), can technically be detected on-chain, but as of yet no efforts have been made to do so. While it may be possible to use blockchain data to detect and potentially prevent fraud, efforts need to be made to research this and develop proper tooling. Making blockchain data more accessible is a key step toward this goal; data protocols such as The Graph,[14] who provide easier access to on-chain data, look promising for this purpose.

Protocol design

Anyone can create a decentralized finance protocol, and anyone can use it. Protocol designers should strive to provide a user experience design that minimizes fraud, that is ethical and honest in its presentation of data, and clear is in its communication of risk. Decentralized finance allows for a high degree of composability, with new protocols being able to leverage existing ones. This allows for experimentation and the development of entirely new financial primitives, but also has fraud implications which should be carefully considered. Protocol incentives also need to be deliberately designed to prevent malicious use, as even well-intentioned features could be abused for fraud.

Education

Education is a sector-wide responsibility and will likely play an important role in preventing cryptocurrency fraud. When using cryptocurrencies and decentralized financial protocols, users are dealing with intricate financial tools that offer a degree of control over finances that many are not used to having. Education is often considered as a key tool for preventing cybercrime (Martin & Rice, 2011; McQuade, 2007; Sarre et al., 2018), and it could be that fostering self-reliance and financial literacy are helpful in preventing low-hanging fraud such as fake services, phishing, and token impersonation in the crypto sector as well.

Regulation

Regulation of cryptocurrencies has been increasing throughout different parts of the world at different rates, and there is no global standard. Compliance with regulation has largely been placed on the shoulders of centralized exchanges, which often require know-your-customer (KYC) documents in order to comply with anti-money-laundering regulations. There are some concerns that KYC information poses a privacy risk, not necessarily because users are required to offer sensitive information, but because they are being asked to store that data with an increasing number of services, widening the attack vector for potential hacks and leaks (Johnson, 2019). Digital identity solutions, where users have more control are appearing e.g. BrightID (BrightID, 2021), but nothing has become standard thus far. It has also been argued that decentralized currencies deserve decentralized regulation (Nabilou, 2019), positing that regulation would be more effective when applied to the "application" layer or the middlemen, rather than directly to the protocols themselves. Indeed, this seems to be what many countries do (with exchanges), since other measures may induce regulatory arbitrage: where services simply leave the countries with poor regulation. Key regulatory challenges include finding the balance between and effective regulation.

Conclusion

The cryptocurrency ecosystem offers new opportunities for fraud, but also for fraud detection, prevention, and mitigation. We have described how the field is emerging, under-researched, and lacks development standards and regulation. With this in mind, we highlighted four key areas for focus in relation to cryptocurrency fraud prevention: data integrity and tooling, fraud-first protocol design thinking, educational resources, and smart regulation.

Data is prevalent in the cryptocurrency space; it is one of the things that defines and separates it from traditional finance. It provides transparency, but we need to continue to develop our data tooling and how we present our findings to make this transparency accessible. Developers in the space should take a fraud-focused approach to protocol design, critically thinking about how each piece of their system could be used for fraud. This is no easy task, especially with the modular nature of decentralized finance allowing different protocols to interact with each other in a permission less fashion. Education will also be important in reducing fraud from a personal standpoint. Cryptocurrencies offer self-custody of funds, and there are currently many intricacies and steps where things could go wrong if users are not aware of all the details and responsibilities that come with this. From a regulation standpoint, decentralization is a goal of most cryptocurrency protocols, and thus traditional regulation and fraud prosecution methods that rely on a centralized entity may not suffice. If these are applied with a heavy hand, it may stifle the industry leading to regulatory arbitrage.

Reversing crypto fraud can be more difficult because there is no central authority through whom all transactions flow. It follows that a focus on prevention is key to mitigating cryptocurrency fraud, and we have proposed that the transparency cryptocurrencies provide supports such a focus. Cryptocurrencies provide a unique financial sandbox with exciting possibilities for the future of finance and for the future of fraud prevention.

Acknowledgements

Josh Kamps: This research was funded by the Dawes Centre for Future Crime at UCL.

Arianna Trozze: This work was funded by the UK EPSRC grant EP/S022503/1 that supports the Centre for Doctoral Training in Cybersecurity at UCL.

Notes

1 The requirements and software for becoming a full node on the Bitcoin network can be found at https://bitcoin.org/en/full-node.
2 The rules of a Ponzi scheme (with many variations) can be coded into a smart contract meaning it can be deployed pseudonymously and cannot be shut down.
3 For more information about PlusToken see: https://blog.chainalysis.com/reports/plustoken-scam-bitcoin-price.
4 https://chain.link.
5 https://bandprotocol.com.
6 https://sushi.com.
7 https://tokenlists.org/.
8 https://makerdao.com/en/.
9 For an example, consider this dashboard created for MakerDAOs expenses made using on-chain data: https://bit.ly/3rJpSl7.
10 https://www.getmonero.org.
11 https://z.cash.
12 https://en.bitcoin.it/wiki/CoinJoin.
13 https://tornado.cash.
14 https://thegraph.com.

References

Alexandre, A. (December 25, 2018). *Altcoin Bitcoin Private Confirms Additional 2 Million Coins Secretly Premined*. Cointelegraph. https://cointelegraph.com/news/altcoin-bitcoin-private-confirms-additional-2-million-coins-secretly-premined

Ante, L. (2019). *Market Reaction to Exchange Listings of Cryptocurrencies*. https://doi.org/10.13140/RG.2.2.19924.76161

Antonopoulos, A. M. (2015). *Mastering Bitcoin* (First edition). O'Reilly.

Bach, L. M., Mihaljevic, B., & Zagar, M. (2018). Comparative analysis of blockchain consensus algorithms. *2018 41st International Convention on Information and Communication Technology, Electronics and Microelectronics (MIPRO)*, 1545–1550. https://doi.org/10.23919/MIPRO.2018.8400278

Badawi, E., & Jourdan, G.-V. (2020). Cryptocurrencies emerging threats and defensive mechanisms: A systematic literature review. *IEEE Access*, *8*, 200021–200037. https://doi.org/10.1109/ACCESS.2020.3034816

Banton, C. (December 16, 2020). *Stop Hunting*. Investopedia. https://www.investopedia.com/terms/s/stophunting.asp

Bartoletti, M., Carta, S., Cimoli, T., & Saia, R. (2020). Dissecting Ponzi schemes on Ethereum: Identification, analysis, and impact. *Future Generation Computer Systems*, *102*, 259–277. https://doi.org/10.1016/j.future.2019.08.014

BBC. (November 24, 2019). Cryptoqueen: How this woman scammed the world, then vanished. *BBC News*. https://www.bbc.co.uk/news/stories-50435014

Benedetti, H., & Nikbakht, E. (2021). Returns and network growth of digital tokens after cross-listings. *Journal of Corporate Finance*, *101853*. https://doi.org/10.1016/j.jcorpfin.2020.101853

Bitcoin Wiki. (2021). *Full node—Bitcoin Wiki*. https://en.bitcoin.it/wiki/Full_node#What_makes_a_full_node.3F.

BitMEX. (2020). *Introducing the Quote Value Ratio Trading Rule*. https://blog.bitmex.com/introducing-the-quote-value-ratio-trading-rule/

Blakeborough, L., & Correia, S. G. (2017). *The Scale and Nature of Fraud: A Review of the Evidence*. https://assets.publishing.service.gov.uk/government/uploads/system/uploads/attachment_data/file/720772/scale-and-nature-of-fraud-review-of-evidence.pdf

BrightID. (2021). *BrightID*. https://www.brightid.org/

Chainalysis. (2020). *The Chainalysis 2020 Crypto Crime Report*. https://go.chainalysis.com/2020-Crypto-Crime-Report.html

Chavez-Dreyfuss, G. (May 11, 2019). U.S. investor awarded $75 million in cryptocurrency crime case. *Reuters*. https://www.reuters.com/article/us-crypto-currency-lawsuit-idUSKCN1SG2CO

Chen, W., Zheng, Z., Cui, J., Ngai, E., Zheng, P., & Zhou, Y. (2018). Detecting Ponzi schemes on Ethereum: Towards healthier blockchain technology. *Proceedings of the 2018 World Wide Web Conference*, 1409–1418. https://doi.org/10.1145/3178876.3186046

Cimpanu, C. (February 7, 2018). *Ethereum Scammers Make $5,000 in a Night by Impersonating Celebs on Twitter*. BleepingComputer. https://www.bleepingcomputer.com/news/cryptocurrency/ethereum-scammers-make-5-000-in-a-night-by-impersonating-celebs-on-twitter/

CipherTrace. (2020). *Spring 2020 Cryptocurrency Crime and Anti-Money Laundering Report—CipherTrace*. https://ciphertrace.com/spring-2020-cryptocurrency-anti-money-laundering-report/.

CipherTrace. (February, 2021). *Cryptocurrency Crime and Anti-Money Laundering Report, February 2021—CipherTrace*. https://ciphertrace.com/2020-year-end-cryptocurrency-crime-and-anti-money-laundering-report/

CME. (2021). *Wash Trades—Definition of a Wash Trade—CME Group*. https://www.cmegroup.com/content/cmegroup/en/education/courses/market-regulation/wash-trades/definition-of-a-wash-trade.html

Coin Bureau. (February 19, 2018). Stop-loss hunting: Crypto whales are making a killing on your stops. *Coin Bureau*. https://www.coinbureau.com/analysis/stop-loss-hunting-crypto-whales/

CoinGecko. (February 7, 2021). *CoinGecko: Cryptocurrency Prices and Market Capitalization*. https://www.coingecko.com/en

CoinMetrics. (December 23, 2018). Don't trust, verify: A Bitcoin Private case study. *Coin Metrics*. https://coinmetrics.io/bitcoin-private/

Cong, L. W., Li, X., Tang, K., & Yang, Y. (2020). *Crypto Wash Trading* (SSRN Scholarly Paper ID 3530220). Social Science Research Network. https://doi.org/10.2139/ssrn.3530220

Conti, M., Gangwal, A., & Ruj, S. (2018). On the economic significance of ransomware campaigns: A bitcoin transactions perspective. *Computers & Security*, *79*, 162–189. https://doi.org/10.1016/j.cose.2018.08.008

Daian, P., Goldfeder, S., Kell, T., Li, Y., Zhao, X., Bentov, I., Breidenbach, L., & Juels, A. (2019). Flash Boys 2.0: Frontrunning, transaction reordering, and consensus instability in decentralized exchanges. *ArXiv:1904.05234 [Cs]*. http://arxiv.org/abs/1904.05234

DeFi Pulse. (February 10, 2021). *DeFi Pulse | The DeFi Leaderboard | Stats, Charts and Guides*. https://defipulse.com

Duhaime, C. (January 14, 2020). *Bitcoin SIM Swapper Charged with Stealing $50 Million, Arrested in British Columbia | Duhaime's Anti-Money Laundering & Financial Crime News*. https://www.antimoneylaunderinglaw.com/2020/01/bitcoin-sim-swapper-charged-with-stealing-50-million-arrested-in-british-columbia.html

Dunn, J. (July 2, 2014). *Ransom Trojans Spreading beyond Russian Heartland—Techworld.com*. https://web.archive.org/web/20140702211354/http://news.techworld.com/security/3343528/ransom-trojans-spreading-beyond-russian-heartland/

ENISA. (October 20, 2020). *ENISA Threat Landscape 2020—Cryptojacking* [Report/Study]. https://www.enisa.europa.eu/publications/enisa-threat-landscape-2020-cryptojacking.

Eskandari, S., Leoutsarakos, A., Mursch, T., & Clark, J. (2018). A first look at browser-based Cryptojacking. *ArXiv:1803.02887 [Cs, Econ]*. http://arxiv.org/abs/1803.02887

FCA. (February 5, 2019). *FCA Warns Public of Investment Scams as over £197 Million Reported Losses in 2018*. FCA. https://www.fca.org.uk/news/press-releases/fca-warns-public-investment-scams-over-197-million-reported-losses-2018

Foxley, W. (October 26, 2020). *Harvest Finance Token Plummets 65% after Attack Saps DeFi Site of TVL*. CoinDesk. https://www.coindesk.com/defi-platform-harvest-finance-exploit

Gemini. (December 21, 2020). *Our Take on YouTube Bitcoin Scams*. Gemini. https://www.gemini.com/blog/our-take-on-youtube-bitcoin-scams

Gervais, A., Karame, G. O., Wüst, K., Glykantzis, V., Ritzdorf, H., & Capkun, S. (2016). On the security and performance of proof of work blockchains. *Proceedings of the 2016 ACM SIGSAC Conference on Computer and Communications Security*, 3–16. https://doi.org/10.1145/2976749.2978341

Haig, S. (August 19, 2020). *Fake Tokens Continue to Plague Uniswap*. https://cointelegraph.com/news/fake-tokens-continue-to-plague-uniswap

Hamrick, J. T., Rouhi, F., Mukherjee, A., Feder, A., Gandal, N., Moore, T., & Vasek, M. (2018). *The Economics of Cryptocurrency Pump and Dump Schemes* (SSRN Scholarly Paper ID 3303365). Social Science Research Network. https://papers.ssrn.com/abstract=3303365

Harrigan, M., & Fretter, C. (2016). The unreasonable effectiveness of address clustering. *2016 Intl IEEE Conferences on Ubiquitous Intelligence Computing, Advanced and Trusted Computing, Scalable Computing and Communications, Cloud and Big Data Computing, Internet of People, and Smart World Congress (UIC/ATC/ScalCom/CBDCom/IoP/SmartWorld)*, 368–373. https://doi.org/10.1109/UIC-ATC-ScalCom-CBDCom-IoP-SmartWorld.2016.0071.

Hileman, G., & Rauchs, M. (2017). 2017 global cryptocurrency benchmarking study. *SSRN Electronic Journal*. https://doi.org/10.2139/ssrn.2965436

Hong, G., Yang, Z., Yang, S., Zhang, L., Nan, Y., Zhang, Z., Yang, M., Zhang, Y., Qian, Z., & Duan, H. (2018). How you get shot in the back: A systematical study about cryptojacking in the real world. *Proceedings of the 2018 ACM SIGSAC Conference on Computer and Communications Security*, 1701–1713. https://doi.org/10.1145/3243734.3243840

Johnson, A. (April 3, 2019). *Is Privacy Under Threat From All the Know-Your-Customer Documents Stored with Countless Services?* Forbes. https://www.forbes.com/sites/alastairjohnson/2019/04/03/is-privacy-under-threat-from-all-the-know-your-customer-documents-stored-with-countless-services/

Kamps, J., & Kleinberg, B. (2018). To the moon: Defining and detecting cryptocurrency pump-and-dumps. *Crime Science*, 7(1), 18. https://doi.org/10.1186/s40163-018-0093-5

Keoun, B., Godbole, O., & Sinclair, S. (September 8, 2020). *First Mover: SushiSwap's Billion-Dollar 'Rug Pull' Is Thriller to Crypto Geeks*. CoinDesk. https://www.coindesk.com/sushiswap-rug-pull-thriller-crypto-geeks-bitcoin

Kharraz, A., Ma, Z., Murley, P., Lever, C., Mason, J., Miller, A., Borisov, N., Antonakakis, M., & Bailey, M. (2019). Outguard: Detecting in-browser covert cryptocurrency mining in the wild. *The World Wide Web Conference on - WWW '19*, 840–852. https://doi.org/10.1145/3308558.3313665

Kshetri, N., & Voas, J. (2017). Do crypto-currencies fuel ransomware? *IT Professional, 19*(05), 11–15. https://doi.org/10.1109/MITP.2017.3680961

La Morgia, M., Mei, A., Sassi, F., & Stefa, J. (2020). Pump and dumps in the bitcoin era: Real time detection of cryptocurrency market manipulations. *ArXiv:2005.06610 [Cs, q-Fin]*. http://arxiv.org/abs/2005.06610

Lee, E. J., Eom, K. S., & Park, K. S. (2013). Microstructure-based manipulation: Strategic behavior and performance of spoofing traders. *Journal of Financial Markets, 16*(2), 227–252. https://doi.org/10.1016/j.finmar.2012.05.004

Lee, K., Kaiser, B., Mayer, J., & Narayanan, A. (2020). An empirical study of wireless carrier authentication for SIM swaps. *Sixteenth Symposium on Usable Privacy and Security (SOUPS 2020)*, 61–79. https://www.usenix.org/conference/soups2020/presentation/lee

Levi, M., & Burrows, J. (2007). Measuring the impact of fraud in the UK: A conceptual and empirical journey. *British Journal of Criminology, 48*(3), 293–318. https://doi.org/10.1093/bjc/azn001

Liu, B., & Szalachowski, P. (2020). A first look into DeFi oracles. *ArXiv:2005.04377 [Cs]*. http://arxiv.org/abs/2005.04377

Mansourifar, H., Chen, L., & Shi, W. (2020). Hybrid cryptocurrency pump and dump detection. *ArXiv:2003.06551 [Cs]*. http://arxiv.org/abs/2003.06551

Martin, N., & Rice, J. (2011). Cybercrime: Understanding and addressing the concerns of stakeholders. *Computers & Security, 30*(8), 803–814. https://doi.org/10.1016/j.cose.2011.07.003

Martinez, A. (June 18, 2020). DeFi protocol compound pumps after coinbase listing, COMP prices double. *Crypto Briefing*. https://cryptobriefing.com/defi-protocol-compound-pumps-after-coinbase-listing/.

McGuire, M., & Dowling, S. (2013). *Cyber Crime: A Review of the Evidence*. https://ncvc.dspacedirect.org/handle/20.500.11990/871

McMillan, R. (August 31, 2010). Alleged ransomware gang investigated by Moscow police. *PCWorld*. https://www.pcworld.com/article/502841/article-2702.html

McQuade, S. C. (2007). We must educate young people about cybercrime before they start college. *Chronicle of Higher Education, 53*(14), B29.

Meiklejohn, S., Pomarole, M., Jordan, G., Levchenko, K., McCoy, D., Voelker, G. M., & Savage, S. (2016). A fistful of bitcoins: Characterizing payments among men with no names. *Communications of the ACM, 59*(4), 86–93. https://doi.org/10.1145/2896384

Mirtaheri, M., Abu-El-Haija, S., Morstatter, F., Steeg, G. V., & Galstyan, A. (2019). Identifying and analyzing cryptocurrency manipulations in social media. *ArXiv:1902.03110 [Cs, Stat]*. http://arxiv.org/abs/1902.03110

Möser, M., Böhme, R., & Breuker, D. (2013). An inquiry into money laundering tools in the Bitcoin ecosystem. *2013 APWG ECrime Researchers Summit*, 1–14. https://doi.org/10.1109/eCRS.2013.6805780

Nabilou, H. (2019). How to regulate bitcoin? Decentralized regulation for a decentralized cryptocurrency. *International Journal of Law and Information Technology, 27*(3), 266–291. https://doi.org/10.1093/ijlit/eaz008

Nakamoto, S. (2008). *Bitcoin: A Peer-to-Peer Electronic Cash System, 9*.

Narang, S. (February 19, 2020). *Cryptocurrency Scams: Fake Giveaways*. https://www.tenable.com/blog/cryptocurrency-scams-fake-giveaways-impersonate-followers-of-political-and-other-notable

NCSC. (September 11, 2020). *National Cyber Security Centre: Mitigating Malware and Ransomware Attacks*. https://www.ncsc.gov.uk/guidance/mitigating-malware-and-ransomware-attacks.

Ning, R., Wang, C., Xin, C., Li, J., Zhu, L., & Wu, H. (2019). CapJack: Capture in-browser crypto-jacking by deep capsule network through behavioral analysis. *IEEE INFOCOM 2019 - IEEE Conference on Computer Communications*, 1873–1881. https://doi.org/10.1109/INFOCOM.2019.8737381

Nomics. (August 5, 2019). *Transparency Must Be Trustless: The Nomics Manifesto*. https://nomics.com/blog/essays/manifesto

Nomics: Crypto Market Caps – Prices, All-Time Highs, Charts. (2021). https://nomics.com

NonFungible. (August 18, 2020). *What Is "Wash Trading" and Why Is It Negative for Non-fungible Tokens?* NonFungible.Com. https://nonfungible.com/blog/wash-trading-and-why-its-negative-for-non-fungible-tokens

Oggier, F., Datta, A., & Phetsouvanh, S. (2020). An ego network analysis of sextortionists. *Social Network Analysis and Mining, 10*(1), 44. https://doi.org/10.1007/s13278-020-00650-x

O'Malley, R. L., & Holt, K. M. (2020). Cyber sextortion: An exploratory analysis of different perpetrators engaging in a similar crime. *Journal of Interpersonal Violence*, 0886260520909186. https://doi.org/10.1177/0886260520909186

Osborne, C. (February 4, 2021). *Discord Servers Targeted in Cryptocurrency Exchange Scam Wave*. ZDNet. https://www.zdnet.com/article/discord-servers-targeted-in-cryptocurrency-exchange-scam-wave/.

Palmer, D., & De, N. (September 11, 2020). *'I F**ked Up': SushiSwap Creator Chef Nomi Returns $14M Dev Fund*. CoinDesk. https://www.coindesk.com/sushiswap-creator-chef-nomi-returns-dev-fund

Paquet-Clouston, M., Haslhofer, B., & Dupont, B. (2018). Ransomware payments in the bitcoin ecosystem. *ArXiv:1804.04080 [Cs]*. http://arxiv.org/abs/1804.04080

Paquet-Clouston, M., Romiti, M., Haslhofer, B., & Charvat, T. (2019). Spams meet cryptocurrencies: Sextortion in the bitcoin ecosystem. *ArXiv:1908.01051 [Cs]*. http://arxiv.org/abs/1908.01051

Peltier, T. R. (2006). Social engineering: Concepts and solutions. *EDPACS, 33*(8), 1–13. https://doi.org/10.1201/1079.07366981/45802.33.8.20060201/91956.1

Petrov, I., Invernizzi, L., & Bursztein, E. (2020). CoinPolice: Detecting hidden cryptojacking attacks with neural networks. *ArXiv:2006.10861 [Cs]*. http://arxiv.org/abs/2006.10861

Qin, K., Zhou, L., & Gervais, A. (2021). Quantifying blockchain extractable value: How dark is the forest? *ArXiv:2101.05511 [Cs]*. http://arxiv.org/abs/2101.05511

Qin, K., Zhou, L., Livshits, B., & Gervais, A. (2020). Attacking the DeFi ecosystem with flash loans for fun and profit. *ArXiv:2003.03810 [Cs]*. http://arxiv.org/abs/2003.03810

Qureshi, H. (January 19, 2021). *Flash Loans: Why Flash Attacks Will Be the New Normal*. Medium. https://medium.com/dragonfly-research/flash-loans-why-flash-attacks-will-be-the-new-normal-5144e23ac75a.

Redman, J. (January 15, 2019). Crypto impersonation scammers on social media raked in millions in 2018. *Bitcoin News*. https://news.bitcoin.com/crypto-luminary-impersonation-scammers-on-social-media-raked-in-millions-in-2018/.

Robinson, D. (September 21, 2020a). *Ethereum Is a Dark Forest*. Medium. https://medium.com/@danrobinson/ethereum-is-a-dark-forest-ecc5f0505dff

Robinson, D. T. (July 23, 2020b). *Tracing the Twitter Hack Bitcoins—An Update from Elliptic*. https://www.elliptic.co/blog/tracing-the-twitter-hack-bitcoins-an-update-from-elliptic.

Sarre, R., Lau, L. Y.-C., & Chang, L. Y. C. (2018). Responding to cybercrime: Current trends. *Police Practice and Research, 19*(6), 515–518. https://doi.org/10.1080/15614263.2018.1507888

Schär, F. (2021). *Decentralized Finance: On Blockchain- and Smart Contract-Based Financial Markets*. https://research.stlouisfed.org/publications/review/2021/02/05/decentralized-finance-on-blockchain-and-smart-contract-based-financial-markets

Schultz, J. (October 31, 2018). *Anatomy of a Sextortion Scam*. http://blog.talosintelligence.com/2018/10/anatomy-of-sextortion-scam.html

SEC. (August 28, 2017). *Investor Alert: Public Companies Making ICO-Related Claims | Investor.gov*. https://www.investor.gov/additional-resources/news-alerts/alerts-bulletins/investor-alert-public-companies-making-ico-related

SEC. (February 4, 2021). *SEC.gov | SEC Charges Investment Adviser and Others with Defrauding over 17,000 Retail Investors*. https://www.sec.gov/news/press-release/2021-24

Singer, A. (July 29, 2020). *Cleaning Up Crypto Exchange Wash Trading Will Take Global Regulation*. Cointelegraph. https://cointelegraph.com/news/cleaning-up-crypto-exchange-wash-trading-will-take-global-regulation.

Spagnuolo, M. (2013). *BitIodine: Extracting Intelligence from the Bitcoin Network* [Thesis, University of Illinois at Chicago]. /articles/thesis/BitIodine_Extracting_Intelligence_from_the_Bitcoin_Network/10842314/1.

Tahir, R., Huzaifa, M., Das, A., Ahmad, M., Gunter, C., Zaffar, F., Caesar, M., & Borisov, N. (2017). Mining on someone else's dime: Mitigating covert mining operations in clouds and enterprises. In M. Dacier, M. Bailey, M. Polychronakis, & M. Antonakakis (Eds.), *Research in Attacks, Intrusions, and Defenses* (pp. 287–310). Springer International Publishing. https://doi.org/10.1007/978-3-319-66332-6_13

Thompson, P. (December 31 2020). *The DeFi Hacks of 2020*. CoinGeek. https://coingeek.com/the-defi-hacks-of-2020/

Tiwari, M., Gepp, A., & Kumar, K. (2020). The future of raising finance - a new opportunity to commit fraud: A review of initial coin offering (ICOs) scams. *Crime, Law and Social Change, 73*(4), 417–441. https://doi.org/10.1007/s10611-019-09873-2

Twomey, D., & Mann, A. (2020). Fraud and manipulation within cryptocurrency markets. In C. Alexander, & D. Cumming (Ed.), *Corruption and Fraud in Financial Markets: Malpractice, Misconduct and Manipulation* (pp. 206–249). Wiley.

Vasek, M., & Moore, T. (2015). There's no free lunch, even using bitcoin: Tracking the popularity and profits of virtual currency scams. In R. Böhme, & T. Okamoto (Eds.), *Financial Cryptography and Data Security* (pp. 44–61). Springer. https://doi.org/10.1007/978-3-662-47854-7_4

Victor, F. (2020). Address clustering heuristics for ethereum. In J. Bonneau, & N. Heninger (Eds.), *Financial Cryptography and Data Security* (Vol. 12059, pp. 617–633). Springer International Publishing. https://doi.org/10.1007/978-3-030-51280-4_33

Werner, S. M., Perez, D., Gudgeon, L., Klages-Mundt, A., Harz, D., & Knottenbelt, W. J. (2021). SoK: Decentralized finance (DeFi). *ArXiv:2101.08778 [Cs, Econ, q-Fin]*. http://arxiv.org/abs/2101.08778

Xia, P., Wang, H., Luo, X., Wu, L., Zhou, Y., Bai, G., Xu, G., Huang, G., & Liu, X. (2020a). Don't fish in troubled waters! Characterizing coronavirus-themed cryptocurrency scams. *ArXiv:2007.13639 [Cs]*. http://arxiv.org/abs/2007.13639

Xia, P., Zhang, B., Ji, R., Gao, B., Wu, L., Luo, X., Wang, H., & Xu, G. (2020b). Characterizing cryptocurrency exchange scams. *ArXiv:2003.07314 [Cs]*. http://arxiv.org/abs/2003.07314

Xu, J., & Livshits, B. (2019). The anatomy of a cryptocurrency pump-and-dump scheme. *ArXiv:1811.10109 [Cs, q-Fin]*. http://arxiv.org/abs/1811.10109

Yousaf, H., Kappos, G., & Meiklejohn, S. (2019). *Tracing Transactions across Cryptocurrency Ledgers*, 837–850. https://www.usenix.org/conference/usenixsecurity19/presentation/yousaf

Zimba, A., Wang, Z., & Mulenga, M. (2019). Cryptojacking injection: A paradigm shift to cryptocurrency-based web-centric internet attacks. *Journal of Organizational Computing and Electronic Commerce*, *29*(1), 40–59. https://doi.org/10.1080/10919392.2019.1552747

Zmudinski, A. (April 15, 2020). *Google Removes 49 Phishing Extensions That Steal Cryptocurrency Data*. Cointelegraph. https://cointelegraph.com/news/google-removes-49-phishing-extensions-that-steal-cryptocurrency-data.

Zoltu, M. (August 25, 2020). *How to Turn $20M into $340M in 15 Seconds*. Medium. https://medium.com/coinmonks/how-to-turn-20m-into-340m-in-15-seconds-48d161a42311

Index

For Product Safety Concerns and Information please contact our EU
representative GPSR@taylorandfrancis.com
Taylor & Francis Verlag GmbH, Kaufingerstraße 24, 80331 München, Germany

www.ingramcontent.com/pod-product-compliance
Ingram Content Group UK Ltd.
Pitfield, Milton Keynes, MK11 3LW, UK
UKHW022017180926
475701UK00005B/891

* 9 7 8 0 3 6 7 8 6 1 4 4 5 *